LADINO REVERIES

Tales of the Sephardic Experience in America

by Hank Halio

The Foundation for the Advancement
of Sephardic Studies and Culture
New York

Second Printing – November 1999
Printed in the United States of America

ISBN 1-886857-01-6
Library of Congress Catalog Card No: 95-60423

Cover design by Linda Pierro & Robert Bedford
Cover photograph by Stuart Fishelson

Foundation for the Advancement
Sephardic Studies and Culture, Inc.
34 West 15th Street, 3rd Floor
New York, NY 10011

P.O. Box 2
Atlantic Beach, NY 11509

Dedicated to all those whose life work
preserved the history, culture and lore
of the Sephardim – the Jews of Spain,
and to all those of future generations who
will continue along the path.

PREFACE

With this edition of ***Ladino Reveries – Tales of the Sephardic Experience in America,*** the *Foundation for the Advancement of Sephardic Studies and Culture* resumes its thirty-year tradition of publishing works recording and preserving the Sephardic heritage. Over the years, the *Foundation* has been instrumental in paving the way for many writers and scholars who have contributed toward what can only be called a Sephardic cultural "Renaissance." In keeping with this tradition, we are pleased to present this latest publication, an anthology of stories and anecdotes by noted Sephardic columnist Hank Halio.

Preserving the remnants of a vanishing culture is a difficult task, and it is mainly through the work of several dedicated individuals that any progress has been made at all. Among the more prominent of those who dedicated their lives to promoting the history and culture of the Sephardim are the late Albert Amateau, a leader in the Sephardic community for over 80 years, founder of numerous Sephardic organizations from the earliest societies to the most recent; David N. Barocas, philosopher and linguist, the single most influential leader in Sephardic studies in the latter part of this century; M.J. Bernardete, professor of Romance Languages and Literature at the City University of New York, the foremost secular Sephardic scholar of our time; Henry V. Besso, prominent leader of the Sephardic community in America, a linguist for the *Voice of America* and bibliographer for the Library of Congress; Albert Matarasso, educated and trained in Salonika, the foremost Sephardic rabbinical scholar and teacher in America; Joseph Papo, social worker, executive director of the *Central Sephardic Jewish Community of America* and author of the comprehensive work, Sephardim in 20th Century America; and Albert J. Torres, journalist, editor, and staff member of every Ladino newspaper published in the U.S., publisher and printer of ***La Vara,*** the last Ladino newspaper in America.

Finally, one must add to the list the late Louis N. Levy, impresario to these giants, who worked tirelessly to promote and publicize their causes and helped to found such organizations as *Sephardic House,* the *American Association of Jewish Friends of Turkey,* and the *Foundation for the Advancement of Sephardic Studies and Culture.*

Despite the collective lifetime works of these pioneers, there is still much to be done in the field of Sephardic studies. As we approach the new millennium, we must remind ourselves of our responsibility to preserve the rich heritage, culture and language of our parents, grandparents and ancestors. It is hoped that this publication will encourage further interest and studies in our Sephardic culture and the Judeo-Spanish language. It is only through such interest that our heritage, which has survived for hundreds of years, will truly survive for future generations.

Joe Halio, M.D., President
Robert Bedford, Vice-President
Stuart Fishelson, Secretary

Foundation for the Advancement
of Sephardic Studies & Culture, Inc.

ACKNOWLEDGEMENTS

The first column of ***Ladino Reveries*** appeared in the December 1986 issue of the *Sephardic Home News.* Since then I have had a multitude of reveries, but I have not had them alone. Over the years many wonderful people, both living and departed, have inspired me to write more and more columns. To all those, I am grateful.

I wish to thank the many people to whom I am indebted in gathering the material for this book. First and foremost, I thank my parents Sultana (Susie) and Yusef (Joe) Halio, of blessed memory, for remembrances of growing up in a Sephardic household. My thanks to the *Sephardic Social Club of Florida* for giving me the start in its monthly newsletter and to the wonderful people from all over the United States who took the time to write, encouraging me to continue with the column. They were hearty with their praise and extremely generous in sharing their experiences and anecdotes with me.

I am grateful to Mark Alhadeff, the first editor of the *Sephardic Home News* with whom I worked; to Charles Pesso, the Editor in Chief; Ike Amira for his voluminous letters, challenging me and expanding my knowledge of Ladino; Ike Beresid for his patience in translating many of the Turkish words and idioms I heard so often as a youngster, but did not know the exact meaning of; Sol Elias, Marilyn Mayo, Phyllis Modiano and June Rousso for their photographs; Pete Colan for his original **Djoha** cartoons; Susan Alouette Rich for writing the very first letter of encouragement; Vickie Chiprut for her many colorful letters; my golfing partner, Dr. Jack Crespin, who took out his golf frustrations with Ladino expletives that fit those bad shots; to Rabbi Abraham Deleon Cohen and Rabbi Lester Hering for transcribing and translating the Hebrew portions; and to Rabbi Morris Cassorla for his assistance in proofreading.

Special thanks to Bob Bedford for his tremendous help in formatting and preparing the book, photographs and artwork; to Stuart Fishelson, my son-in-law, for his work with Bob in reproducing the photographs and for tirelessly pursuing the completion of this work, and to the Media Arts Department of L.I.U., Brooklyn; to Linda Pierro for generously offering the use of her graphics facilities and for her invaluable advice on graphics and layout.

My everlasting gratitude to my children: Susan, who doubled as my very caring editor; Joe, whose vast knowledge of his grandfather's newspaper, ***La Vara,*** contributed much towards the material in this book; Stacey, for the many hours she spent drafting this work; and to my granddaughter, Phoebe, whose childhood inspired me to think of my own. And finally to my cherished wife of 48 years, Phyllis, without whose infinite patience, steadfast support, and Sephardic sensibility this work would never have come to fruition.

Hank Halio
Delray Beach, August 1995

CONTENTS

FOREWORD

Mi Padre Komia Roskas y Yo Muero De Ambre

My father used to tell me that I am the doctor who made him famous. Now I tell him that he is the writer who made me famous. I have many older friends, mostly Sephardic (Turks, Greeks, etc. – Americans all), but lately my younger friends, also Sephardic, have been greeting me with what I have been saying for almost twenty years now: **"Mi padre komia roskas y yo muero de ambre."** ("My father used to eat cake, and I am dying of hunger.") Why? Because my father's generation, first-generation Americans, had this culture at their fingertips and we are starving for more.

Your mothers and fathers, though they spoke Spanish, were mostly Turks. Born and raised in the Ottoman Empire, their lifestyles were Turkish. Once here, they sympathized with Turkey deeply and even went to her aid from time to time. I have often thought they were no more Spanish Jews than they were Turkish Jews (Turkish 'subjects' they used to say). But first-generation Americans paid little attention to all that. Struggling to learn English, to make a living, to fight a war and establish beyond a doubt that they were Americans, they naturally partook of the beauty of their parents' culture and neglected just as naturally to pass it on to us. Now when nostalgia brings it back, it makes us yearn for more. I have always felt that I was robbed by twentieth-century American life of the rich culture my grandparents left behind in Turkey.

Turkey was good to the children of Israel, welcoming them from their expulsion from Spain, protecting religious freedom for 500 years, during which time they were unwelcome everywhere else. Our culture still lives in Turkey. Moslem and Jew live together in peaceful coexistence with equal opportunity for those who seek it. If you travel to Turkey, you will see how vibrant our culture is there, in an unassimilated environment. Five hundred years following the Spanish Inquisition and subsequent expulsion, Turkey's haven is unmatched in history, except in the USA. Yes, **mi padre komia roskas,** and I ask for more. We are proud of our Sephardic history, and we must work to keep it alive.

Joe Halio, M.D.

INTRODUCTION

Kiss me, I'm Sephardic!!!

The ***Ladino Reveries*** column that appeared in the December 1992 issue of the *Sephardic Home News,* celebrated six of the most enjoyable years of my life. Back in 1986, Mark Alhadeff, at that time the assistant editor of the *Sephardic Home News,* asked for permission to reprint an article that he had read in the newsletter of the *Sephardic Social Club of Florida, Inc.* Permission was gladly granted. Little did I know then that **en mi viejes** (in my old age) I would be making a new career for myself.

Writing the columns all these years has been tremendously enlightening for me. The contributors have been enormously provocative in challenging me with words and phrases, asking if I ever heard of this word or that expression, would I define this or that for them? Many wonderful people who have written to me have expanded my knowledge of Ladino and, in many cases, have taught me numerous Turkish words. Over the years I have received a great number of compliments, and my readers have generously shared their experiences and anecdotes with me. Some of you have asked if a collection of all the columns exists in one volume. The answer to that is, HERE IT IS!!!

In these pages I hope to share with you my appreciation of the beauty and wisdom of the Ladino language, including personal experiences and those of my friends and relatives. My earliest recollection is that **Djudeo-Espanyol** (Ladino) was mostly spoken at home, interspersed with Turkish, Hebrew, French, Greek, Italian, and believe it or not, English. It always amazed me how easily the adults switched from one language to another. One thing we "younger" Sephardim noticed was that sometimes words of three or more languages were used in one sentence. To illustrate, I will quote a passage from *Tract Number XI, "The Sephardic Storm Lamp,"** written by David N. Barocas: "In the early 1920's, it was my custom to meet my father at the [subway] station after work. On one occasion it rained heavily, and I did not go to meet him. I knew that he would understand. When my father came home, drenched from the rain, he said, **'Me digo de mi para mi,**

* David N. Barocas. *A Study on the Meaning of Ladino, Judezmo and the Spanish Jewish Dialect. The Sephardic Storm Lamp, Tract No. XI.* The Foundation for the Advancement of Sephardic Studies and Culture, New York, 1976.

si David me esta esperando al stashon, ishmish var.' Translated it means: "I say to myself, if David is waiting for me at the station, we have a problem." In this dialect my father used three different languages to express a thought. Besides the Spanish phrases, the word ***stashon*** is from the English and the expression **Ishmish var** is a Turkish idiom, which means literally, "We have our business" [We have a problem]."

Oh, that our foresight were as good as our hindsight. We did not realize how linguistically rich our parents were. They weren't bilingual; they were multilingual. I visited with Dr. Albert Menache* when he was 93 years old and still very alert. During our conversation he interjected words in Greek, French, Turkish, Spanish, and Hebrew. When I questioned a word I did not understand, he would say, "You Americans, you are so poor. I feel sorry for you." Today, anyone who speaks more than one language is admired. Dr. Menache passed away shortly after my visit with him in 1992.

For many years, Ladino has been dying in America. It is not spoken at home anymore as a result of intermarriages between first-generation Americans of Sephardic descent with members of other ethnic groups, especially Ashkenazim. From 1922 to 1948, the newspaper ***La Vara*** was very important to the Sephardic household. Ever since the suspension of ***La Vara*** in 1948, nowhere has written Ladino been in use.

This book does not hope to bring about a renaissance of our **Djudeo-Espanyol**. It is not an attempt to give an in-depth history of the Spanish Inquisition, nor of the events leading up to the eventual Edict of Expulsion. The plight of the Jews who were expelled from Spain has been documented by such scholars as Rabbi Marc Angel, David N. Barocas, Henry V. Besso, Joseph Papo, Dr. David Raphael, and many others. Rather, this book recalls for the benefit of many middle-aged, first-generation Americans of Sephardic extraction – and all others who wish to be enriched – our culture, language, and folklore. The object is to remind you of our glorious recent past, to bring back loving memories of our parents and grandparents who spoke Ladino.

The Sephardic Social Club of Florida, to which in large part this book owes its existence, came into being in 1978, when a handful of Sephardim led by Hymie and Tillie Elias met. The result has been a resurgence of interest in our heritage. The Club in South Florida has grown to a mem-

*Dr. Albert Menache was a prominent physician in Salonika, Greece before WWII. A concentration camp survivor, he was a leader of the Sephardic Community in Salonika in Post-War Greece. He emigrated to the U.S. after the war with his second wife, Julia, and became the Resident Physician at the *Sephardic Home for the Aged* in Brooklyn, NY until he retired in 1976.

bership of nearly one thousand. Our problems were commensurate with our growth. We could not find places large enough to accommodate the tremendous response to the affairs we sponsored: annual 'Oriental Night,' the yearly weekend outings and our annual picnics. Hardest of all was to find a place large enough for our monthly meetings.

Organizations that manage to get an attendance of ten percent of their membership at their meetings consider themselves lucky. With a membership of close to one thousand, we have anywhere from three to five hundred in attendance at any one time. That is a testimonial to the popularity of the club, and you can imagine how much noise so many 'Turks' in one place can generate.

We come together, hungrily experiencing the delight in meeting friends that had been lost and all but forgotten. All the conversations start with "Do you remember?" "I don't believe it. Is that ________? How long has it been? Thirty, forty years?"

I first became interested in writing these columns after an article that I wrote as a fill-in for the newsletter of the *Sephardic Social Club of Florida* created a ripple of interest among its members. I had been motivated to write it by the constant referral to Ladino words and proverbs at gatherings of Sephardim. Someone was always asking, "How do you say ______ in Ladino?" Or, "Do you remember this proverb?" I began to comb my memory for happenings, rituals, folklore, old wives' tales, superstitions, and **refranes** (proverbs) that I had heard during my childhood at home, in the synagogue, at parties and at other get-togethers. From then on it was just a steady flow of ideas that arose, by-and-large, from walking around at our meetings and listening in on conversations that took place. Thus, ***Ladino Reveries*** came into being. The first article appropriately made its debut by quoting the By-Laws of *The Sephardic Social Club*. Here's how it started:

"Through our newsletter we have the means to share our unique language, and our Sephardic experiences that can enrich us all. Our By-Laws specifically state in Article 2, Section 1: "The purpose of this club shall be to preserve, promote and encourage our heritage, culture and customs." (We have been delinquent in this respect by the non-use of our beautiful Ladino in our newsletter.)

The next few articles drew such a pleasantly surprising response that I was inspired to continue. A big boost came when the *Sephardic Home for the Aged,* Brooklyn, New York, asked for permission to print the articles in the *Sephardic Home News,* which has a readership of about 10,000. The response from the readers of that publication, I am delighted to say, has been phenomenal. The *Sephardic Home News* is distributed throughout the United States, Israel, and much of Europe. Almost all the subscribers have Sephardic ties. Letters and telephone calls have poured in, both from Sephardic Club members and *Sephardic Home News* readers; and many will be included in these pages.

My friends ask, "How do you remember all that stuff you write about?" My answer is that I was an only child; my parents, Sultana (Susie) and Joe Halio operated a sewing factory, and I was raised among adults. I spoke Ladino before I spoke English, as I am sure most of my contemporaries did. With each column I wrote, so much of what I saw and heard as a child started coming back to me and so many long-forgotten memories surfaced that I went a step further and started asking questions of friends and relatives. So intriguing were the questions asked by the people who wrote to me that I was compelled to do some research in order to answer them. As a by-product, I personally have been enriched. In short, I've listened a lot and have done a lot of follow-up.

I don't expect to cover all the customs, proverbs, home cures, etc., for the simple reason that no one person can be completely knowledgeable – much has been lost forever with the passing of most of the generation of immigrants of the early part of the century. Here in America, the generation that had emigrated from Turkey set out to become American citizens. Some of the better educated Sephardim here urged and helped the new arrivals in applying for citizenship and integrating themselves into the American way of life. The children of these immigrants, my contemporaries, soon realized that we were Americans, even though we spoke Ladino at home. The schools played an important part in instilling patriotism within us. The singing of the National Anthem, the observance of the Fourth of July, and other holidays cemented our loyalties as Americans.

Many of us still remember our home-lives as youngsters, the wonderful ways that our parents greeted friends and relatives, the ethnic foods that were served on a daily basis, the delicacies that were prepared for our holiday celebrations, and the rites that were conducted when in mourning.

Intermarriages with the Ashkenazim and other ethnic groups eroded much of our culture. Yet those who strayed still have a yearning to hear, read and remember the culture that was lost to them, lamenting that their children and grandchildren will have no knowledge of their heritage. Sad to say that the progeny of first-generation Americans will only hear of our wonderful Sephardic family experiences, but never truly appreciate them. It is in the hope of preserving this rich and beautiful heritage that I offer these tales, folklore and proverbs.

GUIDE TO PRONUNCIATION AND SPELLING

I have been forced to take a defensive position regarding my interpretation of the proverbs, the spelling, and the meaning of the words I use. The interpretations are interrelated. I have done fairly extensive research in this area and have learned a bit more each time. To name a few localities where the same words have different meanings and different words have the same meanings, we have Monastir, Kastoria, Rhodes, Izmir, Chanakale, Salonika and Istanbul, examples of which appear in a following chapter.

One good example appears in *Bar-Misvah Speeches* written by Rabbi Robert Ouziel and Mr. Albert Matarasso, both learned, scholarly, and respected men in the Sephardic Community. They were diverse in their spelling of the same words, yet both were correct, and the messages they conveyed were clearly understood.

As for my spelling of **Djudeo-Espanyol**, or Ladino, or whatever you choose to call our dialect, there is no doubt in my mind that many of you will question it throughout this book. Many of the first- and second-generation Sephardim here in America have studied Spanish in high school and in college. To them the spelling may be abominable, but these columns are not written in an academic manner. Furthermore, the writing of Ladino should not be compared with that of present-day Castillian Spanish, which is written in Roman characters and has its own historically based system of spelling. Ladino is classically written in the Hebrew alphabet, which has no letter *"q"* or *"c."* Thus, the Ladino that appears in this book is actually a transliteration.

I don't think that I am doing anything original or unusual with my method, only writing the language as the words sound to me, using our Roman alphabet with consistency to produce a phonetic transliteration, as interpreted from my readings of the newspaper, ***La Vara,*** which I used as a guide (***La Vara,*** a Sephardic newspaper which my father-in-law, Albert Torres, published from 1922 to 1948, employed the Hebrew alphabet to transmit faithfully the proper pronunciation of our beautiful Ladino). The Hebrew alphabet, in which the Ladino ***La Vara*** was written, was universally accepted as the written language of the Sephardim.

Unfortunately, no written form can truly duplicate the flavor of a tongue, as no written work can capture the intonations and color of everyday communication in **Djudeo-Espanyol.**

In the Hebrew alphabet there are no artificial groupings of letters to produce a desired sound such as **"que"** to effect the *"k"* sound. Hebrew employs the letter **"kaf"** as in **"kien," "ke," "komo,"** etc. The letter *"c"* is never used. In conventional Spanish the *"c"* is used interchangeably as an *"s"* and a *"k"* and as a *"th"* as well. I will be using the letter *"s"* for all *"s"* sounds, i.e., **"sien"** for **"cien"** and *"k"* for all the *"q"* sounds.

You will have no difficulty in reading the transliterations if you follow some ground rules regarding the pronunciation of the vowels as they are laid out below:

"a" to sound as in *"ah," "car"* (Spanish, **"nada"**)
"e" to sound as in *"neck"* (Spanish, **"negro"**)
"i" to sound as in *"eat"* (Spanish, **"vida"**)
"o" to sound as in *"owe"* (Spanish, **"otro"**)
"u" to sound as in *"boot"* (Spanish, **"uno"**)

The letter *"h"* is used where the Hebrew uses the letter **"het"** as in **Hanuka** and sometimes at the end of a Hebrew word, such as **Pesah**. The letter *"a"* is mostly used for the Hebrew letter **"heh,"** which is often silent as in **Aaron**.

To produce the *"Zsa Zsa"* (as in Zsa Zsa Gabor) sound of *"j,"* as the Sephardim use it, I will use the letter *"j"* for such words as **mujer, ijo, bavajada, pujar, handrajo,** etc. Lastly, the letters *"dj"* are used in tandem to produce the hard *"j"* sound as in **Djoha, Djudio, Djugar**.

Since Ladino has no history as a written language in the Roman alphabet, please keep in mind that the spellings here are a transliteration of a spoken language and there is great variability and no set rules. Since I have not found a single dictionary that can serve as an authority, I hope this book will become the basis for one.

SPANISH JEWS

The Sephardic saga has spanned over 1,500 years. Starting in Spain, it has extended to many other countries as well, evolving into a unique culture, rich in spirit. Among its primary characteristics has been the retention of Spanish as the language of the family and the synagogue. Concurrently, there has been the incorporation of the conventions, foods, and family traditions, originating in Spain and subsequently modified in accordance with the customs of the lands in which the Sephardim lived. These were passed on from generation to generation, as our fleeing ancestors settled in Constantinople, Salonika, and other parts of the Ottoman Empire.

Our ancestors had lived in Spain for almost 1,000 years, side by side with Muslims and Catholics peaceably. True, there were instances of persecution, but Spain had become our homeland. Then, on March 31, 1492 the Edict of Expulsion was signed. It reads in part: "Thus we grant permission to said Jews and Jewesses to take their goods and belongings out of our reigns, by either sea or by land, with the condition that they not take out either gold or silver or minted money or any other items prohibited by the laws of the kingdom." In other words, the only valuables with which Jews were permitted to leave Spain were the clothes on their backs, their language, and their culture. Many carried the keys to their houses with them in the belief that some day they would return.

There were not many places that the exiles could turn to for refuge. Yet, 500 years after the expulsion, the Sephardim are alive and well, thanks to Sultan Bayazid II of the Ottoman Empire. The good and wise Sultan is reputed to have said, "I welcome all the Jews of Spain to Turkey. These people have helped build and strengthen Spain. King Ferdinand and Queen Isabella are fools for ejecting them. They will impoverish their country and enrich mine." He sent ships to Spain to transport them to Turkey.

One would think that the memory of the cruel and unjust treatment inflicted upon the Spanish Jews would have resulted in a strong desire to erase any memory of the country of their persecution. One must wonder why, then, after the terrible ordeal of the Inquisition and subsequent expulsion, did our ancestors hold on to the customs of Spain for the more than four centuries following, during which time they lived elsewhere? **Y porke, asta este dia, kinyentos anyos despues de muestra expulsion de Espanya, mosotros, los Sephardim, dayinda avlamos muestro Espanyol?** (And why, until this day, 500 years after our expulsion from Spain, do we, the Sephardim, still speak our Spanish?) Is it simply that the essence and energy of the millennium during which the Jews lived in Spain was too deeply ingrained to be forgotten? The answer to these questions holds the secret of our passage as a people into the the 20th century and the state in which we find ourselves today.

My supposition is that even though they were accepted and given sanctuary, Jews were not given any kind of national status. Turkey, being a Muslim country, could not offer citizenship to a non-Muslim. Although they were never assimilated into Turkey as Turks, the Sephardim were allowed the freedom and were even encouraged to practice their religion without government interference, to go into any profession, and to participate in some governmental affairs. And while most of their liberties were subject to the whims of each succeeding Sultan, not being Muslims, they were not required to serve in the armed forces. Of course, there really never was the feeling that "this is my own, my native land." They were always **Djudios Espanyoles** (Spanish Jews).

As the 19th century waned, so did the strength of the Ottoman Empire. Parts of Turkey broke away into independent enclaves, Salonica, Monastir, Kastoria, Rhodes and Macedonia among them. While independence may have favored the average citizen in those lands, the benefits to the Sephardic Jew, and the Sephardic community, were questionable.

In 1908 a revolution led by the *Young Turks* – members of various liberal groups – arose within the Ottoman Empire, demanding that the Sultan restore the constitution and parliament of 1876 and rule democratically. (The name *Young Turks* is sometimes used for insurgents within various organizations, such as political parties, that are unrelated to Turkish politics.) The uprising of the *Young Turks*, curtailing the powers of the Sultanate, brought about many changes. New laws were enacted in order to unify the country. All inhabitants of Turkey, regardless of religion or former nationality, were to become Turkish subjects. One of the laws passed mandated that all able-bodied men were to serve in the armed forces. However, for Jews, that service would be one of subservience. With all the benevolence that Turkey exhibited towards us, there still were restrictions. An incident I will not forget was that upon my being commissioned a Second Lieutenant in the United States army during World War II, my father remarked, **"En Turkiya, ijo de Djudio nunka se azia zabit en la armada."** (In Turkey, the son of a Jew could never be an officer in the army.) The dietary laws were another factor that deterred Jews from enlisting. Although Muslims do not eat pork, there are enough differences to make it difficult to serve in the Turkish Army. With all due respect to the Turkish government, the Jewish people were never imbued with national pride. Jewish men felt no obligation to serve and possibly die for the country that had always considered them as Spanish Jews, and not full-fledged Turkish subjects. Thus, governmental change in part motivated the exodus in the early 1900s, and the lure of America was irresistible.

Here in the United States, we are Americans. Shortly after arriving here, most Sephardim applied for and received their first papers toward American citizenship. We, the offspring of these hardy people, were immediately integrated into the American way of life, having no knowledge of past hardships, except through conversations heard at home. Many of us spoke Spanish before we spoke English, but were quick to learn once we got out onto the streets. My first experience outside the home was in kindergarten, where the kids teased me and made me cry because I didn't speak English!

It was once thought that Ladino would thrive in Latin America where Spanish is the native tongue of almost all. But the Jewish Community is no longer as isolated as it once was. Like any ethnic group that is free to assimilate into the native population, Jews naturally began to speak the Spanish of their secular national identity. Today very few of the Sephardim in South America, Mexico, Cuba, and other Spanish-speaking countries, speak the Spanish of their immigrant parents and grandparents.

KE SIGNIFIKA "SEPHARDIC"
WHO ARE THE SEPHARDIM?

Since the inception of my column, ***Ladino Reveries,*** I have always tried to give an example of Sephardic life as we lived it from the time our folks came over from Turkey. I seldom wrote anything of a heavy nature, but lately, I have been hearing erroneous statements about our language, and that anyone who is not an Ashkenazi is Sephardic. This is a recent development, as only since the Six Day War of 1967 have all Jews of non-Eastern European descent come to be known as Sephardim.

The late David N. Barocas wrote many tracts on Sephardism, and I am lucky that my son, Dr. Joe Halio, had a very close relationship with this erudite Sephardic man. Joe gave me some of Mr. Barocas's books to read, and I am going to quote directly from some of his writings to substantiate my beliefs.

Mr. Barocas dedicated part of his *Tract Number-XI,* entitled *The Sephardic Storm Lamp: Ladino, Judezmo And The Spanish Jewish Dialect,* to Henry V. Besso's essay, *Judeo-Spanish, Its Growth And Decline.*

In this essay, Henry Besso examines the origins of Judeo-Spanish, and of those who speak the language. One must not confuse the Jews who spoke Ladino, he writes, whose origin must be found in the Iberian Peninsula, with the other 'Oriental' Jews whose ancestors never set foot upon the soil of Spain. Quoting a former president of Israel, Besso declares that "Jews of the latter type [Oriental] should be referred to as Jews from Islamic countries whose vernacular language is Arabic, or Aramaic or Persian."

Besso continues: "Another distinguished scholar of our time, Dr. Joseph B. Schechtman, believes that there is a definite distinction between the 'Oriental' and 'Sephardic' immigrant groups. Dr. Schechtman says, "They are by no means identical, and it is erroneous and misleading to use these terms indiscriminately and interchangeably. The Sephardim are Jews originating from Spain (Sepharad), who lived in various parts of Turkey, Greece, Egypt, Italy and North Africa. They form a category by themselves and exhibit marked differences from other

Oriental groups. Neither the Jews of Yemen, nor those of Iraq, Iran, Afghanistan or Libya are Sephardim, and by far not all immigrants from North Africa, Syria and Lebanon are of Sephardic origin." "

On the subject of our language, Ladino, Henry Besso quotes Maximo Jose Kahn, who was Consul General of Spain in Salonica: "The Spanish language is a sacred language to the Sephardic Jew. When in the past centuries, the Rabbis used the Spanish classical translations of the Old Testament and of other religious books to educate the people, they gave the name Ladino to the language of these translations; they called it Ladino because it was to the Jews what Latin is to the Catholics. Even today, scholars think of Ladino as the early pure Castilian such as it was imported from Spain."

Henry Besso goes on to say, "Whether the language used by the Spanish Jews is called Ladino, Judeo-Spanish, or jargon, it has been agreed that this dialect when stripped of the Portuguese and some foreign words, is in reality, the authentic, beautiful, melodious as well as the divine language of Spain. It is the language with which to communicate with God, as the Spanish Jews and the Spaniards would say."

THE BEAUTY OF DJUDEO-ESPANYOL

Ladino is a very genteel language, full of beautiful, pithy, impressive and courteous expressions of salutation and consolation. In some cases, it is almost impossible to translate. It is true that everything can be translated in its literal sense, but much of the poetry is lost. While the literal meaning is easily expressed in English, the real flavor and feeling of many words and phrases go astray in translation. Only to one who is steeped in the language and culture is it understandable and meaningful.

Did you ever hear your mother say, when she saw you in some sort of a bad situation, **ojos de la kara,** or **ijo/ija de la madre?** What do these phrases mean? Eyes of the face, or, son/daughter of the mother. Actually, they mean a mother's most prized possessions. If you had a stiff neck or a sore shoulder, she would say, "**Es de sudor yelada, no te akavidates** ("It's from cold sweat, you did not take care of yourself").

If someone mentioned something that was distasteful, such as a murder, robbery or an accident, Mama would say, **"Leshos,"** literally meaning: "Far away;" but it was meant for any of these happenings to occur far from us. If someone was going to make an off color remark at the dinner table, it would be prefaced by **afuera de las karas** (away from our faces). If anyone had a coughing spell, or tripped and fell, you would hear: **oras buenas** (good hours), or **malahim ke te akompanyen**. I admit I don't know how to translate **oras buenas** to relate to someone having a coughing spell or falling, but it was always used. I can relate to **malahim ke te akompanyen,** because that means, "May the angels accompany you." In my estimation, it was meant that something trivial should happen, nothing serious. We do know that in the five hundred years since the expulsion from Spain, Ladino has been infused with other languages. Many of the words my family used in our everyday speech are not Spanish. This led me to hunt down the origin of these words. The discovery that many of these words were Turkish should not have seemed peculiar to me, but it did.

Having been expelled from country to country throughout history, it is not surprising that our people adapted themselves to their ever-changing environment. It is a testament to our tenacity that Ladino has survived throughout the ages.

I wonder if you will be as surprised as I was to learn that many of the words used in the following sentences are Turkish? Have a little fun with your friends by turning some sentences around; substitute English words for Turkish words. Many of us are so rusty in our Ladino that we do it just as a matter of course. Have you ever found yourself saying, for instance:

Ke es el hurry?	What is the **adjile**?
Dame el pencil.	Give me the **kalem**.
Ande esta the paint?	Where is **boya**.
Lo kierro right away!	I want it **pishin**!
No **te mixeyes**.	Don't **karisheye**.
Mete ice **en el vaso**.	Put **booz** in the glass.
Ya pagates el rent?	Did you pay the **kira**?

The language with which the Sephardim left Spain was de-hispanisized over the 500 years they lived in Turkey and further modified in the years they lived in the United States. There were some differences in the language that each community claimed to be correct. A person from Monastir will say **taralikos** (round sesame cookies) for what an Istamboli will say **biskochos**. One from Ankara will say **pishtamal** (towel) and one from Izmir will say **tovaja**. The word **guzano** in Ladino and in conventional Spanish means a worm (Fidel Castro uses the word in a derogatory way, referring to those who leave Cuba as **guzanos** – worms). We call anyone who is digging for information a **guzano**. **"Es guzano, todo kierre saber. Te va eskarvar asta ke le digas todo lo ke kierre saver."** ("He's a worm, he wants to know everything. He will dig until you tell him everything you know.") Who can tell me where the expression, **Dale show, esta perdiendo** (Give him a break, he's losing), came from? This demonstrated the elasticity and, in some cases, the rigidity of the Sephardic mind.

We first-generation Americans inherited this culture and use it to this very day. Having acquired the language from our parents, we maintain, as they did, that their meaning and pronunciation of a word was the proper way. Quite a few Sephardic discussion groups have emerged in the last fifteen or so years and a lot of fun has been generated as a result. The following words and phrases are sprinkled with many languages, and I trust you can relate to them. See if you can pick out the different languages.

El Dyo ke te guadre de nazar (May the Lord protect you from the evil eye). **Me va murir del sar** (I am going to die of fright). A sharp guy is said to be able to **kitar al guerko a baylar** (make the devil dance). This same 'sharpie' is said to be **fuido de la kuedra** (to have escaped the noose, or one step ahead of the sheriff). **Riko o prove es bueno tener paras** (Rich or poor, it's good to have money). **Aziya hamalik** (He worked as a laborer).

PROVERBS

Aze lo ke te digo, no lo ke ago.
Do as I say, not as I do.

Kien avla la vedrad, piedre la amistad de sus amigos.
He who speaks the truth loses his friends.

La boka aze y la boka dezaze.
The mouth builds and the mouth destroys.

La palavra estado en ti sos tu el patron.
You are the master of the words you speak.

La tinta del savio es mas sagrada ke la sangre de martirio.
The ink of the wise man is holier than the blood of the martyr.

Regreto siempre aver avlado, nunka aver kayado.
I always regret having spoken, never having been silent.

KOMO SE DIZE...

At an impromptu gathering of friends and relatives someone asked, **"Komo se dize *ceiling* en Espanyol?"** That started an avalanche of questions. The rest of the evening was spent with everyone asking **Komo se dize** – how do you say? Do you remember this proverb, or this expression? I'll bet many of you have had the same experiences. Now, whenever Sephardim gather there is an interjection of our dialect in the conversation. Here are a few proverbs that came out of that visit.

Da el padre, riye el padre, riye el ijo. Da el ijo, yorra el ijo, yorra el padre. The father gives, the father laughs, the son laughs. The son gives, the son cries, the father cries. That one is my all time favorites. I think it is one of the first proverbs I remember hearing my father quote.

En boka serrada no entra moshka. A fly does not enter a closed mouth. The American version would be: Silence is golden. Another way of looking at it would be the following: I came home with a black eye one night and my father said, **"Estavas avlando en lugar de oyendo."** You were talking when you should been listening. **Kuando uno avla, serra la boka, y avre los oidos.** When someone speaks, close your mouth, and open your ears. You may learn something, It may keep you out of trouble.

El piadoso no tiene reposo. The merciful one has no rest. How true that is. Once word got around that you were easy, had a soft heart, **todos te topavan**, they all found you.

El haragan es konsejero. The lazy one is an advisor. Don't you just love it? You're breaking your back working at something and someone comes along and says, "Why don't you do this or that." Everyone's a supervisor.

Va ande te arrogan, no ande te arrondjan. Go where you are invited, not where you are chased away. When I was a little kid, I told my mother that I was chased out of a certain place, and she came out with that gem.

Mejor solo de mal akompanyado. Better alone than in bad company. That's a sure way of staying out of trouble.

Ijo sos, padre te aras, lo ke izites te aran. A son you are, a father you will be, as you do, so will they. Remember, kids grow up, get strong, and they don't forget. As ye sow, so shall ye reap.

Una persona espantoso, ni ganansya ni piedrita tiene. A faint-hearted person neither gains nor loses. Nothing ventured, nothing gained. Some might contradict: "Look before you leap."

A point to consider in the translation of words or phrases is that since the Sephardim were scattered over most of the Ottoman Empire for centuries, it was inevitable that our Ladino would be influenced by local words and expressions. Words used in certain localities have different meanings than they have in others. One case in point: In Salonika, they say, **favlar** for **avlar**, not necessarily making one person wrong and another right. Places like Istanbul, Rhodes, Salonika, Izmir, Chorlu, Silivria, Chanakale, Monastir, Kastoria, etc., all had their colloquialisms, claiming their way to be right and the other to be wrong. I don't think any of them are wrong. Here are some differences:

Chamashir	–	**Mudante**	–	Underwear
Putines	–	**Kalsados**	–	Shoes
Churapes	–	**Kalsas**	–	Stockings
Yerno	–	**Nuero**	–	Son-in-law
Aldikera	–	**Djep**	–	Pocket
Suvrino	–	**Primo**	–	Nephew or Cousin
Kanyamazo	–	**Handrajo**	–	a Rag
Pishtamal	–	**Tovaja**	–	Towel
Berendjena	–	**Patlidjan**	–	Eggplant

The flexibility of the Sephardim to adapt to their new environment is demonstrated in their usage of the languages they had to learn in their migrations over centuries of exile from many countries. The best example of 'Ladinoizing' I found was in a tract written by David N. Barocas. "In America we began to form new Ladino-sounding verbs from the English language. The verb 'to park' became ***parkear*** and 'to drive' became ***dravear***. The strangest of these verbs was ***abetchar*** which they had formed from *'I betcha,'* the slang for 'I bet you.' Thus ***abetchar*** became the new Ladino word for "to bet." **Kierres *abetchar?*** You want to bet? ***Parkeya el karro***. Park the car. **Dame un *mech***. Give me a match.

CULTURAL DIFFERENCES

Let's go back a few years to our grade school days. That's when we first became aware that we, as Sephardim, were different from our Ashkenazi co-religionists. The first days in school were not easy for the Sephardic children. I, for one, could not speak English when I entered kindergarten. For the first time, our non-Jewish sounding last names were brought to our attention, and that set us apart. Names like Aboulafia, Abrevaya, Amira, Candiotti, Cherasi, Crespi, Forma, Gormezano, Halio, Massa, Motola, Penso, Roditti, Sarfati, Saporta, Strougo, Susi, Toledano, Varsano, Yohai, and there are many more.

We took off from school on ***Roshana,**** Yom Kippur, Pesah and other Jewish holidays. When we returned to school the next day, our teachers would ask us why we were absent. We said we were absent because it was a Jewish holiday. All the kids would laugh at us, both the Jewish kids and the gentile kids. They didn't believe us. "With your name, how can you say you are Jewish?"

Which of us at the age of six, seven or eight, knew about the Spanish Inquisition, or the Expulsion? Which of us knew how to explain it to our teachers? We just insisted that we were Jewish. The next step was, "Bring a note from your parents." That was when panic set in. Not many of our parents had any schooling and most couldn't read or write English well enough in those days to write a comprehensible letter. With a lot of scrounging around, we managed to get our notes to the teacher. This went on every time we got promoted and changed classes and teachers.

Many of us took a perverse pleasure in not letting on that we were going to be absent from class before a holiday, and we would go through the same rigmarole year after year. Now comes the kicker. When we became old enough to appreciate the charms and fascinations of the opposite sex, our troubles really began. We rarely made dates with Sephardic girls (although many of us married them) because if we were seen with a Sephardic girl more than once, the whole community would have us engaged and ready for marriage. Most of us dated Yiddish girls.

***Roshana** is the typical Ladino short form for Rosh Hashana.

Can't you just hear our folks saying, **"Mira ijo ke se esta indo con una Yiddisha. No puede topar una de las muestras?"** ("Look at this fellow who's going with a Yiddish girl. Can't he find one of ours?") Hardly any of us dated gentile girls.

A new problem arose. The parents of the Yiddish girls would want to meet the 'boyfriend.' Can you picture what happened at the first encounter? We were introduced by our first names only. Then the parents would speak to us in Yiddish. When they saw the blank look on our faces they turned to their daughters and asked, *"Er is nit a yid?"* (**"El no es Djudio?"** "Isn't he Jewish?")

"You say you are Jewish, but you don't speak Yiddish. How can you say you are a Jew?" Some of us had the urge to say, "You don't speak Spanish, how could you be Jewish?" Being well bred Sephardic boys, we didn't. To try to prove we were indeed Jewish we recited some Hebrew prayers, but we pronounced the words differently than they did, and they didn't believe us. Of course, this happened to the Sephardic girls as well. A certain unmentionable thought crossed the minds of some of the wise guys as a source of proof that they were Jewish, but I don't think any of them tried it.

Once it was accepted that the Sephardim were actually Jewish, the language barrier surmounted, and the parties involved convinced we were in fact Jewish, we thought our troubles were over. Far from it – they had only just begun. It was inevitable that there would be 'mixed' marriages. At the turn of the century, this was tantamount to marrying out of the religion. There was much speculation as to how the bride and groom were going to get along. **Komo se van a pasar?** A lot more was said about how the **kosuegros,** or ***mahatunim*** in Yiddish (in-laws), were going to relate and communicate with one another. The Ashkenazim were as apprehensive as the Sephardim in trying to cope with the myriad problems the bride and groom were going to face. The monumental adjustments that had to be made in a so-called mixed marriage touched many of our Sephardic and Ashkenazi brothers and sisters. Our customs and culture were literally continents apart. Our cuisine was different. We, the Sephardim, celebrated the Jewish holidays in a different manner. The way our services were conducted in the synagogue was different, and the way our children were named caused the greatest discord in relations between the husbands, wives, and in-laws. How about the problems the **kosuegros,** the ***mahatunim*** were going to have. When the honeymoon was over, little problems started to crop up. Our different cultures came into play.

Let's start with the food. Keep in mind that since this is being written by a Sephardic, the viewpoint may be slightly biased. In the Ashkenazi home, we were served dishes that were totally alien to us. It took a little doing to get used to dishes such as gefilte fish, potato latkes, tzimmes, kasha varnishkas, borscht, shav, blintzes, kishka, bobka, rogolach, to name a few.

The Sephardim served the following mouth-watering dishes, (which I am sorry to say, we don't see too much of these days): **kodrero al orno** (roast lamb), **avikas** or **fijones kon karne** (navy beans with meat), **pishkado kon guevo y limon** (fish with egg and lemon), **albondigas de patata** (meat patties with potatoes), **pimentonas reynadas** (bell peppers stuffed with meat), **lakerda** (raw salted mackerel – this always raised eyebrows), **bamyas** (okra), **yaprakes** (grape leaves stuffed with rice or meat or both). Now for the real goodies: **masapan, baklava, boorekas, boolemas, kadayif, tishpishti, asoplados, malibi, sutlach,** and of course **kave kon leche a la Turka**. The interchange of food intrigued the parties involved. The boys learned to like them and the girls learned to cook them. I must say that both were enriched by the union.

The greatest conflict in relations between the husbands, wives, and in-laws arose when it came to naming the children. The Sephardim named the progeny for the living and the Ashkenazim, for the departed. With a good deal of research, I was able to understand the merits of both sides of the question. There is no Hebraic law that dictates how the children are to be named in either culture. Simply put, it is strictly a custom that was handed down from generation to generation. I must assume that a certain amount of superstition also comes into the picture. Nevertheless, this is the custom which I consider one of our best. To the Ashkenazim, this custom, to this day is considered sacrilegious. I am always asked, "Why do you name your children for the living?" I answer that question in a typically Jewish manner – with another question: "Why not?" I was named for my grandfather, who was alive at the time. I was born in America, and he was living in Turkey. Even though I had never seen him, I always felt I was somebody. I had identity. I am looking forward to the day when a little Hank will be named for me.

As I have mentioned in my articles, there are many 'Henrys' in my family, all of us having been named for my grandfather. The oldest of my uncles had a factory, and we all worked for him at one time or another. Very often, during the summer months, a half dozen of us worked there at the same time. Whenever he wanted one of us to do something, he would simply yell, "HENRY!" You can picture what happened. We would all come running like there was a fire to be put out.

My mother was very proud when my first daughter was named for her. So was my wife when our first grandchild was named for her. When our second daughter was born, I suggested to my mother-in-law, Sara Pressman Torres, a wonderful Ashkenazi lady, that it was her prerogative to name this child. Her answer was, "By all means give her my name."

It was the custom of the Sephardim for the first-born boy to receive the name of the paternal grandfather, the first-born girl to receive the name of the paternal grandmother, the second-born boy to receive the name of the maternal grandfather, the second-born girl to receive the name of the maternal grandmother. This was done whether those whose names taken were living or deceased; thus the phrase "They name for the living." The naming for the living was the hardest thing for the Ashkenazim to bear, resulting in situations that were very difficult, if not impossible, for them to reconcile.

The last thing I say to anyone who asks why we name for the living is to ask if they believe in the Ten Commandments. If the answer is "Yes," then they must name for the living. The fifth commandment, which says: "Honor thy father and mother so that your days on this earth that God gave to you may be lengthened," seems to be the underlying reason for the Sephardic custom of the naming of the offspring. What better way is there to honor your father or mother? How many times have you seen and heard a proud grandparent point to a toddler and say, **"Tiene mi nombre."** ("He/She has my name.")

Any additional children (and in Turkey there were plenty), were named for deceased members of both sides, starting with the paternal side and alternating with the maternal side. Odds are that the thought of 'male chauvinism' has crossed the minds of many of you. As we can see, the names were given in a pre-determined succession. There were times when an 'irregular' name was given. These departures from the conventional were produced within the families.

In some families, the first-born was named **Behor/Behora**. When death claimed numerous victims in a family, the next child to be born was named **Bension**, or simply, **Sion**. Superstition was the last resort of a family that was left with one child as a result of the death of one or more of the other children. The survivor was **reskatado** (ransomed) by a person close to the family. The ransomer sold the child back to the family for a pittance. The child was then renamed **Merkado** or **Merkada** (bought). This was used as a ruse to pretend that the child was not their natural child, but one that had been purchased, in order to mislead the angel of death. A woman who gives birth to a male child after many years of sterility names the infant ***Rahamim*** (pity, in Hebrew), signifying that God took pity on the woman and blessed her with a child.

A family that has had a constant run of misfortunes may change the name of one of its male children to **Nissim**, in the hope of looking forward to better days.

A person who recovers from a serious illness after a long convalescence, changes his/her name to **Haim** (life, in Hebrew) for a male, or **Vida** (life, in Spanish) for a female.

In the event that a mother-in-law and a daughter-in-law have the same first name, the female child is named **Dudú**. According to custom, a mother and daughter cannot have the same name.

A boy born on Saturday is named **Sabbetai** (Sabbath), one born on a holiday is named **Yomtov**. There probably were many other customs, but that's as far as my research has taken me. Most of these "rules" are now outdated. I doubt that even in Turkey, more than a few are still in practice.

Before my recent illness I had the honor of being invited to speak to the congregation of *Temple Sinai* in Delray Beach, Florida. What do you say to a group of Ashkenazim to hold their attention? I thought a good idea would be to assure them that even though they questioned our Jewishness because we did not speak the same language and because our customs were different, we observe the same laws and we worship the same God. Our pronunciation of Hebrew is different. (Incidentally, our pronunciation of Hebrew is standard throughout Israel today.) Our customs are different. We celebrate some holidays in a different manner than they do.

The talk began with the differences in our synagogues. We both chant in Hebrew. Our ritual is different, but is not contrary to Jewish law; our **teva** (readers' desk), the **bima** (elevated platform from which the **tora** is read), is in the center of the room with benches located all around the **teva**. There is no **hupa** (canopy) – for a marriage, the **taled** (shawl) is wrapped around the couple during the ceremony. When someone is given an **aliya** (opportunity to publically read from the **tora**), his entire family rises as a sign of honor and respect. We do not have **yiskor** services in the same manner as the Ashkenazim, which they have on the holidays. We have this service throughout the year and on holidays. Of course, we also have our **meldados**. It wasn't until recently that we had **Bat-Misvahs**.

THE TEN COMMANDMENTS

I just finished reading *The Road From Babylon,* by Chaim Rafael. The book gives a description of the migration of the Jews from Babylon westward, looking for a place to settle peaceably, eventually settling in Spain after being expelled from many places including England and France. In the book was a painting of the first words of the Ten Commandments in Hebrew and Spanish. We all learned about the Ten Commandments when we went to Hebrew school. Many of us learned our lessons well, but how many of us can recall the wording of each commandment? I confess, I had to do some research to refresh my memory.

Each year on **Roshana,** we look back and reflect on how we could have done things differently, in a better or wiser manner. New Year's resolutions are made and broken. It may not be a bad idea to think about adopting the Ten Commandments as our way of life for the coming year. Most of us live by these precepts instinctively, or is that last statement just wishful thinking on my part?

Here they are in Ladino and in English:

1. **Yo so Adonai, tu Dyo ke te kito de la tierra de Ayifto, de la kaza de servisio.**
2. **No tendras Dyo delantre de mi.**
3. **No tomes el nombre de Adonai tu Dyo en vano.**
4. **Akodra el dia de Shabat para santifikarlo.**
5. **Onra a tu padre y a tu madre para ke te se alargen tus dias sovre la tierra ke tu Dyo te da.**
6. **No mates.**
7. **No fornikes.**
8. **No roves.**
9. **No atestigues kontra tu kompanyero testigo falso.**
10. **No kovidieses la kaza de tu vezino, no kovidieses la mujer de tu vezino, ni su siervo, ni su buey, ni su azno, ni ninguna koza de lo ke es de tu kompanyero.**

1. I am the Lord thy God who brought you out of Egypt, out of the house of bondage.
2. Thou shalt have no other Gods before me.
3. Thou shalt not take the name of the Lord in vain.
4. Remember the Sabbath day to keep it holy.
5. Honor thy father and mother so that your days on this earth that God gave to you may be lengthened.
6. Thou shalt not kill.
7. Thou shalt not commit adultery.
8. Thou shalt not steal.
9. Thou shalt not bear false witness against thy neighbor.
10. Thou shalt not covet thy neighbor's house, wife, manservant, maidservant, ox, ass, nor anything that is thy neighbor's.

PROVERBS

A segun no kieres mal para ti, no kieres mal para tu kompanyero.
Just as you don't wish evil for yourself, you don't wish evil for your companion. *Do unto others as you'd have others do unto you.*

Al aksi le ayuda el Dyo.
God helps the cranky one.

Ayudate y el Dyo te ayudara.
Help yourself and the Lord will help you.

Aze kon el prove, y el Dyo te pagara.
Do with the poor, and the Lord will repay you.

Bendicho el ke tiene, mas el ke da.
Blessed is the one who has, more so the one who gives.

Da al prove, y el Dyo te pagara.
Give to the poor, and the Lord will repay you in kind.

Dar a los proves es emprestar al Dyo.
To give to the poor is to lend to God.

El Dyo apreta, ama no aoga.
God squeezes, but doesn't choke.

El Dyo ke te guadre de vezino malo.
May the Lord protect you from a bad neighbor.

En lo ke estamos, al Dyo bendigamos.
We bless the Lord for what we have.

En mis oras de apretasyon, solo el Dyo es mi salvasion.
In my hours of distress, only God is my salvation.

Kien al Dyo yamo, en vasio no salio.
Whoever called on God, never left empty handed.

Kierres topar las yaves de hohma, pena y lazdra y da sedaka.
To find the keys to wisdom, work, struggle, and give alms.

Kuando el Dyo esta kontigo, no te espantes de tus enimigos.
When God is with you, have no fear of your enemies.

La vedrad es ija del Dyo, la mentira ija del diavlo.
Truth is the daughter of God, the lie the daughter of the devil.

Oy es seguro, manyana solo el Dyo lo save.
Today is sure; tomorrow, only the Lord knows.

Palavras de viejos, palavras de la ley.
Sayings of the elderly, wise sayings of the law.

HOLIDAYS

KIPPUR

These days we celebrate the holidays a little differently than we did when I was a young man. The families were always together. Nowadays, we are scattered all over the country. Last **Roshana** I received a New Year's card from my son, as I do from my two daughters when they aren't in Florida visiting with me. (I didn't start sending my folks holiday or greeting cards until I was drafted into the army during WWII.) This year's card from my son (adapted from ***La Vara***) is worth sharing with you. Here's the translation:

Seyas eskrito y seyado en libros de vidas buenas.
May you be written and sealed into the book of good life.

En Rosh Hodesh elul, Moshe ravenu suvyo al monte de Sinai para resivir las segundas tavlás de la ley y se detuvo

ayi 40 dias de pardon por el pekado de egel de entonses se santifikaron estos dias y son para mosotros dias de regotivos 40 dias de selihot, fin a Kipur.
At the beginning of September, Moses went up to Mount Sinai to receive the second tablets of the Law. He remained there for 40 days of pardon for the sin of the golden calf. Since then, these days have been sanctified and are for us 40 days of prayer until Kippur.

Demandad la pas para Yerushalayim!
Seran prosperados los ke te amen. Sea pas en tu barbakana, sossiego en tus palacios. Por kazade Adonay nuestro Dyo bushkare bien a ti.
Pray for peace in Jerusalem!
May those you love enjoy prosperity. May there be peace all around you, and prosperity in your home. In the House of Adonay, our God, such good I will ask for you.

PURIM

Believe it or not, we observe the holidays more in compliance with the Scrolls than the Ashkenazim do. For example, on **Purim** which is the holiday that I especially enjoy, we exchange gifts and distribute charity.

It always was a special time of the year for me. My mother was very busy baking for days prior to **Purim**. She would make a certain **desayuno** with a hard boiled egg coiled in the dough to signify the rope used to tie **Haman**. For the girls they would make dainty pieces of **masapan** in the shape of little birds. The biggest job of all was to make the **baklava**. In those days one could not go to the store and buy the ready made **fila** dough. It had to be made from scratch. The house was unlivable for several days as the dough was made very thin and stretched over the couch, the tables, and the beds in preparation for the many layers needed to make good **baklava**.

When all the baking was finished and **Purim** finally came around, my mother filled paper bags with these goodies and said to me, **"Aroniko, yeva esta papelera a la Tante Ester, esta a la Tante Bouka, esta a la Tante Zimboul, y esta a la Tante Korrine. Te van a dar purimlik,**

y no te olvides de desir 'Purim alegre, anyo bueno ke tengas.' " ("Aaron, bring this bag to Aunt Esther, this one to Aunt Bouka, this one to Aunt Zimboul, and this one to Aunt Corrine. They will give you Purim money, and don't forget to say, 'Happy **Purim**, have a good year.' ") Being an only child and a very obedient one, I complied. My aunts would all say, **"Tu ke bivas para munchos anyos."** ("May you live for many years.") After a couple of years, I got to know which of my aunts liked me the most, and which were the most affluent, or most generous. The **Purimlik** I got ranged from two cents to a quarter. Can you imagine what it was like for a little boy to get twenty five cents in 1925?

It is possible that **Purim** was celebrated in a different manner in other localities of Turkey and Greece than in the city my folks came from. On those busy holidays, our moms had to be left unencumbered in order to get their cooking and cleaning done. They used several ruses to get us out of their hair for a little while. I have heard of several versions of a ploy our mothers used. I'll relate how my mother got rid of me for a short time. All the mothers used it, but it seldom worked more than once.

Mom: "Aroniko, va ande la nona, y demandale por aliko beni." ("Aaron, go to your grandma, and ask her for **aliko beni**.") When you got to grandma's and said, **"La mama me disho ke venga aki y ke te demande por aliko beni."** ("My mother told me to come here and ask you for **aliko beni**.") Grandma would say, **"Asenta chiko, y espera."** ("Sit, little one and wait.") Like a good little boy I sat and sat and sat. When grandma figured it was the right time she gave you some **bavajada** (something frivolous) and told you to go home. Another version I heard about was, **"Digale a la nona, teneme aka."** ("Tell Grandma, keep me here.")

HANUKA

Hanuka was a problem. The Ashkenazi kids would ask me what I got for **Hanuka**. I never got anything for **Hanuka**. Among the Sephardim **Hanuka** is not a gift-giving holiday. I have never been able to find out where the Ashkenazim came to give gifts on **Hanuka.** I can only assume that it was a way of pacifying the kids, as in having what is called a '**Hanuka** bush' instead of a Christmas tree.

It was a happy holiday where we visited our relatives at candle lighting time. We would sing songs, tell stories, and eat **burmuelos**. We don't eat latkes, or meat balls, or play with a *dredl*. One thing I remember about **Hanuka** was that it was customary for the Sephardim to arrange joint dinners for friends or relatives who had had a falling out, or quarreled during the year in order to bring about a reconciliation. Not a bad idea for today. **Verdad?**

PESAH

Pre-**Pesah** preparation was a very pleasant time at our home. Mom was always looking for something new to buy **para la kaza por Pesah** (for the house for Passover). She would take me from store to store looking for **una tavla mueva, o un mantel ermoso para la mesa, o puede ser ke tengo bastante paras para merkar perdes muevos para las ventanas.** (A new hammered silver tray, or a beautiful table cloth, or maybe I have enough money to buy new curtains for the windows.) Mom would buy a new dress, and my Pop and I would get new suits. That always was a special event. I was very careful not to get my new suit soiled: "Hey watch out, that's my new suit." Of course, with the suits went everything else, new ***shoozes*** (shoes), etc. **Estas ropas muevos mos estrenavamos el primer dia de Pesah** (We would don these new clothes for the first time on the first day of Passover).

Preparations for **Pesah** began at least two weeks before the first Seder. My mother was busy placing her orders with the local grocer and butcher for the many traditional dishes to be prepared for the holiday. Much work went into cleaning and ridding the house of **hamets** (leavened goods prohibited for **Pesah**). All leavened food was generally disposed of by donating it to the janitor of the building, who often was a gentile. Crockery and utensils that had been stored away from year to year for this special holiday were taken out of the closet, washed, polished and set up. The stove was gone over with a 'fine tooth comb' to clean away any vestiges of **hamets**, the bread box was thoroughly washed to remove any trace of crumbs.

On the **Agada** plate there was a mutton shank bone, the bitter herbs, a roasted egg, lettuce, the haroset, a cup of vinegar, three pieces of matza on top covered by an embroidered cloth. Some traditional dishes

I remember were: **kyoftes de prasa** (meat patties with leek), **kyoftes de patata** (meat and potato burgers), **pishkado kon guevo y limon** (fish with egg and lemon), **kebob de kodrero** (lamb casserole), **kwajado de gayina** (baked chicken). Some deserts were: **burmuelos de matza kon miel** (matza fritters with honey), **dulse de bimbriyo** (quince preserve), **dulse de kayisee** (apricot preserve), **dulse de kalavasa** (pumpkin preserve), etc., etc. Positively no gefilte fish.

Our **Pesah** service is different in that it is conducted in Hebrew and in Ladino. The four questions are not questions and are not asked by the children, but recited by the entire assembly. The children are encouraged to ask other questions about **Pesah**. The more provocative the questions, the better. You could see the chests of the proud parents puff up. I always had the feeling that some of the kids weren't smart enough to ask such questions, and that they were prepped by their parents.

We don't eat gefilte fish. For the bitter herbs we had romaine lettuce and vinegar – no salt water. The *Afikomen* was not hidden for the kids to find. I think the Ashkenazim used that ploy to keep the kids from falling asleep during the service.

The part of the ritual I remember best was when **Had Gadya** was sung (in Ladino, of course). See if it brings back some memories.

HAD GADYA

1. **Un kavretiko, ke lo merko mi padre por dos levanim, por dos levanim.**
2. **Vino el gato y se komyo al kavretiko ke lo merko mi padre por dos levanim, por dos levanim.**
3. **Y vino el perro y mordio al gato ke se komyo al kavretiko ke lo merko mi padre por dos levanim, por dos levanim.**
4. **Y vino el palo ke aharvo al perro ke mordio al gato ke se komyo al kavretiko ke lo merko mi padre por dos levanim, por dos levanim.**
5. **Y vino el fuego ke kemo el palo ke aharvo al perro ke mordio al gato ke se komyo al kavretiko ke lo merko mi padre por dos levanim, por dos levanim.**

6. **Y vino la agua ke amato al fuego ke kemo al palo ke aharvo al perro ke mordio al gato ke se komyo al kavretiko ke lo merko mi padre por dos levanim, por dos levanim.**
7. **Y vino el buey y se bevio la agua ke amato al fuego ke kemo al palo ke aharvo al perro ke mordio al gato ke se komyo al kavretiko ke lo merko mi padre por dos levanim, por dos levanim.**
8. **Y vino el Shohet ke degoyo al buey ke se bevio la agua ke amato al fuego ke kemo al palo ke aharvo al perro ke mordio al gato ke se komyo al kavretiko ke lo merko mi padre por dos levanim, por dos levanim.**
9. **Y vino el malakh hamavet ke se yevo al Shohet ke degoyo al buey ke se bevyo la agua ke amato al fuego ke kemo al palo ke aharvo al perro ke mordio al gato ke se komyo al kavretiko ke lo merko mi padre por dos levanim, por dos levanim.**
10. **Y vino el Santo Bendicho El y mato al malakh hamavet ke se yevo al Shohet ke degoyo al buey ke se bevyo la agua ke amato al fuego ke kemo al palo ke aharvo al perro ke mordio al gato ke se komyo al kavretiko ke lo merko mi padre por dos levanim, por dos levanim.**

1. One kid, one kid, my father bought for two coins, two coins.
2. Then came the cat that ate the kid that my father bought for two coins, for two coins.
3. Then came the dog that bit the cat that ate the kid that my father bought for two coins, for two coins.
4. Then came the stick that beat the dog that bit the cat that ate the kid that my father bought for two coins, for two coins.
5. Then came the fire that burned the stick that beat the dog that bit the cat that ate the kid that my father bought for two coins, for two coins.
6. Then came the water that quenched the fire that burned the stick that beat the dog that bit the cat that ate the kid that my father bought for two coins, for two coins.

7. Then came the ox that drank the water that quenched the fire that burned the stick that beat the dog that bit the cat that ate the kid that my father bought for two coins, for two coins.
8. Then came the Shohet who slaughtered the ox that drank the water that quenched the fire that burned the stick that beat the dog that bit the cat that ate the kid that my father bought for two coins, for two coins.
9. Then came the angel of death who slew the Shohet who slaughtered the ox that drank the water that quenched the fire that burned the stick that beat the dog that bit the cat that ate the kid that my father bought for two coins, for two coins.
10. Then came the Holy One, Blessed be He who smote the angel of death who slew the Shohet who slaughtered the ox that drank the water that beat the dog that bit the cat that ate the kid that my father bought for two coins, for two coins.

THE TRADITIONAL BLESSING: AFTER MEALS

Ya komimos y bevimos, y al Dyo santo barehu baruh shemo bendizimos ke mos dio y mos dara pan para komer y panyos para vestir, y anyos para bivir. El padre, el grande ke manda al chiko asegun tenemos de menester para muestras kazas y para muestros ijos. El Dyo mos oiga y mos aresponda y mos apiade por su nombre el grande, ke somos almikas sin pekado. Hodu l'adonai ki tov ki le-olam hasdo. Siempre mejor, nunka peor, nunka mos manke la meza del Kriador, Amen.

We ate, we drank, and we bless the Holy One blessed be He and His holy name, Who has given us and gives us bread to eat, clothes to wear, and years to live. The Almighty Father Who provides for the littlest one, He grants us the necessities for our homes and for our children. May God hear us and respond to us, and have pity on us for the sake of His great name, for we are little souls without sin. Praise the Lord, for He is good, for His kindness is everlasting. May things always be better, not worse, may the Creator's table never be lacking for us, Amen.

KIEN SUPIENSE Y ENTENDIENSE ALAVAR AL DYO KRIENSE

Kien supiense y entendiense	Who knows and understands
Alavar al Dyo kriense	Praise the Lord, our Creator
Kualo es el uno?	Which is the one?
Uno es el Kriador	One is the Creator
Bareh u baruh shemo	Blessed be He and His holy name
Kien supiense y entendiense	Who knows and understands
Alavar al Dyo kriense	Praise the Lord, our Creator
Kualos son los dodje?	Which are the twelve?
Dodje tribos de Israel	Twelve are the tribes of Israel
Onze son las estreyas	Eleven are the stars
Del suenyo de Yusef	Joseph saw in his dream
Diez mandamientos son	Ten are our Commandments
Mueve meses de la prenyada	Nine months of pregnancy
Ocho dias de la mila	Eight days of circumcision
Siete dias kon shabat	Seven days with the Sabbath
Sesh dias de la semana	Six days of the week
Sinko libros de la ley	Five books of our Law
Kuatro madres de Israel	Four, the mothers of Israel
Tres muestros padres son	Three, our fathers
Dos Moshe y Aron	Two Moses and Aaron
Uno es el kriador	One is our Creator
Bareh u baruh shemo	Blessed be He and His holy name

LA NOCHE DE SEDER Y LOS DOS AZNOS

Avia de ser un marido y mujer rezin kazados. La mujer era muy bien edukada y el marido era sin edukasion. Vino la primera noche de pesah y la mujer vido ke el marido no savia meldar la agada y pasaron una noche muy negra.

Al anyo ke vino la mujer le disho al marido en la noche de seder, "Al salir del kal bushka un ajeno ke no tiene ande azer la Agada, y traelo a kaza para ke melde la Agada en tu lugar." El marido, despues del servisio en el kal enkontro un ajeno ke no tuvo ande ir, y lo kombido a su kaza.

Kuando ya vino la ora de dezir la Agada, el patron le disho al musafir, 'behavod,' y el musafir respondio, "No, no, behavod al patron de la kaza." Esto kontinuo de uno al otro asta ke se entendio ke ni el musafir savia meldar. La mujer ke ya avia perdido la pasensia, tomo el libro y disho, "Yo digo la Agada," y empeso, "Kuanto fue demandada la noche la esta, mas ke todas las noches? En todas las noches tenemos un azno en la mesa, y en esta noche tenemos dos! Y agora ya puedemos empesar a komer!"

Once upon a time there was a newly married couple. The wife was very well educated and the husband, uneducated. The first night of Passover came and the wife realized that her husband was unable to read the *Agada* and they passed a very unpleasant evening.

The next year she told her husband on the night of the Seder, "On leaving the synagogue, look for a stranger who has no place to go for a Seder, and bring him home so that he may read the *Agada* in your place." Her husband, after the service in the synagogue, found a stranger who had no place to go, and he invited him to come to his house.

When the time came to recite the *Agada,* the master of the house said to the visitor, "It is your honor." The visitor answered, "No, no, the honor belongs to the master of the house." This went on until it was clear that not even the visitor knew how to read. The wife, who had lost all patience, took the book and said, "I will read the *Agada* – "Why is this night different from all other nights? On all other nights we have one jackass at the table, but on this night we have two! Now we can commence to eat!"

MUSAFIRES: GUESTS, VISITORS

Musafires. Do you remember the frantic preparations that took place in the house when guests were expected? Everything had to be ship-shape. Nothing could be out of place. All the finery that was stored away for just this occasion was taken out, inspected, washed and ironed, and put in its proper place. There were hand-embroidered tablecloths with matching napkins. The 'good' silverware and special glassware were taken out of storage and they were cleaned and displayed.

Do you recall the beautiful words of greeting that our folks used when we got **musafires?** It was the custom of our folks to welcome the visitors with old world courtesy. Sephardic hospitality has always been warm and gracious. **Entra en buena hora, bouyroon, merhaba, vishita alegre, barouh haba,** etc. Notice that three languages were used to say *"Welcome."* Spanish, Turkish and Hebrew.

It didn't take long for the elegant operation to begin. Out came **la tavla de dulse** (the tray of sweets). The **tavla** was a very ornate tray generally made of hammered silver. It was used only on special occasions: **vijitas** (visits). The hostess, **la balabaya**, would arrange a variety of bowls (generally of cut glass) with **dulses** (home made sweets). The guests would show their appreciation by remarking, **"Bendichas manos, mira tanto ke lavoro Madam Sultana."** ("Blessed hands, look how hard Madam Sultana worked.") The greater the variety of **dulses**, the greater the compliment to the guests: **bimbriyo** (quince), **kayisi** (apricot), **mandarina** (tangerine), **portokal** (orange), **gazo** (grapefruit), **vijna** (Bing cherries) – they were the **dulses de alegria** (sweets of happiness).

The proper number of **kucharas** (spoons), one for each guest, was placed on the tray with the proper number of glasses. There was always an extra glass on the tray for the used spoons.

The honor of serving the **dulses** was given to the eldest daughter. The compliments to the hostess were beautiful. Depending on the reason for the visit, they went something like this: **Dulses de alegria** (Sweets of happiness); **Afyet olsun** (Turkish for 'May it do you good'); **El kasamiento ke seya largo y provechoso** (May the marriage be enduring and fruitful); **Kaza de amor y alegria** (House of love and happiness); **Otro tanto de los chikos** (Likewise to the little ones); **Ke te bivan por sien**

anyos (May they live for a hundred years); **Munchas grasias Madam Sultana** (Many thanks, Madam Sultana); **Kon grande plazer** (With great pleasure); **Ke kaza tan ermosa** (What a beautiful home); **Mashala, mira kriaturas tan ermosas, y mira komo se komportan** (May the Lord preserve, look at such beautiful children, and how well behaved).

Then **kave turko** was served. On happy occasions the remark, **Kave de alegria** (Coffee of happiness) was always made, because coffee was also served on sad occasions. The maker of the coffee was judged by the richness of the **kaimahk** (the creamy foam) at the top of the cup. The coffee was made in a brass **librik** (Turkish coffee pot), and served in **fildjanes** (demi-tasse cups). My father would take a cigarette out of the pack and offer one to each of the men and to the elderly ladies. Smoking was taboo among the younger women, but it was considered a courtesy to offer cigarettes to the **nonas** (grandmas), especially when drinking **kave turko**. When introduced to someone, the acknowledgement would be, **"Me da muncho gusto de konoserte."** ("It gives me great pleasure to know you.") **Konoser** means to recognize or know. Another word of acknowledgement that was used is **enkantado** (enchanted, charmed).

On greeting friends and relatives, some expressions are: **Buenos dias** (Good morning), **Buenas tadres** (Good afternoon), **Buenas noches** (Good evening or good night). **Vengan en buena ora**. How does one translate that expression? Come in the good hour? Enter in the good hour? A good translation might be, "I'm so glad to see you." The answer was "**Munchas gracias.**" ("Many thanks.") As our folks became more Americanized, they said, ***"Tenk you verry mahch."*** On taking leave of someone, the saying was, **Salud y vida** (health and life). If any danger was involved, the words would be **El Dyo ke te guadre** (May the Lord watch over you). Instead of saying goodbye when departing, the saying was **Kon bien ke amaneskas** (May your dawn be good), and the response was **Y ke amaneskas** (May your dawn also be good) – the English equivalent of 'likewise.' My mother used to say, ***"De sem to you."***

Kon salud ke lo gozes (Enjoy it in good health). That was said when someone **se estrena una koza mueva** (wore something for the first time). I used to say to my children, "Tear it in good health."

The young would show **merced** (respect) to their elders in the manner they addressed them. My mother was referred to as **Madam Sultana**, and my father as **Senyor Yusef**. Our revered Rabbi was called **Senyor Haham**, and they were always spoken to in the third person. Expressions were heard, like **"Le puedo dar al Senyor Yusef un sigariko?"**

("May I give Mr. Joseph a cigarette?"), or **"Le gustaria a Madam Sultana un vazo de agua?"** ("Would Madam Sultana care for a glass of water?") It was an honor to **bezar la mano del Haham** (kiss the rabbi's hand). He would place his hand on your head and utter a **bendision** (a blessing).

My mother made sure that I would address her first cousins as **tante** or **tio**, never by their given names. Friends of my parents were always Mr. or Mrs. **Fulano de tal** (Mr. or Mrs. so and so).

Many greetings were also expressed in Hebrew. **Shalom alehem** (Peace on you). The response was, **Alehem shalom** (On you peace!). On the Sabbath it was **Shabbat shalom** (a Sabbath of peace), the answer was **Shabbat shalom mevorah** (a Sabbath of peace and blessings).

RECIPE FOR KAVE TURKO

2 heaping teaspoons of Turkish coffee, 2 teaspoons of sugar, 2 **fildjanes** (Turkish coffee cups) of water. Mix the coffee, sugar and water in a **librik** (pot) and bring to a boil, remove from heat. Stir gently. Return to heat and bring to a boil. Cooking time 5 minutes. Serves two.

* * *

DJOHA – SAVIDO

Komo Djoha era el mas savido en la sivdad en ke el biviya, la djente siempre se ivan onde el por konsejo. Un dia un ombre muy viejo le demando a Djoha, "Es posible para un ombre de ochenta anyos de edad ke tenga kriaturas?"

Djoha le respondio, "Si, es posible si este ombre tiene vezinas ke son de vente o trenta anyos de edad."

WISE ONE

As Djoha was the wisest man in the city where he lived, the people always went to him for advice. One day a very old man asked Djoha, "Is it possible for a man of eighty years of age to have a child?"

Djoha answered him, "It is possible if this man has neighbors who are twenty or thirty years of age."

* * *

MELDADOS

Me akodro komo si fuera ayer (I remember as though it were yesterday). **Meldados** were held at home in remembrance of our dear departed. They were beautiful, memorable, solemn, and elaborate occasions. I was so profoundly impressed when the family got together for the purpose of formally remembering a deceased loved one, that I remember saying to myself, **"Kuando yo me ago grande, yo va azer lo mismo para mi padre y madre."** ("When I grow up, I am going to do the same thing for my father and mother.")

Several **meldados** were held each year, and the same rabbi was called to officiate. He was very old, had a long grey beard and an ever-present benevolent smile on his beautiful, wrinkled face. His name was **Haham** Sedacca. I was always warned, **"Kuando el Haham viene serka de ti, tomale la mano, bezala y el te va dar una bendision."** ("When the rabbi comes near you, take his hand, kiss it, and he will bless you.") There always seemed to be plenty of prayer books and yarmulkes in the house, but the rabbi brought some with him in case there was a shortage. The women covered their heads with scarves and, of course, shed a few tears.

Today, **meldados** are hardly, if ever, held at home. The practice now is to attend Saturday services in the synagogue and to make a donation in their memory. In the old days, instead of a **meldado**, some families went to the synagogue **para echar azete al kal** (to pour oil), light a **mecha** (wick) and make a donation in name of the deceased. My recollection of this gesture was as an expression of thanks in the event of a birth, a recovery from an illness, or a happy event.

The **meldados** had to be performed before the anniversary date, usually on the night before. Once the day was passed, it had to wait until the following year. The table was set with a beautifully embroidered table cloth that was used for holidays and the special occasions such as this one. A cut glass bowl partly filled with water and partly with oil was placed on the table with a three-pronged floating wick (**mecha**). They had figured out exactly how much oil and how much water to put in the bowl so that it burned for as long as it was supposed to. The **mecha** was lit when the name of the deceased was mentioned. It was permissible for a non-family member who was present to ask the rabbi to intone a prayer for a loved one. **"Senyor Haham, me aze el favor de echar hashkava por mi padre."** ("Esteemed Rabbi, would you please recite the prayer for my father.") It was customary to unobtrusively slip a token of appreciation to the rabbi for the service.

Rarely was it ever a problem to get a **minyan** (a quorum of 10). On the rare occasion that we would be short of a **minyan**, we knocked on doors in the building or my father sent me to the **kavane: "Aroniko, vate a la kavane y di le al kavanedji ke se kierre unos kuantos ombres para minyan en la kaza de Yusef Halio."** ("Aaron, go the coffee house and tell the owner that a few men are needed for a minyan at Joe Halio's house.") Half the **kavane** would empty out. My father was known as **hoovarda** (generous), and my mother was renowned for her **desayuno**. Once when a delivery boy came to the house to deliver a package, my father asked him if he was Sephardic and said that we needed a **minyan.** The fellow was very happy to accommodate. He knew the feast he was in for. After the services, out came the **burekas, filikas, kashkaval, keso blanko, biskochos, azetunas, la kerda, karpoose, raki** and of course **kave turko**.

Luto (mourning). **Asentar en siete** literally means to sit in seven; **Shiva** is the Hebrew word for seven. It was and still is proper to make a condolence call as a sign of respect to the family of the deceased. On greeting the bereaved members, phrases of consolation were expressed: **Mas ke no vos de el Dyo** (May the Lord give you no more of this); **Vosotros ke bivesh por munchos anyos** (May you live for many more years); **En paz deskanse** (May he rest in peace). At meal time all who were present were invited. **Es una onor asentar y komer kon la famiya en luto** (It is an honor to eat with the family in mourning).

* * *

DJOHA – DEDIKASION

Djoha estaba ensima de su azniko y el azniko estaba kaminando muy avagar. El amigo, memet le demando, "Djoha, ande te estas indo ensima de este azniko viejo?" Djoha le respondio, "me esto indo al servisio de orasion. Memet le disho, "Loko estas?

Oy es Martes. El servisio no es asta Viernes. Djoha le respondio, "En este avagaroso azno, kale ke empeses en Martes para arrivar en Viernes."

DEDICATION

Djoha was on his donkey and the donkey was walking very slowly. His friend, Memet asked him, "Djoha, where are you going on that old donkey?" Djoha answered, "I am going to the prayer services." Memet said, "Are you crazy? The prayer service isn't until Friday." Djoha's response was, "On this donkey, I have to start on Tuesday if I want to get there on Friday.

* * *

PROVERBS

Ande te vas, aze lo ke veras.
Wherever you go, do as you see.
When in Rome, do as the Romans do.

Este mundo es un molino, bravo al ke lo puede aboltar.
This world is a mill, kudos to the one that can turn it around.
In today's vernacular one could say, "It's a rat race."

Mira kon ojos en kuatro.
Look with all four of your eyes.
Be extra careful, totally alert – have eyes in the back of your head.

BON VIVANT

That's what my Pop was, a 'Bon Vivant.' *Roget's International Thesaurus* gives many definitions of a 'Bon Vivant.' For example: polished, cultured, elegant, jovial, hale fellow, well met, man about town, devoted friend, lives the good life, etc., etc. Just to show that he was also human, I must say that many a time he was called **aksi** (cranky). A 'Bon Vivant' may also give the impression that he is a philanderer. Not my Pop. He was an 'eat, drink and be merry guy,' but he adored my mother. I have 8mm films to prove it.

Throughout the ages, songs, poems, ballads, and the like, have praised our Moms: *My Yiddisha Momma, Mother Machree, Mammy, Madre Mia* – all great songs. But how about dear old Dad? "I want a girl just like the girl that married dear old Dad," is about the only lyric I know about Dads. And that song refers to Dad only as an afterthought.

We must remember that Mom was with us twenty-four hours a day, while Pop was out making a living. We had Pop only for a few hours at the most. I have written about my Pop on occasion, but it has always been in a sort of comically affectionate way, and not with the heavy sentimentality of my writings about my Mom. Here's what I remember hearing when we acted up and Mom found it difficult to control us. **"Mira komo estos animalikos se estan koudouriando!! Agora los va fixearlos. Amoudisyon!! Si no vos kedash kayados, se lo vo a dezir a tu padre komo me estash kitando la alma kuando viene a kaza esta noche."** ("Look at how these little animals are carrying on! Now I'm going to fix them. Quiet!! If you don't keep quiet, I am going to tell your father that you are taking my soul out when he comes home from work.")

Okay, what does that tell you? Mom was a goody two-shoes, and that Pop was a villain! Not so. She never told Pop, although we imagined all kinds of wild punishments Pop was going to deal out, and we were scared to death in anticipation of what he was going to do to us. It never happened. Pop was a pussy-cat. When I was small and living in Harlem, in the summer my father sometimes came home during daylight hours. I used to play on 117th Street between Madison and Fifth Avenues. He'd stand on the corner and blow a special kind of whistle. I always heard it. No matter where I was – on first base, at bat, or wherever – I would drop everything, run to the corner and jump into his arms. He would carry me home. As time went by, I got too big for that and I came to realize it the day I almost knocked him over. That was the last time I ever did it.

Pop always had a little **raki** with **meze** (liquor and hors d'oeuvres) before dinner. If any of my cousins were around at that time, he would give them a taste of whatever **salata** (salad) he had prepared that evening. One of my little cousins loved the sliced boiled potato that was immersed in a vinegar and oil preparation. This little cousin used to say, "Uncle Jofes (Joseph) give me **mas** (more)." Pop would **untar** (dip) some bread into the salad and give it to him.

Back in the 1930's, most Sephardic families lived in neighborhoods like Bronx River Avenue, New Lots, Sea Beach, etc. My family lived on Bronx River Avenue in the East Bronx. This was one long street. When I say 'my family,' I mean my mother's brothers and sisters and their kids, my father's brothers and sisters and their kids and their **patriotis**. The whole **mispaha** (clan) celebrated and mourned together.

One night after a family celebration and a good bit of **vino, champagnya,** and **raki**, my father and my Uncle Joe, two legendary drinkers, feeling no pain, were walking home on Bronx River Avenue. Uncle Joe stopped at a lamp-post and started knocking on it with his knuckles, yelling, **"Jek, avre la puerta. El garon esta seko. Kierro ke me dez un poko de raki."** ("Jack, open the door. My throat is dry, I want you to give me a little **raki**.") My father said to him, **"Ke estas aziendo? Ya es tadre, vas a despertar a todos los vezinos. Ven a mi kaza, y te do todo el raki ke puedes bever."** ("What are you doing? It's late, you will wake all the neighbors up. Come to my house and I'll give you all the **raki** you can drink.") Uncle Joe wasn't going anywhere. He kept yelling, **"Jek si no me me deshas entrar, te va romper la puerta."** ("Jack, if you don't let me in, I'm going to break the door.") And he could do it. My father, who wasn't as far gone, said, **"Mira Pepo, Jek no te va avrir la puerta porke no esta en kaza."** ("Look Joey, Jack is not going to open the door because he's not home.") Uncle Joe pointed to the light at the top of the lamp-post and said, **"Ke estas avlando? No puedes ver la luz ariva? No me digas ke no esta en kaza."** ("What are you talking about? Can't you see the light up there? Don't tell me he isn't home.")

When pop had a 'glow on,' he used to say to me things like, **"Ijo mio, yo te va azer a ti un ombre del mundo. Te va ambezar a**

bever, komer y gozar, komo un verdadero kavalyero. Embezate de tu padre. Kuando te vaz a azer grande me vaz a bendizir. Y nunka te vaz azer sawree." ("Son, I am going make you a man of the world. I am going to teach you how to eat, drink and be merry, like a true gentleman. Learn from your father. When you get older you will bless me and you will never be sorry.") Man, did he ever do that!

After World War II, when many of the eligible bachelors returned home from the service, it was not uncommon for everyone who knew an unmarried man to get on his back to get married. All we ever heard was **"Tengo una ijika para ti!"** ("Have I got a girl for you!")

I lived on the Grand Concourse in the Bronx in those days. I had two cousins who also lived there and, of course, we would walk up and down the Concourse on nice days or evenings. That wouldn't last too long as it got embarrassing to hear the comments from our well-meaning friends and relatives. **"Mira a estos chapkines** (**chapkin** is a Turkish word for vagabond, rascal or single fellow on the prowl), **se van a azer viejos antes ke se van a kazar. Ya tendran serka de trenta anyos y mas. Ke estan esperando? Aye tantas ijikas ermozikas de las muestras sin kazar."** ("Look at them, they will become old men before they get married. They must be thirty and older. What are they waiting for? There are so many pretty girls of our own that are single.")

My father was the one dissenting voice. He would say, **"Una vez ke se kazan, van a ser enterrados en kazamiento por lo ke les keda de la vida. Deshalos ke bivan un poko."** ("Once they get married, they will be buried in marriage for the rest of their lives. Let them live a little.")

Whoever wrote the song **'La vida do por el raki'** ('I give my life for **raki**') had to have had a man like my father in mind. This is what people said about my Pop when he passed on: **"Halio se murio, in paz deskanse. Este era un ombre ke en vida, supo bivir."** ("Halio has died, may he rest in peace. This was a man who in life knew how to live.") People did not have to say Joe, or Yusef Halio, all they had to say was 'Halio.' He was one of a kind.

PICNICS

The great migration of Sephardim from Turkey occurred from around 1910 to 1920. The majority of these emigrants were men in their twenties and thirties, with little money and scant education. Yet in the space of one generation, with backbreaking effort, they were able to hammer out decent lives for themselves and their families. Very few of them accomplished anything in the academic field. That development was reserved for us, the first-generation Americans.

I must say that I had the good fortune to come into direct contact with some very well-educated Sephardim such as Mr. Albert Matarasso, Mr. David N. Barocas, Mr. Joe Kattan, Rabbi Robert Ouziel, and Mr. Albert J. Torres, who I am proud to say was to become my father-in-law. There were many other men of that caliber whom I did not have the honor of knowing personally.

In retrospect, I marvel at how my parents, relatives, and their friends grew with the times, however difficult. The businesses they went into required common sense rather than technical expertise. Many a fortune was made in the garment industry. Some became restauranteurs and fast-food operators, opening up hot dog stands and luncheonettes. Others went into retailing and door-to-door sales. I remember hearing one budding entrepreneur tell another, **"Yo puedo vender arena a un arabo!"** ("I can sell sand to an Arab!")

All their work was not for personal gain. They built synagogues on the Lower East Side, in Harlem, the Bronx, New Lots, Sea Beach and Queens. They formed burial societies – *The Sephardic Brotherhood* and *The Source of Life,* to name two; they formed social clubs – the *Broome and Allen Boys,* the *Sun-Ray Boys,* and more. They organized a theatrical group that staged plays in Ladino. Wouldn't that be an idea for today? The crowning achievement was the founding of *The Sephardic Home for the Aged* in Brooklyn.

It wasn't 'all work and no play' for them. They were a fun-loving people, always finding time to **enjoyar**. I remember one time my uncle Jack announced, **"Yo me merki una mashina mueva y este Alhad mos vamos a ir a Van Cortland Park y yo va traer la komida y**

bevienda." ("I bought a new car, and this Sunday we are going to Van Cortland Park and I am bringing the food and drink.") No one had ever heard of this park. **"Ande es este *pahk?*"** ("Where is this park?") His answer was, **"No te espantes ya lo topamos, la mashina mia save el kamino."** ("Don't be afraid, I'll find it. My car knows the way.") We drove around for over an hour. It was hot in the car. There was no air conditioning in those days and everyone was getting edgy. **"Ande mos estas yevando? A djenem yolu?"** ("Where are you taking us? On the road to hell?") **"Ya me va morir de ambre antes ke lo topes el lugar."** ("I'll die of hunger before you find this place.") My father said, **"Jeck, demanda a uno ke dravea taxi si save ande esta este maldicho *pahk*."** ("Jack, ask a taxi driver if he knows where this damned park is.") At the next light my uncle pulled up alongside a taxi and said, **"Hey, ijo de un azno** (Hey, son of a donkey), you know where is Van Cortland Park?" The cabby turned around and said, **"Las muelas ke te kaigan. Kien te disho ke yo so ijo de un azno?"** ("Your teeth should fall out. Who told you I was the son of a donkey?") They both got a big laugh out of it, and the cabby said, **"*All right* hamor** (donkey, in Hebrew), **ven detras de me y yo te yevo, ama kale ke me des a komer y bever."** ("All right donkey, get behind me I'll take you there, but you must give me food and drink.") One never knows, does one?

Prior to my uncle's acquisition of his new car, we used to go to Bronx Park, which wasn't too far from where we lived on Bronx River Avenue. In those days we traveled by hired truck. Practically the whole family lived in the same neighborhood. As many as thirty of us piled up in the back of the truck. We took our folding tables and chairs and enough food and drink to last a week. My father never went anywhere without his **raki** and **meze.**

If we got to the park early enough, our choice of a picnic area was near the waterfall. We carried a specially designed basket filled with a **karpooz** (watermelon), bottles of soda, beer, and **kezo blanko** (white cheese). Anything that needed to stay cold we lowered into the Bronx River. It worked better than the icebox we had in those days. What great times they were! The folks made their own music. All they needed was an **ood** (an oversized Oriental mandolin), a **pandero** (tambourine), and Uncle Nissim's clarinet. It didn't take long before all within earshot gathered around, swayed and clapped hands to our Oriental rhythm. The remarks I heard were, "Who are these people? Where do they come from? They don't look like Gypsies. They sure know how to enjoy themselves."

DJOHA – PERLAS DE AMOR

Djoha tenia dos mujeres. En akeyos dias era permitido tener dos mujeres. Despues de un poco de tiempo realizo ke kierriyan saver a kuala de eyas el amava mas. Para mantener pas en la famiya, las yamo a kada una separadamente y a kada una le dio una perla muy ermosa. En el mismo tiempo les disho a kada una ke no diga nada a la otra. Ke esto iva ser "muestro sekreto." Unos mezes pasaron y las dos mujeres lo konfrontaron a Djoha, y le demandaron, "a kuala de mosotros amas mas?" Djoha les disho, "Yo amo mas a la ke le presenti una perla muy ermosa."

PEARLS OF LOVE

Djoha had two wives. In those days it was permissible to have two wives. After a little time, he realized that they wanted to know which one he loved the most. In order to have peace in the family, he spoke to each one separately and gave each one a beautiful pearl. At the same time, he admonished each of them not to say anything to the other, that this would be "our secret." A few months passed and the two women confronted Djoha and asked him, "Which of us do you love the most?" Djoha's answer was, "The one I gave the beautiful pearl to."

* * *

MOM'S WASHBOARD

Our washer and dryer went on the blink, and my wife felt it was time to replace them rather than to try to have them repaired again. It happened just before the Labor Day weekend. Phyllis didn't like having unwashed laundry around for any length of time, and she still doesn't, but it brought back memories.

I remarked that my mother would not have had a problem with that. She was her own washer and dryer. She would take off her corset, roll up her sleeves, and go to work. Of course, times were different then.

The tenements we lived in on the Lower East Side of New York were railroad flats. The rooms ran one behind the other from front to back. The toilets were in the hall and were shared by all the tenants who lived on the same floor. The entrances to the apartments were almost always through the kitchen.

The kitchen was the main room of the house, except when we had company. Then we went into the 'parlor.' The kitchen served several functions. It contained the usual appliances, plus a washtub that was used to bathe in and wash clothes. We also had, if you remember, an electric meter that would put us all in shock when we had a 'power failure.' That happened if we didn't put a quarter into it at the proper time. If my father didn't have a quarter he would yell, **"Kien tiene un *kawreh*?"** ("Who has a quarter?") But I'm getting away from the story.

The washtub was divided into two sections. One section would be filled with boiling hot water and out of the closet would come the trusty old corrugated washboard. There were no detergents in those days. They used good old-fashioned Octagon soap, blueing (which came in a small blue bag), and backbreaking elbow grease to do the job. A broom stick handle was used to move the wash around, loosen up the dirt, and help cool the water so that they could start scrubbing the wash on the washboard. The washboard was very effective, especially when Mama put her 'back power' into it. The other section was filled with cool water to rinse the soap off.

The part Mom enjoyed most was when she went to the window in the back of the house to hang the wash out to dry. There was a clothes line attached to a pole about fifty feet away facing another building.

Do you remember the smell of the clothes after they were dried in the sun? The linen, the underwear, the starched shirts? Mom used to iron the underwear in those days. The shirts cost a nickel if they were sent to the Chinese laundry to be washed and starched, but when you have one boy, a husband and three of Mom's brothers living with you, it adds up to a lot of nickels. Mom found much better use for those nickels she saved.

Mom enjoyed hanging the wash on the line because it gave her a chance to gossip with her neighbors, especially when Pop wasn't around. A typical conversation went something like this:

Mama: Sehoula, ke ay de muevo? Ke mos kontas? Tu marido topó lavoro dayinda? Y tu ija komo esta? (Sehoula, what's new? What can you tell us? Your husband, has he found work yet? And your daughter, how is she?)

Sehoula: Todo esta bueno. Mi marido no esta eyelak mas. Topo lavoro ayer. Mi ija, el Dyo ke la guadre de nazar, esta prenyada otra vez. Y tu komo estas? (All is well. My husband is no longer unemployed. He found work yesterday. My daughter, may The Lord protect her from malevolence, is pregnant again. And how are you?)

Mama: Por lo mas esto buena. Solo ke me va y viene lo ke yaman aki en al Amerika un *migrate headek* ke me esta kitando loka. (Mostly, I'm all right. Only it comes and goes what they call here in America a 'migraine headache' that is driving me crazy.)

Sehoula: Vate al doktor pishin. Puede ser ke tienes un toomoh en el meyoyo. (Go to the doctor immediately. You may have a tumor of the brain.)

Mama: Loka estas? Yo no tengo toomoh en el meyoyo. Mira yo no tengo ora de avlar oy. Kuando eskapo de enkolgar la ropa me va vestir y me va ir al kal. Yo me ize '*society leddy*.' Me izyeron la presedente de el *Seesterhoo*. Y te kierro ver a ti y a todas tu amigas en el kal. (Are you crazy? I don't have a tumor of the brain. Look, I don't have time to talk today. When I finish hanging the clothes, I'm getting dressed, and I am going to the synagogue. I am now a 'society lady.' They made me the president of the sisterhood. And I want to see you and all your friends in the synagogue.)

BAR-MISVAH

Ladino Reveries is looking for old Bar-Misvah speeches written in Djudeo-Espanyol. If you have your old Bar-Mitzvah speech, please send it to Hank Halio, c/o the Sephardic Home For The Aged. We will print as many as we can with the proper credits.

The above notice appeared in the May/June 1987 issue of *The Sephardic Home News.* The following gentlemen graciously responded and sent me photocopies of their speeches. Sol Hattem, Tamarac, Florida; Morris Tarragano, New York City; and Morris Capeluto, Seattle, Washington. Mr. Hattem's speech was written by Rabbi Robert Ouziel; Mr. Tarragano's speech was written by Mr. Albert Matarraso; and Hazan Nessim Yeuda Israel wrote Mr. Capeluto's.

The translations are my interpretations of what these learned men had in mind at the time they were written. I knew and respected Rabbi Ouziel and Mr. Matarraso all my life. Rabbi Ouziel was a close friend of my parents and Mr. Matarraso was my Hebrew teacher. They were known and esteemed by all Sephardim in New York and probably in much of the United States. I did not have the honor of knowing Hazan Nessim Yeuda Israel of Seattle, Washington. In reading the original speeches you will notice the beautiful employment of our dying **Djudeo-Espanyol**. The flowery phrases, the almost forgotten niceties, the reverence and the constant use of the Hebrew phrases emphasize a feeling the writers wanted to project. We don't hear that type of talk anymore. As a matter of fact, the second-generation of American-born Sephardim have been totally robbed of this beautiful heritage.

Also observe the differences in the spelling of the same words in the speeches. Since there is no uniformity, it is evident that there was no formal arrangement of lexicography. Each scholar wrote phonetically, and I don't think any of these learned gentlemen would have found fault with one another. The pronunciation guide in the beginning of this book is influenced somewhat by these scholars. I've reproduced the spelling based on their original documents.

Hebrew translations are by Rabbi Abraham Deleon Cohen, and Rabbi Lester Hering.

Solomon Hattem, May 4, 1927

Rabbi Robert Ouziel
Shabbat, Iyar 2, 5674. May 4, 1927

Onorada asistencia i keridos parientes:

Oy es oun dia santo para mi. Yo vengo de coumplir mis treje anios, so oun בַּר מִצְוָה. De oy endelantre yo so contado como oun vero Joudio, gozando de los mezmos privilegios, ma tambien asoumando la responsabilidad de mis actos verso el Dio i la jente. Mientres ke mi kerido padre bendize al Dio de aver escapado de mi responsabilidad en diziendo בָּרוּךְ שֶׁפְּטָרָנִי מֵעָנְשׁוֹ שֶׁל זֶה. Yo en este dia entro en la grande i bendicha עֲדַת ה׳ so considerado como oun ermano de la compania de יִשְׂרָאֵל?

Mi corason es yeno de alegria i en mezmo tiempo yeno de favor. So mouy orozo de aver arivado a este momento en avansando oun paso mas adelantre en la vida. De oy endelantre so endependiente i responsable de mis acciones. Este cargo ke pezza sovre mi de agora endelantre aze levantar mis ojos a los cielos i rogo por la proteccion del Dio.

Mis keridos parientes no son mas mis guardianes espirituales, i yo siendo tierno de edad i sin experiensa en la vida, rogo al Dio santo de conservar mis mouy keridos padre i madre por longos anios para ser giado por sus buenos consejos, para ser giado en el camino derecho i devinir oun ombre bueno para el Dio i bueno por la jente.

Keridos parientes, a mi es imposivle de dizirvos mis sintimientos de amistad i no se como rengraciar vos por todas vuestras buendades ke izitesh i azesh con mi. Vuestros sacrificios fueron grande para presentarme oy delantre del Dio como oun ijo de la bendicha nasion de יִשְׂרָאֵל?

Prometo en este momento sacro de afirmar el comando de כַּבֵּד אֶת אָבִיךָ וְאֶת אִמֶּךָ en siendovos fiel, amarvos i respectarvos siempre. Mas tambien prometo delantre el Dio santo i delantre esta respectar congregasion de ser oun vero Joudio de caminar en el camino derecho i azer mi dover como desendiente de esta noble i alta rasa.

Los תְּפִילִין ke visto de agora endelantre me aran acodrar mis sinceras prometas i rogo al Dio de darme la fuersa por acoumplirlas. El Dio בָּרוּךְ הוּא nos amostro dos caminos el bueno i el malo, i mos dio la libertad de escojer el ke mos gousta.

רְאֵח נָתַתִּי לְפָנֶיךָ הַיּוֹם אֶת הַחַיִּים וְאֶת הַטּוֹב אֶת הַמָּוֶת וְאֶת הָרָע ma El con sou amistad i kerensia nos conseja de seguir el camino bueno, derecho i jousto, el camino de las vidas buenas וּבָחַרְתָּ בַּחַיִּים לְמַעַן תִּחְיֶה אַתָּה וְזַרְעֶךָ.

O Dio de אַבְרָהָם יִצְחָק וְיַעֲקב muestros padres i Dio de todo el ouniverso, acorda a mi, oun corason bueno i limpio para ser oun vero Joudio i oun ombre onesto.

לֵב טָהוֹר בְּרָא לִי אֱלֹקִים וְרוּחַ נָכוֹן חַדֵּשׁ בְּקִרְבִּי. Dame la oportounidad durante mi vida de ser provechozo para mi pueblo i ser tambien oun sincero sivdadino para mi bendicho payis.

O Dio santo i piadozo manda tous bendiciones sovre mis keridos padre i madre i parientes, acordales vidas largas con saloud i bien.

O Dio yeno de mercedes bendize a todos los ke estan aki recojido i coumple demandas buenas de sous corasones, Manda tou salvaciones i rigme tou puevlo יִשְׂרָאֵל?

אָמֵן. (Amen)

Solomon Hattem, May 4, 1927

Honored Congregation and Dear Parents:

Today is a sacred day for me. I have completed thirteen years of life, I am **Bar Misvah** (I am of age). From this day forward I am considered a true Jew, enjoying the same privileges, but at the same time assuming the responsibility of my actions before God and our people. My dear father thanks God for my having reached the age where I am no longer his responsibility in saying **Baruh shepetarani meonsho shel ze** (Praised be he who hath released me from the responsibility of this one). On this day I enter the great and blessed **Adat Ashem** (Congregation of God). I am considered a brother of the company of **Israel**.

My heart is full of joy and at the same time full of love. I am very proud to have arrived at this moment, to have advanced another step forward in my life. From this day on I am independent and responsible for my actions. This burden that weighs on me from now on makes me raise my eyes heavenward and pray for the Lord to protect me.

My dear parents are no longer my spiritual guides and I, being of a tender age and without experience in life, pray to God to sustain my dear parents for many years so that I may be guided by their good counsel to help me choose the right path in order to become a man for God and our people.

Dear parents, it is impossible for me to relay my sentiments of love, and I don't know how to repay you for all your goodness toward me. Your sacrifices were many in order to introduce me today before God as a son of our blessed nation **Israel**. I promise in this sacred moment to affirm the commandment, **Kabed et aviha veet imeha** (honor thy father and thy mother), to be loyal, to love and respect you always. I further promise before God and this respected congregation to be a true Jew, to walk the righteous path and to do my duty as a descendent of this noble and exalted race.

The **tefilin** (phylacteries) that I will wear from this day on will be a reminder of my sincere promises, and I pray to God for the strength to execute them. God, **Baruh U** (Blessed be His name) shows us two paths, the good and the evil, and grants us the liberty to choose whichever we wish.

Re'eh natati lefaneha hayom et ahayim ve'et hatov et hamavet ve'et ara (Behold, today I am giving you the life and the good, the death and the evil...), but He in His wisdom and love advises us to choose the good path, the straight and narrow path of the good life. **Uvaharta bahayim lema'an tihye ata vezareha** (And you shall choose life in order that you will live, you and your generations to come). Oh God of **Avraham, Yitzchak, Veyakov** (Abraham, Isaac and Jacob) our fathers and God of all the Universe, grant me a good clean heart to be a good person and a true Jew.

Lev tahor birra lee elokim vorvah nahon hadesh bekirbee. (God has created within me a pure heart and a proper spirit.) Grant me the opportunity during my lifetime to be productive for my people and to be a sincere citizen of my blessed Nation. Oh, Heavenly Father convey your blessings upon my dear father, my mother and relatives. Grant them long and healthy lives. Bless all who are gathered here today, grant them the good wishes of their hearts, and send salvation to our people **Israel**.

Amen.

Morris Murray Tarragano, January 14, 1933

Honorable Albert Matarasso
Shabbat, Tevet 16, 5693. January 14, 1933

Karo Padre, Madre, Nono, Nona, i Onorada Asistensya:

Azen tredje anyos ke yo vidi la looz de este moondo. Myentres estos anyos vooestros penseryos eran sovre mi. Kon mootcho goosto yo miro atras a estos anyos de la tchikes, anyos ke me velatesh kon mootcho kooydo. Dias ke me fueron aklarados por los ojos senseros de mi kara madre i guiados por los konsejos de mi karo padre. Oy yo entyendo todo el lavoro ke ash etcho por mi, asta agora. Kooanta pena i ansya yo vos kavzi.

Tredje anyos de mi vida an passado. I sigoon la ley Djoodia yo devengo Bar Mitsvah. Oon ijo de la aliansa de Israel. I so kontado entre los responsables. Oy yo bolto oona oja enteramente noeva en la estorya de mi vida.

Delantre de mi se avre el kamino de doveres i aktividades. La tchikes, kon soos doolses esfooenyos se va de mi. La seryedad de la vida, kon soos myedos i esperansas se aserka de mi. En la vida ay defikoltades. Kooalo devra todavia sostenerme a bivir kon amor i dinyidad? Kooalo devra salvarme de kayer en pekado? Nada ke solo la fey i kreensa en Dyo, i doovido a esto yo ádresso a Dyo la orasyon sigooente.

Meldamos en la biblia ke kooando el Rey Salomon devino rey en Israel. Dyo se le aparesyo en esfooenyo i le disho, "Demanda kooalo dezeas a ke yo te de" i el Rey Salomon no demando ni longa vida, ni rikezas, ni glorya. Solamente el demando por oon לֵב חָכָם וְנָבוֹן לְהָבִין בֵּין טוֹב לְרָע oon korasson savyo i de entendimyento por apartar entre lo booeno i lo malo. Dyo estoovo mooy kontente de la demanda de Salomon i le Dyo no solo lo ke demando ma i lo ke no demando.

Tambyen i yo en esta santa ora, rogo a Dyo por oon לֵב תָכָם וְכָבוֹן oon korasson savyo i de entendimyento, por pooeder konosser entre lo booeno i lo malo. Por pooeder apresyar las ermoozooras de nooestra santa ley. Az de mi o Dyo! oon ombre pertenesyente a nooestra rassa. La ke tyene oona estorya de glorya, i nobleza. Inspirame de los exempyos de nooestros grandes

ombres. Ombres ke soos nombres estan escritos kon letras de oro en las ojas de nooestra istorya. Deshame ser oon verdadero Jidyo i oon booen ombre. Dame el poder de ovedesser too santa ley. Deshame ser oon sensero sivdadino de este gloryozo paez. Deshame engrandesser por realizar las esperansas de mis paryentes. Por ke ansi soos lavoro no sea en vazio.

I vosotros mi karo padre i kara madre! Messajeros de Dyo en la tyera me protejatesh. Me kooydatesh! I izitesh todos los sakrefisyos por mi byen estar. No ay byervos por agradesservos. Pardonadme todas mis koolpas i yeros.

O Padre de syempre! Manda toos bendisyones i salood a mi karo padre i kara madre, alarga soos vidas de mi respektado Nono i Nona. Por ke ansi vean en lo booeno de soos ijos. Bendize a mis ermanas i a todos los de mi famia. Ansi ke a todos los reoonidos aki i a todo too Pooeblo Israel.

Amen.

Morris Murray Tarragano, January 14, 1933

Dear Father, Mother, Grandfather, Grandmother and Honored Guests:

Thirteen years ago I first saw the light of this world. During these thirteen years your thoughts have been on me. I look back on the years of my childhood with great pleasure. For years you watched over me with great care. Days that were enlightened for me through the sincere eyes of my dear mother, and guided through the advice of my dear father. Today I understand all the work you have done for me until now and how much work and anxiety I caused you.

Thirteen years of my life have passed and according to Jewish law, I am **Bar Misvah** (of age), a son of the Alliance of Israel, and I am considered among the responsible. Today I turn an entirely new page in the story of my life. A path of duty and activity is unfolded before me. Childhood, with its sweet dreams, is no longer with me. The solemnity of life with its fears and hopes confront me. There are difficulties in life. What will support and sustain me to live with love and dignity? What will save and prevent me from falling into sin? Nothing but the faith and belief in God.

In this regard, I dedicate the following prayer to God: We read in the bible that when Solomon became king of Israel, God appeared in a dream and said to him, "Ask for what you wish me to give you." Solomon did not ask for long life, nor riches, nor glory. He asked for **Lev haham venavon lehavin ben tov lera**. (A wise, understanding heart and knowledgeable men to help him distinguish between good and evil.) God was very pleased with Solomon's request and gave him not only what he asked, but also what he did not ask for. I, also in this sacred hour, pray to God for **Lev haham venavon** (a wise and understanding heart), in order to distinguish between good and evil, so that I may appreciate the beauty of our sacred law.

Make of me Oh Lord, a man worthy of this race that has a history of glory and nobility. Inspire me to exemplify our great men, men whose names are inscribed in letters of gold on the pages of our history. Allow me to be a true Jew and a good person. Grant me the power to obey thy sacred law. Permit me to be a sincere citizen of this glorious nation. Let me grow to attain the hopes of my family. For in that manner their labor shall not have been in vain.

You my dear father and dear mother, messengers of God on earth, you protected, cared for me and made sacrifices for my well being. There are no words with which I can express my appreciation. Please pardon my errors and transgressions.

Oh, Everlasting Father, send thy blessings and health to my dear father and dear mother so that they may enjoy the fruits of their labor. Bless my sisters and everyone in my family. Lengthen the lives of my dear grandparents. Bless all who are here today, and all the people of Israel.

Amen.

Morris Capeluto, February 18, 1944

Hazan Nessim Yeudah Israel

Shabbat, Shevat 24, 5704. February 18, 1944.
Seattle, Washington

Ermanas y Ermanos:

Oy a la occasion de el complimiento de los tredge anios de mi vida, yo me paro enfrente de Dios y de esta Santa Congregation. Con grande humilidad y sinceridad yo tomo sovre mis ombros la carga y responsabilidad de un ombre Judio, la cuala fue llevada por mi querido padre desde el dia de mi nacimiento.

Esta es una responsabilidad que traye honor y denyidad a aquel Judeo que la accepta con lleno entindimiento y buen corason. Enshalshado es aquel miembro de la communidad Judia que assiduosamente practica la ley, las tradiciones y las encomendansas sigun ordenas de Dios y de nuestros Hahamim. Puesto en sia de honor es aquel precioso anio de la cadena que forma la nacion Judia, que siempre esta pronto a luchar por el bien estar de sus coreligionarios esparsidos en las cuatro partes de el mundo.

Oy en estos dias en los cualos, trajedia y dolor covre el seno de la tierra, en estos dias en los cualos suffriensas encreivles son afflictadads sovre nuestros hermanos Judios en el inferno que oy es la Evropa, la importansa de mi complimiento de minian assuma un grado mas serioso. Y es que en addision a los doveres religiosos que son demandados de nos por el santo Dios y nuestros Hahamim, se ajunta la enorme responsabilidad de tomar entereso y prestar ayuda en todas las maneras possibles a los millones de nuestros hermanos que son persecutidos por el onico cremen de ser nacidos de parientes Judios, como lo so yo y lo sosh vosotros.

Como miembro de idad de la Communidad Judia yo meto mis ombros con los vuestros allevar esta carga que nos pesga y nos va pesgar por muchos anios de el avenir, y ansi hacer lo que es possible para salvar cada alma Judia. Siendo solo en perpetuando la rasa Judia puedremos ser dinios de ser yamados pueblo escojido de el Dio.

Hermanos: Avrid el santo livro de Tehilim y bushcad el salmo hermoso que leye (Ine Ma Tov U Ma Naim Shevet Ahim Yam Yah-ad) Cuanto bueno y cuanto hermoso es la union y la hermandad. La verdadera riquesa de una communidad no se topa en la possession de valores materialas, sino que en la hermandad que existe entre sus miembros. Y este prencipio se applica a nuestra familla, a nuestra communidad, a nuestra nacion. Si y ala humanidad entera. Si la concordia, el amor y la ermandad penetrava entre todas las naciones de el mundo, cuanto mejor seria la suerte de la humanidad entera.

Yo como ombre Judio y miembro de esta Santa Congregation, Ezra Bessaroth, prometo de basar mi vida sovre encomendansas de el Santo Dio y de nuestros savios. Yo prometo de regular mis acciones en mis relaciones con el mundo en tala manera a trayer honor i allegria a vosotros i a mi querida famiya. Y sigiere siempre los caminos derechos sigun prescribe nuestra ley santa y ansi trayer contentes a mis queridos padre y madre.

Senioras y seniores: Antes de acavar mi chico descorso, me ago el sagro dover de publicamente rengrasiar a mis queridos padre y madre. Vosotros que siempre estovitesh prontos a hacer todo sacrificio disde el dia de mi nacimiento por asigurarme el cudio physical, moral y educasional, como todos buen padre y madre se esforsan a dar. Vos prometo en la presencia de el Santo Dios y de esta sagrada communidad que yo sere el ijo y el buen Judio que vos dezeash verme.

A mis queridos Gran Papa y Mama rogo que el todo poderoso les accorde vidas largas y contentes. Que la maldicha guerra sea acavada con victoria y vos retorne a vuestra casa sano y bivo a nuestro querido David, y tambien a todos los miliones de hombres en el servisio de la nacion.

A mis queridos tios y tias, los vijitadires de Portland y los de Seattle, los rengrasio por todos los cudios y las affecciones que siempre tuvieron por mi persona. En fin rengrasio a todos parientes y amigos que tuvieron el plaser de onrarme con sus presencia. A mis instructores y a nuestro venerable Rabbino, y rogo que el santo Dio vos accorde a todos vidas largas y allegres.

Beshiva Tova Deshenim Veraananim Yihiu Laad Amen. I Pray God to grant all long and happy lives. **Amen.**

Morris Capeluto, February 18, 1944

Brothers and Sisters:

Today on the occasion of the completion of thirteen years of my life, I stand before God and this sacred congregation. With great humility and sincerity I embrace the responsibilities and duties of a Jew, which have been carried by my dear father from the day of my birth.

This is a responsibility which brings honor and dignity to that Jew who accepts it with full knowledge and a good heart. Enshrined is that member of the Jewish community who assiduously practices the Law, traditions, and the commandments as ordered by God and our Rabbis. Placed on the throne of honor is that precious link of the chain that forms the Jewish nation, which is ever ready to strive for the well being of its co-religionists scattered throughout the four corners of the earth.

Today, in this time of tragedy and pain that cover the bosom of the earth, these days of incredible suffering that is being inflicted on our fellow Jews in the inferno that is Europe, the importance of my **Bar Misvah** (coming of age) assumes a very serious tone. And it is in addition to the religious duties that are asked of us by God and our Rabbis, the enormous responsibility further arises to take an interest and to help in every possible manner the millions of our brothers who are being persecuted solely for the crime of being born of Jewish parents as you and I are.

As a person of age and a member of the Jewish community, I join arms with you in order to carry the responsibility which will weigh heavily upon us for many years to come, and in this manner to do what I can to save every Jewish soul. Only by perpetuating the Jewish race can we deserve to be called the "Chosen people of God."

Brothers, open the holy book of **tehilim** (psalms) and find the beautiful Psalm that says **Hine ma tov uma naim, shevet ahim gam yahad** (How good and beautiful it is when brothers live in peace and harmony). The true richness of a community is not found in the possession of material assets, but rather in the brotherhood that exists within its members. And this principle is applied to our family, our community, our nation, yes, to all of humanity. When agreement, love and brotherhood spreads to all the nations of the world, how much better the fate of all humanity will be.

I, as a Jew and a member of this sacred congregation, *Ezra Bessaroth,* promise that my life's work will be based on the Commandments of God and our Elders. I promise to regulate my actions in my relations with the world in a manner that will bring honor and happiness to you and my dear family. I shall always follow the straight and narrow path as prescribed by our holy Law and in that manner bring contentment to my dear father and mother.

Ladies and Gentlemen, before I end my small speech, I make it my sacred duty to thank my dear father and mother publicly. You have always been prepared since my birth for any sacrifice to assure my physical, moral and educational well-being, as all good parents are dedicated to be. I promise you in the presence of our Sacred God and this sacred community to be the son and good Jew that you desire of me.

To my dear grandparents, I pray that our all merciful God grant you long and happy lives. That this cursed war end with victory and return to your house safe and sound our dear David, and all the millions of men in the service of our nation.

To my dear uncles and aunts, visitors from Portland and Seattle, I thank all for the care and affection you have had for me. Lastly, I wish to thank all the relations and friends who were kind enough to honor me with their presence. To my instructors and to our venerable Rabbi, **Besheva tova deshenim vera'ananim yihyiu laad amen** (I pray God to grant all long and happy lives).

Amen.*

*Note that in Seattle by 1944, writing Ladino in English characters was influenced by both modern Spanish and Ashkenazi Hebrew.

EL HAHAM Y EL PAPAZ

The Sephardim have a great sense of humor as illustrated by the **Djoha** stories and the folklore our folks handed down to us. In order to lighten up the atmosphere in a house of mourning, the more resourceful rabbis would often tell a lightly humorous story to prove a point: **La riza no se puede kontener** (The smile, or a laugh, cannot be withheld).

A good many years ago I paid a condolence call at the home of one of my cousins. After the third or fourth day of the **siete (shiva)**, the rabbi told this story:

Un haham y un papaz se enkontraron en un treno, en kamino de Izmir a Istanbol. Se pasaron muy bueno echando lashon sovre munchas kozas, ama tomando muncho kudyado para no avlar de los deferentes religiones ke representavan. Despues de unas oras, le vino ambre al papaz. El kito de su aldikera una papelera ke tenia un pedaso grande de karne ke era de puerko. De la otra aldikera, un pedaso de pan, y una ridoma de leche kon un vazo.

Viendo ke el haham no estava komiendo, el papaz le ofresio al haham la mitad de la karne, el pan, y la leche. Al haham le vino boulanteez, y iva a gumitar. Ama siendo un ombre muy kebar, se kontenyo. Le Dio las grasias al papaz y le disho, "Komo tu saves, yo so Djudio y la ley Djudia dize ke no se puede komer karne kon leche y espesialmente karne de puerko."

El papaz le disho al haham, "Esta karne es muy savrosa y tu no saves lo ke te esta mankando en la vida por no poder komerla."

El haham le disho al papaz ke ay deferentes leyes en las religiones y kada uno deve soportar sus leyes. "Por ejemplo, la religion Djudia desha al haham ke se kaze y ke tenga kriaturas."

El haham le demando al papaz, "Diga me, komo esta tu mujer?" El papaz le respondio, "Tu saves ke yo no tengo mujer. Es prohibido en la religion mia para un papaz ke se kaze, y no deve de tener kriaturas."

El haham, riendose, le disho al papaz, "Ke pekado, ke no te deshan kazar y tener kriaturas. Tu no sabes lo ke te esta mankando en tu vida!!"

THE RABBI AND THE PRIEST

A priest and a rabbi met on a train on the way from Izmir to Istanbul and conversed about many things, both being very careful not to discuss the different religions they represented. After a few hours, the priest got hungry. He took out of his pocket a paper bag that had a big piece of meat that was pork, out of the other pocket, a piece of bread and a bottle of milk with a glass.

Seeing that the rabbi was not eating, he offered the rabbi half of the meat, bread, and milk. The rabbi became nauseated and was about to throw up. But being a man of good breeding, he contained himself, thanked the priest and told him, "As you know, I am a Jew and Jewish law says that we cannot eat meat with milk, and especially meat from a pig."

The priest told the rabbi, "This meat is delicious, and you don't know what you are missing in your life by not being permitted to eat it."

The rabbi told the priest that there are different laws in the religions, and each one is obligated to support his own. For instance, the Jewish religion allows a rabbi to marry and have children. The rabbi asked the priest, "Tell me, how is your wife?"

The priest answered, "You know I have no wife. My religion forbids a priest from marrying and having children."

The rabbi laughingly told the priest, "What a pity. Since you are forbidden to marry and have children, you don't know what *you* are missing in your life!!"

PROVERBS

Kien es riko? El ke esta kontente kon si.
Who is rich? The one who is happy with himself.

Lo ke es ermoso es lo ke plaze a ti.
Beauty is in the eyes of the beholder.

Un dia en la silya del rey es un dia.
One day on the throne of the king is one day.

ENLIGHTENMENT: TURKISH IN LADINO

One of the most enlightening and fascinating discoveries I made in researching and writing the columns for this book was the number of words we use in everyday Ladino that are actually Turkish words. Some of them are as follows: **mashala, patladear, kyoutouk, atavanado, ugursoos.** There are many others, but let's see what we can do with these.

Mashala: Means 'May the Lord preserve.'

Patladear: The true meaning of **patladear** is 'dying.' In most cases that I have heard the word, the connotation is 'to bust.' The best example that I can give is when a fish is caught and placed on the floor of the boat, it flip-flops gasping for air, until it dies. **Se esta patladeando**, means that it is dying.

Kyoutouk: A Turkish word meaning a 'tree stump.' Generally considered very hard wood. When someone is referred to as a **kyoutouk**, the reference is to his hard head. A stubborn, or thick person is called a **kyoutouk. Kyoutouk de bano** was the wood that was used to heat water for the bath (in those days there were no water heaters), since it was very hard and slow burning. My mother used to refer to me in exasperation (but with affection) as **"kyoutoukito de bano!"**

Atavanado: Construed as someone who is eccentric or off-beat. In a column I wrote that a person who was **atavanado** was 'off the wall.' My friend, Abe Capon, set me straight in suggesting that since **tavan** is 'the ceiling,' **atavanado** has to be someone who is 'off the ceiling!'

Ugursoos: If someone was referred to as **un ugursoos**, we knew he was a bad person. A little research turned out to be very rewarding. **Ugur** in Turkish means 'luck.' **Ugursoos** carries the connotation of 'an evil, luckless person, or a bad omen.' Hence, one called an **ugursoos** is someone to be avoided.

We go an entire lifetime using words that we really do not know the true meanings of. For instance, we have all heard the expression, **'Es un Lehli.'** I, of course, 'knew' that it referred to an Ashkenazi. We all know that when you add **'li'** to a person it indicates the city the person was born in: such as **Izmirli, Stambuli,** and so on. That in itself should have given me a clue as to the origin of the word. A Turkish dictionary provided the answer. Lo and behold, I discovered that **Leh** is the Turkish word for Poland. Thus **Lehli** means a person from Poland.

* * *

POSTEMAS DE UN PADRE

Dos amigos se enkontraron por la kaye y uno le demando al otro, "Ke tal esta tu ijo? Esta estudyando?"

"Si, me dize ke esta estudyando shimistra."

"Y ke lavoro puede azer kon este estudyo?"

"El me dize ke va tomar lodo y lo va pueder azerlo oro."

"Kreyes ke va a reushir?"

"Esto es lo ke te puedo dezir, yo le esto dando oro, y el lo esta aziendo lodo."

THE PROBLEMS OF A FATHER

Two friends met on the street. One asked the other, "How is your son? Is he studying?"

"Yes, he says he is studying chemistry."

"And what kind of work can he do with this study?"

"He says he will make gold out of mud."

"Do you believe he will succeed?"

"This is what I can tell you, I am giving him gold and he is making mud out of it."

* * *

SHEETS

The old folks had a rough time with the English language. One day, when I was in grade school, my mother was talking with my **Tante** Zimbul (later changed to **Tante** Jenny). To the best of my recollection, here's how the conversation went:

Mom: Mira Zimbul, me alegro ke venites por aki agora. Tienes tiempo para venir kon mi? Ya se ke kale ke te vayas a kaza temprano para dar a tu familya a komer, ama tengo de *shapear* por unas kuantas kosas y kierro ke vengas kon mi. Tengo de menester savanas y fundas de kavesales, y unas bavajadas. (Look Zimbul, I'm glad that you came by now. Do you have time to come with me? I know you have to get home early in order to feed your family, but I have to shop for a few things. I need sheets, pillow cases, and a few knik-knaks.)

Tante Zimbul: Seguro ke tengo tiempo. Vamos! (Of course I have time. Lets go!)

Mom: Las savanas y las fundas de los kavesales se estan arazgando kada vez ke las lavo. Ya se izyeron viejas y kale ke merke muevas. Ama no se komo se dize savanas y fundas de kavesales en Ingles. Puede ser ke Aroniko save. Ven, le demandamos. Aroniko, ven aki, komo se dize savanas y fundas de kavesales en Ingles? (The sheets and pillow cases are tearing every time I wash them. They are getting old and I must buy new ones. But I don't know how to say sheets and pillow cases in English. Maybe little Aaron knows. Come, we'll ask him. Little Aaron, come here, how do you say sheets and pillow cases in English?)

Me: Ma, por funda de kavesal, se dize, *'pillow case,'* y por savana, la palavra es *'sheet.'* (Ma, for **funda de kavesal**, you say *'pillow case,'* and the word for **savana** is *'sheet.')*

Mom: Ke estas avlando? (Disho con kara soflamada.) Aroniko se esta burlando de mosotros. Esta palavra, *'sheet'* es palavra suzya. Me demando: Tu saves lo ke estas diziendo? What are you saying? (She said this with a red face.) Aaron is making fun of us. This word *'sheet'* is a dirty word. She turned back to me and asked, do you know what you are saying?

Me: Ma, kreye me. La palavra por savana, es *'sheet.'* La otra palavra ke estas pensando, es muy semejante, ama es diferente. (Ma, believe me. The word for **savana** is *'sheet.'* The other word you are thinking of is very similar, but it is different.)

Mom: (Abolto a su ermana y disho:) Ah si biva yo, yo no puedo ir al estor y dezir, *'Please meester geev me sheet.'* Les van a pareser ke so mujer de las kayes. Ke vamos a azer? (She turned to her sister and said: As I live and breathe, I cannot go into the store and say, 'Mister please give me *'sheet.'* They are going to think I am a woman of the streets. What are we going to do?)

Tante Zimbul: Mira Sultana, traelo a Aroniko kon mosotros. Deshalo <u>a el</u> ke demande por las savanas, y veremos ke va pasar. (Look Sultana, bring little Aaron with us, and let <u>him</u> ask for the *'sheets,'* and we'll see what happens.)

It took a long time to get Mom to understand the difference between the two words (I hope you all know the <u>other</u> word I am referring to). I don't think she ever really did believe there was a difference. Mom's conclusion was that English is a crazy language. She remarked that neither in Spanish nor in Turkish are there any words interchangeable with two such meanings. When my Mom and my aunt thought I was not around, I overheard them pronouncing *'sheet'* over and over again.

STANTON STREET

My friend, Sam Zalma, sent me an audio cassette tape relating his experience as a young boy growing up on the Lower East Side. Some of you may have had the same experience.

Sam lived at 85 Stanton Street on the sixth floor. One day his friend, David Saragossi (he called himself *Syracuse*), picked up an empty pack of Murad cigarettes. Those cigarettes were one of the few packs of cigarettes, in those days, that were packed in a hard box.

Sam and Syracuse, who lived across the street from each other, each took one half of the box of Murads up to his own house. Each punched a hole at the bottom of the inside of his box and knotted a long string in them. They each lowered the other end of the string to the street below where Sam's sister was waiting. She tied the two pieces of string together, and both boys pulled the tied string until it was stretched across the street.

Sam's words: "Would you believe it? We actually spoke to each other. We made up a set of signals as to when we would talk to each other over our own communication system. When one spoke, the other would hold the Murad box to his ear and listen, and visa versa. It was like having our own private telephone. I don't remember where the idea came from. It may have been something we heard about in school. Pretty soon, every building on Stanton Street had strings strung across the street from one building to another. It wasn't long before an official from the city came around and made everyone take the strings down."

My friend, Ike Beresid, passed away on January 4, 1994. He was not only a dear friend, he was a great source of inspiration to me. He would, in his gentle and congenial way, prod me with phrases like:

"Aroniko, ke te akodras de tus djenetores kuando te estavas engrandesiendo?" ("Hank, what do you remember about your parents when you were growing up?") **"Komo era la vida biviendo *dahntahn* kuando eras chiko?"** ("How was life living down on the Lower East Side when you were small?") **"Kuando te embezates a avlar en Ingles?"** ("When did you learn to speak English?")

He would very often speak to me in Turkish, knowing that I didn't speak Turkish. He knew me well enough to know that eventually I would learn enough Turkish to give him an answer – which I did and am still doing.

On paying a condolence call to his beloved wife, Gertrude Beresid, I had a very interesting conversation with Ike's son-in-law, Sol Almira. Sol was born in Turkey and is fluent in Turkish. We had a little fun trying to converse in Turkish; it was no contest, but as usual, I learned something.

During the conversation we talked about religion. Somehow the trend went toward the holidays. Sol said something about **Roshana** that I had never heard. We all know that we celebrate **Roshana** for two days. The belief I had was that the exact date was not known, so in order to make sure that the holiday was properly celebrated, it was observed for two days.

Sol enlightened me with his version: **No ay errores, la ley es muy definitiva. El dia de Roshana nunka era en duda. De el tiempo de nuestro rey, Salamon, Roshana fue selebrada por dos dias. La razon siendo ke avia djente ke bivian en las sivdades, y djente ke bivian en los kampos. La djente de los kampos venian kon arabas y si avia luvya les tomavan mas tiempo porke los kaminos se azian de lodo. Y era muy duro para las arabas ke kaminen, entonses, lo izyeron por dos dias para akomodar la djente ke venian de leshos. Agora uno puede preguntar, "Si esto era el kavzo, porke no selebraron todos los dias santos por dos dias?" Buena pregunta, y yo no tengo la repuesta.**

There are no errors. The law is very definitive. The day of **Roshana** was never in doubt. From the time of our King Solomon, **Roshana** was celebrated for two days. The reason was that some of the people lived in the cities and others lived out in the fields. Those that lived out in the fields could only travel by wagon and that made it very difficult to attend the services, and if it rained, the country lanes became muddy, making it time-consuming and very difficult to travel. Now, one could ask, "If that were the case, why weren't all the holidays celebrated for two days?" Good question, and I don't have the answer!

DJOHA – AMBRETITIS

Un dia Djoha paso por la eskola de medisina. Dos estudiantes salyeron de la eskola para ir a komer. Los dos estudiantes lo vieron a Djoha kaminando serka de eyos, y vieron ke no esta podiendo kaminar bueno. La konversasion fue ansina:

Memet: "Saves ke hazinoora tendra este ombre?"

Selim: "Si. Este ombre tiene artritis."

Memet: "No puede ser, tiene rumatitis."

De uno al otro disheron, "Artritis." "Rumatitis."

Memet: "Mira, si tiene artritis, yo pago por la komida, si tiene rumatitis, tu pagas por la komida.

Selim: "De akuedro."

Los dos se aserkaron a Djoha y le demandaron: "Senyor, mos puedes azer el favor de darmos una repuesta?" "Digame," les responde Djoha. Le demanda el uno, "Mosotros somos estudiantes de medesina, y keremos saver la hazinura ke tienes. "Es vedrad ke tienes artritis, o rumatitis?"

Djoha: "Si vos vash a komer, kumbidame a mi, y despues de komer vos digo lo ke tengo."

Los dos lo yevaron kon eyos, le dieron a komer y a bever, y esperaron la repuesta.

Selim: "Es vedra ke tienes artritis."

Djoha: "No senyor."

Memet: "Vez? No te lo dishe? El tiene rumatitis!"

Djoha: "No es vedrad. Los dos estash yerrados. Estava muerto por komer. Agora ke tengo la tripa yena, no tengo ninguna maldad. Yo tenia ambretitis."

HUNGERITIS

One day Djoha passed by the school where people studied medicine. Two students were on their way to lunch. They spotted Djoha walking near them, and they saw he was having trouble walking. Their conversation went as follows:

Memet: "Do you know what malady that man has?"

Selim: "Yes, that man has arthritis."

Memet: "It can't be. That man has rheumatism."

They kept going back and forth, arthritis, rheumatism.

Memet: "Look, we'll ask him. If he has arthritis, I'll buy lunch, if he has rheumatism, you pay for lunch."

Selim: "Agreed."

They approached Djoha and they asked him: "Sir, could you do us the favor of giving us an answer?" "Tell me." Djoha said.

One of them asked Djoha, "We are medical students and we would like to know what malady you have. Is it true that you have arthritis or rheumatism?"

Djoha: "If you are on your way to lunch, invite me, and after lunch I'll tell you what I have."

They took him with them, and after eating and drinking, they waited for his answer.

Selim: "Is it true that you have arthritis?"

Djoha. "No sir."

Memet: "Didn't I tell you? He has rheumatism."

Djoha: "It isn't true. You are both wrong. I was dying of hunger. Now that my stomach is full, I have nothing wrong with me. I was suffering from hungeritis."

* * *

SUPERSTITION

Superstition played a dominant part in the everyday lives of the Sephardim who migrated to this country in the early part of the century. **Ajos** (garlic) was important in averting **nazar** (evil eye). I'll bet if you look in the glove compartment of a car owned by a Sephardic, you will find a clove of garlic. **Klavos** (cloves) and a gold coin had a place in the crib of a new born baby. My earliest recollection, when I was old enough to understand, is the following: When my mother was in a hurry and had to sew a button or anything on clothing I was wearing, she would have me recite this poem with her:

Mom: Ensima de kien kusgo? (Upon whom am I sewing)?
Me: Ensima del rey de Fransia. (Upon the king of France).
Mom: Ansi ke no es verdad, (Since this is not true),
Me: El ke tenga mis ansyas, y yo ke tenga sus ganasyas.
(He should have my problems, and I should have his wealth).

I have a feeling there was more to it than that, but I can't recall the rest. When I was old enough to ask questions, Mom told me that it was something that her mother did for her when she was a little girl and she wouldn't feel comfortable if she didn't carry on with the tradition. I found out later on that the reason for the poem was to ward off evil. The only time anything was sewn on a person was when the **mortaja** (shroud) was sewn.

The Sephardim had a very interesting custom regarding life and death in their custom of preparing their own **mortaja.** Preparing the **mortaja** was a ritual dating back many centuries and was practiced in their old age.

Era el kustumbre de los Djudios de las Balkanas, de uno ke tuvo el mazal de kumplir sesenta anyos de edad, para selebrar kon el preparasion de la mortaja. (It was the custom of the Jews of the Balkans that one who had reached the ripe old age of sixty would celebrate by preparing for his/her shroud.) The logic behind the custom probably was to celebrate a long life.

Their outlook was not one of defying death, but one of courage. **Miravan al ojo de la muerte sin espanto** (They stared death in the eye not in defiance, but without fear), and that death would bow its head before them. I surmise that in those days, at sixty, people were considered very old. The ceremony was a festive one, with many members of the family present, singing, dancing and feasting. The recipient was made to lie on the floor, while the attendants cut and sewed the material to be used for the shroud, which, by the way, was always white. Those not involved in the actual sewing were busy having a good time. Strangely enough, the **mortaja** was sewn with a pocket in it. Why would a pocket be sewn on a shroud? Good question. Believe it or not, the pocket was used for a bar of soap.

I dug into my files and came up with a letter from Murray Tarragano asking if I ever heard of **mortaja**. I had, but I was reluctant to introduce any morbidity into my stories. Murray's letter, however, lent some levity to the subject.

"In the late twenties and thirties, my mother, Rachel Tarragano, was a member of the Women's Sewing Circle at *The Sephardic Jewish Center* on 115th Street in Harlem. The major project of each member was to sew her own **mortaja**. Its completion was the signal for the members to celebrate. They threw **konfites** (Jordan almonds) and other items customarily used in these celebrations. Years later, when cousins got together at our house in the Bronx, we swapped stories. My cousin [Murray's] Alice Amira, on hearing this story, laughed and asked with tongue in cheek, **"Kuando se les eskapa la mortaja, se les dizen, kon salud?"** ("When the shroud is finished, do you say to them, wear it in good health?")

Another old custom: It was incumbent upon the newly-wedded bride to bear children as quickly as possible. That was the desire of the parents on both sides. Especially the paternal in-laws, since the first male and female babies would receive their first names; and we can't forget the husband – he would want the family name perpetuated.

In the event that a birth was not forthcoming in a reasonable time and sterility was suspected (never in the male, in those days), certain steps would be taken. One of the more common methods was to hang three jars between two heavily laden fruit trees. One jar was filled with sugar water, another with rose water and the third with water from a nearby well that had been blessed by the local Rabbi. The lady in question would drink from the three jars, and the local **ichizera** (witch doctor), for a fee, would intone some mumbo-jumbo, probably something like

'Esta maldad agora va a salir de tu puerpo' ('Now this malady will leave your body'), and the sterility would end. This ritual could only be effective if performed on the 15th day of ***Shevat* (Frutas)**, Jewish Arbor day. If it was the wrong time of the year and too long a wait for Arbor Day, there were other, less palatable, 'cures' for infertility.

* * *

DJUDIO BOVO NO AY* – YO VEYO ESTREYAS

Un Djudio estava kaminando en una kaleja en la sivdad de Izmir en shabbat a la tadre. Ensupito vido en basho una koza briyante, y vido ke era una lira de oro. Se aboko para tomarlo, ma se akodro ke era Shabbat. El penso de si para si, "No keda muncho tiempo para ke se eskape Shabbat. Yo puedo esperrar aki asta ke veyo kuando salen las primeras estreyas. Ansina no sera pekado kuando toko la lira." Entonses se metyo el piye ensima de la lira para ke no lo vierran otra djente.

El estava en medio de la kaleja disturbando el pasaje de la djente. Un ombre paso muy serka de el y le dio una buena pizada en el piye ensima de la lira ke vido estreyas, y se disho de si para si, "Agora ke vide las estreyas, ya puedo tomar la lira."

THERE ARE NO DUMB JEWS – I SEE STARS

A Jewish man was walking along the street in the city of Izmir late on Saturday afternoon. All of a sudden he saw on the ground a shiny object and realized that it was a gold lira. He bent down to pick it up, but he remembered it was the Sabbath. He said to himself, "There isn't much time left before the Sabbath is over. I can wait here until I see the first stars. That way it won't be a sin when I touch the lira." He then put his foot on top of the lira so that no other people could see it.

He was standing in the middle of the street disturbing the passage of the people. One man came very close to him, stepping very hard on the foot that was on top of the lira. So severe was the pain of the blow that he saw stars. He said to himself, "Now that I have seen the stars, I can pick up the gold lira."

* * *

Djudio Bovo No Ay** was a weekly feature in the newspaper ***La Vara.

KOZA MUEVA MOS KITARON
A NEW FAD HAS COME OUT

Some of the better educated young Sephardim who migrated to America from Turkey in the 1909-1914 period learned to speak English very quickly by virtue of having been educated by the *Alliance Israelite Universelle.*

In a short time those young men spoke a presentable English, making it easier for them to find good paying jobs. Some of the sharper fellows went into sales, some knocking on doors, some cold canvassing, and I knew one who went to work as an agent for the Metropolitan Life Insurance Company. Who does one go to when starting out in sales? To friends and relatives – who else?

We all know that the marriages performed in Turkey were not all of the kind that were 'made in heaven.' You can imagine what went on in the Sephardic community when the wives heard that **Fulano de Tal** (Mr. So & So) bought life insurance to protect his wife and children in the event of his untimely demise. The prospects of selling life insurance to men who never heard of it were slim. The prospects of a second marriage for a widow with children in those days were even slimmer, unless by a wild coincidence there happened to be a widower with children around at the same time.

From nosing around, I was able to put together how a sales pitch might have gone. Let's call our intrepid insurance man, Nissim.

Nissim: Tio Bohor, yo esto vendiendo lo ke se yama *life insurance*. Aki en la Amerika todos los maridos merkan life insurance, porke kuando se mueren, y tu ke bivas por sien anyos, no kierren ke las mujeres y las kriaturas ke bivan en provedad.

Tio Bohor: Kuanto me va *kostar* esto? (Note the anglicized 'cost.')

Nissim: Es muy barato. Por dos mil dolares de segurita, te va kostar kuatro dolares al mes por vente anyos.

Tio Bohor: Loko estas? Saves kuanto devo de lavorar para ganar kuatro dolares? Y por vente anyos!! Diga me dos kosas; ke pasa si bivo vente anyos, y ke pasa si me muero antes de vente anyos?

Nissim: Si bives vente anyos, y ke bivas mas de sien, la kom-

paniya te da los dos mil dolares kon interes a ti, y si te mueres antes de vente anyos, la kompaniya le da los dos mil dolares a tu senyora, la Tia Boulisa.

Tio Bohor: Tu saves lo ke estas diziendo? Tu me dizes ke si bivo va pedrer, y si me muero va pedrer. En kualker kavso, yo so pedredor.

Nissim: Yo no entiendo esto.

Tio Bohor: Tu sos muy mansevo para entender, yo te lo espliko. Si bivo vente anyos va estar muy viejo para gozar las paras, y si me muero mansevo, el segundo marido de mi mujer se va gozar kon las paras mias.

(Agora la mujer abla.)

Boolisa: Mira, mi kerido, kale ke agas esto. Mira el hal ke le kaiyo zavali, a Sehoula y las kriaturas kuando el marido, Haskiya, se murio, y la desho sin un sentavo.

Tio Bohor: Si, y mira a la povereta Zafira. El marido Nahman, se murio y le desho munchas paras, elya se kazo kon otro antes ke el puerpo de el marido se le izo yelado. Si yo merko esta segurita, kuando yo me muero, tu segundo marido va tener muncha amistad kon mi, porke el se va kazar kon una mujer rika.

Nissim: Uncle Bohor, I am selling what is called life insurance. Here in America, all the husbands buy life insurance so that when they die, and may you live for a hundred years, they don't want their wives and children to live in poverty.

Uncle Bohor: How much will this cost me?

Nissim: It is very inexpensive. For two thousand dollars of insurance, it will cost four dollars a month for twenty years.

Uncle Bohor: Are you crazy? Do you know how hard I have to work to earn four dollars? And for twenty years!! Tell me two things. What happens if I live twenty years, and what happens if I die before twenty years?

Nissim: If you live for twenty years, and may you live more than a hundred years, the company will pay you two thousand dollars with interest, and if you should die before twenty years, the company will give your wife, Aunt Boulisa, the two thousand dollars.

Uncle Bohor: Do you know what you are saying? You are telling me if I live, I lose, and if I die I lose. In any event, I'm a loser.

Nissim: I don't understand this.

Uncle Bohor: You're too young to understand. I'll explain. If I live twenty years, I'll be too old to enjoy the money, and if I die young, my wife's second husband will enjoy my money.

(Now the wife talks).

Boolisa: Look my dear, you must do this. Look at the plight that befell poor Sehoula and her children when her husband, Haskiya, died and left her without a cent.

Uncle Bohor: Yes, and look at poor Zafira, when her husband, Nahman, died and left her a lot of money, she got married before his body got cold. If I buy this insurance, when I die, your second husband is going to love me because he is going to marry a rich woman.

* * *

DJOHA – SIN VER

Al tiempo la djente se kazavan sin ver el uno a otro. Este dezmazalado se kazo kon una mujer muy fea. Kada vez ke le via la kara, le veniya ganas de goumitar. En akeyos dias en Turkiya, las mujeres se tapavan las karas. Un dia la mujer le demando, "En frente de kien ke tenga la kara tapada, y en frente de kien ke la destape?" Djoha le respondio, "Delantre de kien kierres destapada, delantre de mi tapada."

SIGHT UNSEEN

In olden times people got married without seeing each other. Djoha married a very ugly woman. Whenever he saw her face, he felt like throwing up. In those days in Turkey, the women covered their faces. One day his wife asked him, "In front of whom shall I cover my face, and in front of whom shall I keep it uncovered?" He answered her, "You can keep it uncovered in front of anyone you wish, in front of me keep it covered."

* * *

CLEANING DAY

Friday was the usual cleaning day in our Sephardic homes. It also was the day for baking **desayuno**. The kids looked forward to Friday because of the goodies Mom baked. It was hard work, but our moms were young and strong, and could carry the load. As time went by and things got better, our moms started looking for help with their housework. They could use the leisure time to preserve their health and to devote the extra time to the synagogue and other charitable work. The usual arrangement was for the cleaning ladies to come to the house once every two weeks. In those days, for a couple of dollars and a meal, help was available. And they did windows! Do you remember how our Moms used to risk their lives sitting on the window sill five flights up reaching to clean all parts of the window? Thus, they were always on the lookout for someone to help with the housework.

One of the problems they encountered was communicating with the hired help. Their command of English was improving, but at best, it was difficult. One day my mother struck gold. A Mexican couple came to the door looking for work. The lady was hired on the spot, and my mother sent the man to my father's factory. It turned out to be a great setup. Mom got her housework done, and believe it or not, Mom learned a new language, 'Spanish,' albeit the Mexican version. By the same token, the lady learned Ladino. Of course, Mom shared her with the other ladies in the family. It was fun to listen to the women talk about the problems they had making Margarita understand what had to be done using Ladino, and then to hear Margarita speaking her Spanish.

A TYPICAL DAY WITH MARGARITA

Margarita: Senora, donde que empiece? (Madam, where shall I start?)

Mom: Kierro ke empeses kon el *fridjide*. (I want you to start with the refrigerator.)

Margarita: Que es el *fridjide*? (What is the *fridjide?*)

Mom: Aki, ande se enteza la karne, y pishkado para ke no se bozeye y ande se aze bouz. (Here, where the meat and fish is frozen so that they won't spoil and where ice is made).

Margarita: Senyora, ke es pishkado y bouz? (Madam, what is **pishkado** and **bouz**?)

Mom takes Margarita by the hand, leads her to the refrigerator, and says, **"Esto es el *fridjide*."** Mom takes out an ice cube and says, **"Esto es bouz."** Points to the fish in the freezer compartment and says, **"Esto es pishkado."** (This is the fish.) **"Ke es kon ti, no saves avlar Espanyol?"** ("What is it with you, can't you speak Spanish") By the way, fish in modern day Spanish is **pescado** when it is in the sea; when used for food, it referred to as **pez**.

Mom continues, **"Kuando eskapas alimpiando el *fridjide*, metelos chinis en la pila kon los pirones y lava las kucharas y los kuchiyos."** ("When you finish cleaning the refrigerator, put the dishes in the sink with the forks and wash the spoons and the knives.") In Mexican Spanish it should have been as follows: **Cuando acabas** (instead of **eskapas**), **limpiando la nevera** (instead of ***fridjide***), **pone los platos** (instead of **chinis**), **en el fregadero** (instead of **pila**), **con los tenedores** (instead of **pirones**), **y lava las cucharas y los cuchillos.**

"Despues, kierro ke laves la mushama y kuando se seka, mete gazetas en basho para ke se kede limpia." ("Then, I want you to wash the linoleum, and when it dries, put newspapers on it so that it stays clean.") When it appeared to Margarita that the work for the day was finished, she said, **"Si no hay mas trabajo, me gustaria ir a casa."** ("If there is no more work, I would like to go home.") Mom says, **"Kuando sales a la kaye, mete el sierko, y estos handrajos en el *gabich ken* y *tenk you verry mach*."** ("When you go out into the street, put the garbage and these rags in the garbage can, and thank you very much.")

While Mom's usage of Ladino baffled Margarita, she knew Mom was speaking a Spanish dialect of some sort. Still, it didn't take very long for both of them to get to know each others' intent. Some of the words Mom used were Turkish, such as **chini** for a plate; **bouz** for ice; **gazeta** for newspaper. The word **piron** comes from the Greek, for fork. In Ladino, we use the word **eskapar** to mean *to finish.* In modern day Spanish, **escapar** means *to escape.* In thinking about it, there is some reasoning in its use, when you finish something, in a sense, you are escaping from it. The modern word is **acabar**.

I keep referring to 'modern' Spanish. Again, one must remember, our people left Spain five hundred years ago, and we are still speaking the same language our ancestors spoke (15th century Spanish), with the addition of many Turkish words. In that span of time, the Spanish language in Spain itself has changed considerably. When we think of it, the English that was spoken in America in Elizabethan times, is not the same English that is spoken today. One must also take into consideration the fact that in Spain as well as in the U.S. and Turkey, different areas have dialects distinct to each region.

The Confusing Words Between Mom and Margarita

Ladino		English	Spanish
Booz	*T*	Ice	**Hielo**
Bozeyar	*T*	Spoil	**Dañar**
Chini	*T*	Plate	**Plato**
Enbasho	*L*	Floor	**Piso**
Entezar	*L*	Freeze	**Congelar**
Eskapar	*L*	Finish	**Acabar**
Fridjide	*E*	Refrigerator	**Nevera**
Gazetta	*T*	Newspaper	**Periodico**
Handrajo	*L*	Rag	**Trapo**
Mushama	*L*	Linoleum	**Lino**
Pila	*L*	Sink	**Fregadera**
Piron	*G*	Fork	**Tenedor**
Pishkado	*L*	Fish	**Pez**
Sierko	*L*	Garbage	**Basura**

T = Turkish origin *L* = Ladino origin
G = Greek origin *E* = English origin

DE NOVIO AND OTHER SAYINGS

From time immemorial, the newborn baby boy was labeled **el novio.** In the old days the circumcision was generally held in the synagogue. It was the custom that when the Rabbi signaled that he was ready to perform the circumcision, the women in the synagogue would summon the child by calling out, **"Ke salga el novio. Ke salga el novio."** Literally translated this means, 'May the groom emerge.' The intent is, let the baby come out. Then, of course, the regular chanting and ritual would commence.

De Novio, De Novio. From the days before my **Bar-Misvah** and afterward, I always went to the **Kehila** with my father on the high holy days. When I was **Bar-Misvah**, he would bid on the **Misvoth**. He would try to buy the one that offered the **Sefer Torah** so that I would be the one to carry it around the synagogue. It was a great honor, and if a young person was the carrier, the congregation would call out, **"De Novio, De Novio."** The intent being for good wishes to the young man for an early marriage. I would smile sheepishly, not really knowing the significance or the ramifications of such a step. All this led to the next phase which was that every time I attended or was an usher at a wedding, I would hear, **"Otro tanto de ti."** That phrase cannot be translated literally to convey the true meaning. What it means is, "It should happen to you," or "You're next." The trouble with that was that as I got older, the people, relatives and friends, were beginning to ask, **"Ayede bre, kuando?"** (All right already, when?)

For a girl it was a lot tougher. If a young Sephardic girl was past the age of eighteen and still not married or with no prospects in sight, these same well-meaning people would begin to lose patience or all hope that this particular young lady would ever marry. If by the age of twenty-one the situation had not changed, one would hear from some of the not-so-nice people these words about her, **"Este le gole, akel le fiede."** ("To her this one smells and that one stinks.")

As a little boy, I loved going to the synagogue with my father. When he was called to the **Tora,** all the men around him would say, **"Behavod."** (With honor and respect.) He would respond to the salutation by bringing his right hand to his forehead in the manner of the Turkish salute. This probably had its origin in Turkey, a habitual way of showing one's gratitude. On returning to his seat, those in close proximity would say in Hebrew, **"Hazak baruh."** (Be strong.) My father's reply was, **"Hazak tiye."** (May you be strong.) I had an uncle whose name was Izak Barouh. I was bewildered as to why my uncle's name was mentioned so many times in the synagogue, until I made the distinction between Izak Barouh and **Hazak baruh**.

I received a letter from my good friend, Ike Amira, in which he treats me to what he calls his 'random thoughts.' (**Se estavan pishando de la riza** (They were laughing so hard that they were urinating).) He then apologizes by saying, **"Ke suzyedad es esto."** ("What dirt this is.") I am glad he didn't say, **Si beves kave turko, pishas preto.** (If you drink Turkish coffee, your urine will be black.) He goes on to ask, what happened to all the Izaks (Isaacs)?

They started to call themselves, Irwin, Ira, Irving, Edwin, and so forth. He asks, **"Ke akontesyo a todos los Zakitos?"** ("What happened to all the Ikies?") The very few that kept the name, he recalls, are Ike Beresid, Ike Massa, Ike Benbasset and himself... **Avian tantos Yiddishim en *Dahntahn*, ke les paresieron ke eran muestros patrones** (There were so many Yiddish people downtown on the Lower East Side that they thought they were our bosses)... How do you say 'floor' in Ladino? He contends it is **'embasho.'** If someone said, **"Mete lo embasho."** You put it on the floor. Where would you put **la mushama** (the linoleum)? **Embasho** – on the floor – where else? **Se kayo embasho** (He fell to the floor). Included in Ike's letter were a few phrases you may not have heard in a long time:

Es haliz Turko (He's a real Turk). **Es uno de los muestros** (He's one of ours). **Estate kayado** (Be quiet). **Vate a la kaye y da una buelta** (Go to the street and give it a turn). **Si no te serras la boka te va dar uno entre la kara y los mushos** (If you don't close your mouth, I'll give you one between your face and your lips)... **Ke van a dezir la djente** (What will the people say)... **Este es un kademsis** (Turkish: a luckless person)... **No te sikileyes, aki esto yo** (Don't worry, I'm here)... **Porke te estas inyervando?** (Why are you getting angry?)... **Este es un loko y atavanado** (This one is crazy and off the wall). **Ten kudyado lo ke dizes ke te va azer dava** (Be careful of what you say, or I'll sue you)... **No avles muncho, ke te va echar a *La Vara***

(Don't talk so much, or I'll report you to the newspaper ***La Vara)***... **Mira mousho ke esta aziendo el *beby*** (Look at the lip the baby is making)... **El vazo se rompyo y se izo sal y sineeza** (The glass broke and became salt and ashes)... The **'Altizach?'** Remember him? He roamed the back yards yelling, "I cash clothes." He paid good money for the items he purchased. A nickel and a dime.

Does anyone know what it meant when a husband said to his wife, **"Ayede mujer, desha todo y trava banyo."** ("All right wife, drop everything and draw a bath.") He was telling her he wanted to have sex!

PROVERBS

Deshame entrar, y me azere lugar.
Let me enter, and I'll make room for myself.

El kierrer es pueder.
To achieve, one must desire.

La kara es espejo de la alma.
Your face and eyes are the mirrors of the soul.

Las bavas le esta kayendo.
When someone is enjoying something they are said to be drooling. (The Yiddish equivalent would be *'kvelling.')*

No piedres tiempo en bavajadas.
Do not waste time on trivialities.

Tiempo pedrido nunka se topa.
Lost time is never recovered.

THE TURN OF THE CENTURY

When the Sephardim who had no family here came to America at the turn of the century, it was customary to 'put up' our countrymen. Sometimes it was a single person, and sometimes it could be a couple. The usual arrangement was that they would board with you until they found work, and then they would pay you back a little at a time until the account was settled. No one ever defaulted.

Every family on the Lower East Side that came from Europe had at least one boarder. These boarders were always **patriotes** (people from the same city or town in Turkey). One in our house spoke a fairly good English, but was slightly hard of hearing. Whenever anyone spoke to him, his response invariably was, ***"Watch you se?"*** ("What did you say?") His nickname became **'Watch You Se.'** Sometime later the poor fellow got sick and passed on.

One day my father and my Uncle Joe were walking on Rivington Street, and someone approached my Uncle and said something to him in English. My uncle asked him, ***"Watch you se?"*** My father couldn't resist, turned to my Uncle Joe and laughingly said, **"Yusef, *'Watch You Se'* se murio."** It didn't take long for the expression, ***"Watch You Se* se murio"** to catch on. Anytime anyone said, ***"Watch you se,"*** the answer always was, ***"Watch You Se* se murio."** ("*Watch You Se* is dead.") But, indeed, he lives on.

I remember one incident of a countryman coming to live with us. He was a young man from my father's city of Silivria. After a few months he became very ill. His illness was diagnosed as **tikiya** (tuberculosis). In those days it was tantamount to a death sentence. Fortunately, even then there were charitable organizations that one could turn to for help. One I remember was the *Sisterhood of the Spanish and Portuguese Synagogue (Shearith Israel Congregation)*, and another was *HIAS – the Hebrew Sheltering and Immigrant Aid Society.* There were others. I don't recall which organization came to his aid, but I do remember that he was well taken care of.

What stands out vividly in my mind is what this young man said when it occurred to him that he might not have long to live. Since he was here without a family, this is what distressed him:

Kuando me va morir	When I will die
Kien me va yorrar me?	Who will cry for me?
Kien me va kusir la mortaja?	Who will sew my shroud?
Kien me asiendera una kandela?	Who will light a candle for me?

In the early nineteen hundreds, when our folks came over from Turkey, families stayed together. Most started in the Lower East Side, around Orchard, Rivington, Ludlow, Broome, Allen, Forsythe and Essex Streets, to name a few. It didn't take long for them to improve their lot, so to speak, and move to less congested neighborhoods. Some went north, ***Ahptahn*** (Harlem). From there they went further north to the Bronx, eventually graduating to the Grand Concourse. Others went south to ***Brooklee*** – New Lots, Brownsville, and Bensonhurst, then called Sea Beach.

Since land was cheap in what was then considered the outskirts of Brooklyn, most of the societies bought cemetery plots there. The Sephardim, with their mischievous sense of humor, would refer to someone who had passed away as **"Se fue a *Brooklee*."** ("He went to Brooklyn.")

The migration of entire families made for great camaraderie and loyalty within the families. I grew up with enough cousins in the same neighborhood to form a baseball team. We stayed together until World War II. My father, Joe Halio, got along very well with most of his brothers-in-law, but one in particular was his real buddy, my uncle Joe Fintz. As I mentioned, they were legendary **raki** drinkers, practical jokers, and raconteurs.

During a family gathering, my father sneezed, and my Uncle Joe kiddingly said, **"Patla Yusef."** My father said, ***"Tenk you verry mach."*** One of my new aunts, a lovely **Yidishika**, must have made a mental note of that. She was trying very hard to become one of 'us.' As luck would have it, this time my Uncle Joe sneezed, and my new aunt promptly said, **"Patla, Joe."** On hearing this, my mother, who had sort of taken her under her wing, said, **"Miriya** (Miriam), you don't suppose to say that. Is not nice. **Patla** is mean you shoo bust." It didn't take long for her to become one of <u>us.</u>

Most of the kids wouldn't speak Ladino at home. They would tell their folks, **"Estamos en la Amerika, kale ke avlemos en Ingles."** ("We are in America, we must speak English.") Many of them are sorry today, because they forgot their Ladino, and not too many of the older folks really improved their English just from speaking English at home.

As we were growing up in mixed neighborhoods, there were fights between the Jewish and the gentile kids. Invariably we were outnumbered. We had some pretty tough kids, but the odds were always against us. Often we had to run away in order to save our skins. The running away was great training for us – we always won all the medals in the P.S.A.L. (Public School Athletic League) competition. Do you remember those medals?

You all must have heard the expression: **Ya me da eskarinyo**, or **Tengo eskarinyo.** In essence they both mean 'I miss it, him, her, etc.,' or 'I yearn for it.' After a week in the army, in 1942, I started writing home. The one expression that kept running through my head was, **me eskarinyo de ti papa, y de ti mama. Me eskarinyo de esto, me eskarinyo de akeyo** (I miss you dad, and you mom. I miss this and I miss that).

One of the early letters I wrote home was a request for **baklava**. In a couple of weeks I got a cookie tin filled with those delicious tidbits. I, of course, shared them not too reluctantly, but sparingly, with my best buddies.

The time I was assigned to latrine duty, the first words that came to mind were, **Mazal mio, oy me enkasharon en la privada** (My luck, today they stuck me in the john).

Before I was to report for duty in the army, my father laid down some rules he wanted me to follow. He realized it would be difficult to follow the dietary rules, but he did insist that I find some way to attend services during the holidays. Again, I ran into some of the same problems I had when I was in public school. The sergeants would ask, "With your name, you say you're Jewish?" Among a few of the other things my Pop told me was (and this I never forgot): **Nunka te kortes las unyas en Shabat** (Never cut your nails on the Sabbath).

THE FACTORY AND POP'S CITIZENSHIP

Se me fuyo del tino (It ran away from my mind or memory). It actually means, 'It slipped my mind.' **Nunka ke te se tome el tino** (May you never lose your mind or memory). **Lo tengo en el punto de la aluenga** (I have it on the tip of my tongue). **No me akodro** (I don't remember). **Me olvedi** (I forgot).

The loving memories of my dear departed parents, uncles and aunts, makes me understand that I had a far better childhood than I realized. I think that growing into adulthood was easier then than it is now. Reminiscing about those days so long ago when we were young, and how different things are today makes me wonder if our children are better off than we were? Will we be leaving them the legacy our parents left us?

Growing up in suburban areas is a lot different from growing up on the Lower East Side of New York City. The summer heat, the sleeping on the fire escapes, the iceboxes, the brutal winters in cold water flats with no heat, the boxes outside the windows for our perishables (used in the winter only), the garbage thrown out of the windows, the pushcarts, the street hawkers, etc., were all part of our childhood. Will the young people of today look back as fondly on <u>their</u> days in the 'old neighborhood?'

Like many of the newly arrived immigrants in the early 1900's, my father and mother opened up a sewing factory. The crew was composed mostly of family – brothers, sisters, uncles and aunts; and Ladino, with its occasional flurries of Turkish, was the language they spoke among themselves. Some were floor workers, others operated sewing machines. There were single needle, double needle, button hole, button sewers, hemmers and a variety of special machines. The floor workers gathered the work from the machines and brought them to the next stage of production. Wages for the individual operations ranged from one-half cent to ten cents a dozen for the more complicated operations. The very fast operators could earn up to twenty dollars a week, a princely sum in those days.

My earliest years were spent in my parent's sewing factory. As I was an only child, I was with them at all times. Babysitters and day-care centers were unheard of. Until I started school, I saw very little other than the factory and the apartment we lived in. Everyone who worked in the factory was either a relative or a compatriot.

When I was a toddler, I loved climbing on a chair and pulling the chain to turn the lights on. Someone would always say, **"Aroniko, achiliado ke te veya."** ("Aaron, may I see you enlightened.") Electricity was expensive and considered a luxury. **Kuando avrites la luz** (When you 'opened' the light), you had to have good reason for it. In the factory they joked and said, **"Por ke kierres la luz, perlas estas afilando?** ("Why do you need the light, are you threading pearls?") Once in a while I got out of line, interfered with the work, and my father got angry. Mom came to my rescue by saying, **"Tomalo kon buenas."** ("Go easy on him.")

The factory opened early in the morning and closed late in the evening. One day, my father, dressed in his new suit and hat, left the factory around mid-morning. I thought it strange, but I went about my business of pretending to be one of the workers, or making believe I was repairing a broken part on a machine that was not being used or riding my tricycle around the shop. When my father returned early in the afternoon, he was beaming, and I noticed he was carrying what looked like several boxes of candy. On seeing him, my mother shouted **"Reushites."** They hugged, and Pop went from person to person in the shop offering them candy from the boxes. My father had just returned from the Federal Courthouse where he had been granted his U.S. Citizenship papers.

I learned two things that day. I learned a new word that I had not heard before: **reushites** (the infinitive being **reushir)**, to succeed. From my mother's reaction and the congratulatory remarks by the people in the shop, I had to assume that the word had to do with success. The other thing I learned was that I had a sweet tooth. The boxes of candy contained chocolate-covered cherries. I have been addicted to them to this day. Needless to say, whenever I see or hear of chocolate-covered cherries, or hear the word **reushites**, I am reminded of that happy day so long ago in my Pop's factory.

My father always took an interest in the young people who worked for him. They became family to him. One day a former employee of my Pop's opened his own factory and reported pridefully to my father that he was doing so well that he was going to buy a car and a lot of other things.

Pop put his arm around him. He told him how happy he was for him and said, **"Albertiko, te va dar un poko de konsejo y kierro ke me oygas. Agora ke el echo esta kaminando bien, akodrate de estas palabras: Kuando el chorro esta korriendo, inche el kantariko. En otras palavras, ay vezes ke kuando el pozo se seka."** ("Albie, I'm going to give you a little advice, and I want you to listen. Now that the business is going well, remember these words: When the stream is flowing, fill up your jar. In other words, sometimes the well runs dry.") Sage advice that neither he nor his wife ever forgot.

* * *

DJOHA – ALTURA Y LARGURA

Al tiempo, en Turkiya, kuando las mujeres lavavan la ropa, las enkolgavan en una kuedra ke estava atada entre dos palos muy altos. Esto era porke pensavan ke el aire fresko bolava mijor de muy alto. Memet le demando a Djoha, "De ke altura es este palo ande enkolgan la ropa?" Djoha disho, "Yo no se, ama si suvo a la koroniya, puedo saver." Ama ni el ni Memet pudieron suvir a la koroniya. Disho Memet si lo kortamos lo puedemos mezurarlo enbasho." Lo kortaron y Memet tomo la mezura, y disho, "Tiene kuarenta manos de largura." Djoha se inyervo y disho, "Memet tu sos un tokmak. No kierriamos saver la largura – kierriamos saver la altura."

HEIGHT AND LENGTH

In olden times, in Turkey, when the women washed clothes, they hung them to dry on a rope tied between two very tall poles. This was because they thought that the fresh air blew better, the higher the poles were. Memet asked Djoha, "What is the height of the pole that the women hang the clothes on?" Djoha said, "I don't know, but if I can climb to the top, I can tell." Neither one could climb to the top. Memet said, "If we cut it down, we can measure it on the ground." They cut it down, Memet measured it, and said, "It is forty hands long." Djoha got angry and said, "Memet, you are a thick head. We don't want to know the length – we want to know the height."

* * *

FRACTURIZATIONS

My earliest recollection is that **Djudeo-Espanyol** was the only language spoken at home. Our multilingual parents quickly realized that if they wanted to say something not for our ears they could resort to any of the languages at their command.

How many of you remember the phrase, **choodjook var**? (the children are here – in Turkish). That was what my parents used to say when they didn't want us to know what they were talking about. It was a clear signal to switch to one of the many languages at their command, one they knew the kids did not speak. Once that happened, they knew that the children would be 'turned off,' and they would continue on their merry way. There were a few sharp kids around that learned some of the other languages. They were the lucky ones. I am sure that we, who did not learn any of the other languages, lament that now. Unfortunately, for many of us, once we got out into the streets we even forgot our Ladino. Our first months in school were very difficult because many of us couldn't speak English. However, we soon found out that we took to English like ducks take to water. Surely you can guess that the earliest words we learned were some choice 'four-letter words.' The children were not the only ones interested in learning English. Among the adults some learned quickly, others struggled, and some never bothered.

As Mom was learning the English language, she would come to me very often for verification of some of the things she heard. One day she asked me what ***mandja yer own beeznes***, meant. She said it must be something to eat in Italian. Of course, we know how even people born here in America strain the English language. For instance, ***"D'jeet?"*** is very often used for, "Did you eat?" With marriages between the Greek Jews (**Yanyots** or **Romaniotes**) and the Sephardim, we ran into some strange language situations also. My good friend Hy Cohen, who is a **Yanyot**, married Doris Azaria, who is Sephardic. During the courtship Hy heard his future mother-in-law remark to someone in the house, **"Tengo dolor de tripa."** ("I have a pain in my belly.") Hy understood enough Ladino to be a little confused by the statement. While the word

tripa, in Ladino, means belly, in Greek it means *hole*. You can draw your own conclusion as to what may have gone on in Hy's mind.

It was very humorous to hear how some of the adults fractured their English. Once, when an obviously drunk panhandler approached my father, my father's words sounded like something like this: ***Gid de helary***, which was, as any drunken fool could plainly see, "Get the hell out of here. **"Este mundo es *dogee dogee*."** ("This world is dog eat dog.") I always got a kick out of my father when he ordered ***smashed potatoes*** in a restaurant. Mike Sedacca sent these two that his Mom said; ***I noven godda*** (I haven't got it), and ***Ahm gonta Terty Avenoo*** (I'm going to Third Avenue). Annie Cohen sent this one; **La kaza de los viejos esta *'nex da Berrisini Britch.'*** (*The Old Age Home* is next to the Verrazano Bridge). ***En ather way*** (in other words), **Eya es muy *partikoolo*, porke le parese ke es *haya kless*** * (That one is very particular, because she thinks she is high class). Also, ***Ee dem foo*** (You damn fool). Dr. Jack Crespin's father used to say, **"Es nada to *drag abat*."** ("It's nothing to brag about.") These two were sent anonymously: **Kien es este Hy Neely ke estan avlando tanto de el?** (Who is this Hy Neely, that they talking about?) Well, that Hy Neely was her own son Hy, who nearly won the election for the presidency of his class. This same lady wanted to know, **Ke kierre dezir *Beenso*?** She was referring to a hit song that played over and over again on the radio; 'I've Been So Lonely.' Do you remember the song, 'Are You Lonesome Tonight?' Our folks always made a joke out of it by saying, 'Are you ***lonso*** tonight?' In Turkish, **Lonso** means a bear (in Spanish its **oso**). Anyone considered to be stupid was called a **lonso**. By the same token, the center of an iceberg or romaine lettuce is called **troncho**. We also know that one who is a called a **troncho** is considered a hard head, or a dope. There must be hundreds more, and I'll bet you are remembering some right now.

The early years in America (1909 to 1925) were formative years for our folks. I'm sure you can relate to some of the things they did and said when they were learning to use English and Yiddish expressions to impress their Yiddish neighbors. I heard my mother say, **"A shena meddle,"** referring to a pretty girl. I also heard her say **"konna harra,"** a Yiddish expression to ward off evil.

*In Hebrew, **haya** means lowly, like an animal.

When annoyed with me, my Mom would say, ***"I mer on you."*** ("I'm mad on you.") Once after a long walk, she stopped and said, **"Espera un poko, kierro restar *I am* kansated."** ("Wait a while, I want to rest, I'm tired.") Once I took a job that required quite a bit of traveling. Mom wasn't happy about that, but she was proud of it. When someone asked her how I was, she would say, **"Mi ijo esta muy bueno, *tenk you verry mach*, agora esta *ara tahn*."** ("My son is very well thank you, right now he is out of town.") The first time I went to the *Sephardic Home for the Aged* to visit her, she showed me around, and when we got to the recreation room she said, **"Esta kamareta es el *kreashon room*."** Another time, I did something for her, she said, ***"I represheate it."*** Once I even heard her say to my father, **"No esto en de *moo*."** ("I am not in the mood.")

There were a few beauties in Ladino that the folks used: A cranky old man was referred to as, **Un aksi viejo malo**. Pity for someone was expressed as **zavali** (poor thing). My father, who had an eye for beauty, would see an attractive woman and say, "**Mira hanum de mujer. Tan henoza.**" ("Look at that beauty of a woman. So graceful.") An embarrassing situation would bring out the expression **Me vas a echar la kara en lodo** (You are going to throw my face in the mud).

Last month, Phyllis and I went to Port St. Lucie for a weekend with a few of our Sephardic friends. We had a delightful time just shopping, walking around, singing and talking. The talking was the best of all. At one point we decided to speak only in Ladino. Some of the gems that came out of this conversation are priceless.

Someone asked, **"La palabra 'kyutook,' es palavra Espanyola?"** ("The word **kyutouk**, is it Spanish?") In answering, Sonny Lichtman fractured the phrase "I don't know" by saying, **"Yo no savo."**

Kitty Hattem told this beauty: One of her friends brought her future husband home. He was also Sephardic, but knew only a little Ladino. The young lady asked her mother if there was anything to eat. Her mother's answer was, **"No ay muncho en kaza solo un poko sheeshit."** ("There isn't much in the house, just a small variety.") The future husband almost became a memory when he heard **sheeshit**.

Here's another, "Knock, knock." "Who's there?" "Molly." "Molly who?" **"Molly-vanti kon un dolor de kavesa."** ("**Me alavante** – *I woke up* with a headache.")

ESTO Y AKEYO
THIS AND THAT

Lisa Weiss tells how her mom got things fixed at home. **Roto esta? Yo lo fixeyo.** (It's broken? I'll get it fixed.) She would go to the window and yell, ***"Soopy, upystes pliss."*** The superintendent would come up, Lisa's mom would show him a leaky faucet, or whatever was broken and presto, it was fixed. All it cost was some **bavajada** (a small token) for a tip. Lisa also tells about her sister getting married and moving to San Francisco where her new husband's business was. Her Mom said, **"Fin aya se fue, es tan leshos."** ("Up to there she went, it's so far away.") Lisa said, **"Ma, tu deshates tu padre y madre en Turkiya, y Turkiya es mas leshos de San Francisco."** ("Ma, you left your father and mother in Turkey, and Turkey is farther away than San Francisco.")

Some additional contributions from readers are: When someone knocked on the door, this Mom said, ***"Who is you?"***... This one is about the time his father wanted to know how much something cost; he asked the lady clerk, ***"Ha mach you cost."*** The lady had him arrested... Yomtov Crespi gave me this one: When his Mom went shopping and saw something she liked, she said, ***"Gimme dis, ha mach? Okay."*** She always paid with a ten dollar bill and never counted her change... My father wanted cigarettes, and he said to me, **"Aroniko, va merkame sigarikos."** ("Aaron, go buy me cigarettes.") I said, **"Dame paras."** ("Give me money.") My Pop said, **"Kon paras puedo ir yo."** ("With money I can go myself.")... My Uncle Joe asked my Pop, **"Yusef, amigos somos?"** ("Joe, are we friends?") My Pop said, **"Asta el fin, Joe."** ("Until the end, Joe.") Uncle Joe said, **"Empresta me kinyentos dolares."** ("Lend me five hundred dollars.") My Pop said, **"Esto es el fin."** ("This is the end.")... When it was time to go, Mama would say, **"Ayede *goobye*."** Simon Calderon brought home a corner bracket he made in his shop class, and showed it to his mom. Mom looked at it and said, **"Komo de *nize* es esto."** ("How nice this is.")... My father loved fishing; a friend of his who knew this told him that boats go deep sea fishing out of ***Ship Ship Bey*** (Sheepshead Bay) in Brooklyn... Professor David Fintz Altabe told this one about a cousin who migrated to Cuba from Turkey at the time immigration into the United States was curtailed. The cousin remarked to her husband, **"Mira Haim, toda la djente aki son Djudios, mira tan ermoso ke estan avlando Espanyol.** ("Look Haim, all the people here are Jewish, look at how beautifully they speak Spanish.")... A newly arrived immigrant was taken to a cafeteria, and he was impressed with the people carrying trays. He remarked, **"Mira kuantas personas para servirmos ay aki."** ("Look at how many people there are to serve us.") He thought they were all waiters and waitresses... Esther Amira says the way to tell if a woman is pregnant is to look at the base of her throat where the clavicle separates. If it throbs, she's pregnant... Esther Benezra tells us that when her Mom had a problem, she would take a long walk. One time she got lost. This valiant lady didn't panic. She went up to a policeman and said, ***"Me lose."*** The policeman asked, "Where do you live?" Esther's Mom gestured and said, ***"One dolla, one penny, Ellen Estrit."*** The policeman walked her to '101 Allen Street'... Before he learned to read, Uncle Joe got around New York in the subways by counting the stations... Once I must have done something very bad and my Pop was spanking me. I was screaming blue murder when he said, **"Porke estas gritando tanto? Esto me esta tuyendo mas a mi de a ti."** ("Why are you yelling so much? This is hurting me more than it does you.") And I remember saying, **"Si, ama no en el mismo lugar."** ("Yes, but not in the same place.")... When the kids were small we bought a pedigreed dog, and the kids named her Missy. My mother saw the dog and liked her very much, but she asked, **"Komo de nombre por perro is *'Perdido?'* "** ("What kind of a name for a dog is 'Missing?' ")... This one is from Nissim Azuz. He arrived in New York about ten days before Passover in 1920. He was living with his sister, who sent him to the store to buy some Passover wine. Here is Nissim's story: **Entri al lugar ande se vende el sharope y esperi asta todos los mushteris salyeron del lugar, y kuando el patron vino ande mi, me demando, *"War you wan?"* Le dishe 'Sharope, Sharope.' " Este loko me afferro de la yaka, y me echo del lugar a la kaye."** (I entered the store that sold the wine (**sharope**) and waited until all the customers left the place, and when the owner came to me and asked, "What do you want." I said **"Sharope, Sharope."** This nut grabbed me by the collar and threw me out of the store into the street.) The way he said **"Sharope, Sharope,"** it sounded like *"Shut up, Shut up!"*

VISITORS FROM TURKEY

In Turkey, large families were the norm. My mother's family was a large one and my father's family comparatively small. I knew my father's two sisters, as they were here in America, and I had heard of his brothers; one was in Mexico and the other was still in Turkey. I recall that in my mother's family there were fifteen children. Of the fifteen, eight came to America, five had passed away and two remained in Turkey.

The trend in Turkey today is toward smaller families, similar to our lifestyle here in America. The children of my two uncles who remained in Turkey are my first cousins. One of these cousins came to America four years ago, and since I had never seen him, I carried a sign with my name on it in the airport. I am sure many of you must have had the same experience as I when he emerged from the plane. My cousin and I recognized each other immediately because our facial characteristics were so similar that the sign was unnecessary. We smiled, hugged each other, and my cousin said, **"Yo te konosi el punto ke te vide. Pareses entero al Tio Izak."** ("I recognized you the moment I saw you. You look just like Uncle Isaac.")

My cousin had studied English in school and knew enough to get by, but only a native or a long-time resident can readily understand the multitude of idioms in American English. One day my cousin was reading the newspaper ads for restaurants and kept seeing the same thing in most of the ads. *'Early Bird Special.'* He asked me, **"Komo de pasharo es este ke todos los luwares de komer estan sirviendo? Esto no kierre dezir ke es pasharo temprano? Yo nunka tengo oido de pasharo temprano."** ("What kind of a bird is this that all the restaurants are serving? Doesn't it mean a bird that is early. I never heard of a bird that is early.")

Another time as we were riding on the Florida Turnpike, he read all the signs on the billboards and commented on them. He asked, **"Ay lugar de komer en este kamino? Yo tengo ambre."** ("Is there a place to eat on this road? I'm hungry.") I said, **"Seguro, ay uno muy serka."** ("Sure, there is one very near.") At the service area he saw a sign that said, *Eat – Get Gas.* This time he really got excited and said,

"Loko esto? Aki te dizen, 'Kome, y toma gaz.' Yo no kierro komer y ke me de gaz la komida. El Dyo ke no me de, yo tengo bastante problemas kon el estomago sin ellyos ke me den mas, y kon mis paras." (Am I crazy? Here they tell you, eat and get gas. I don't want to eat and they should give me gas with the meal. May the Lord spare me, I have enough problems with my stomach without them giving me more, and with my money.) If that wasn't bad enough, he saw a sign that said, *Hot Dogs, $1.50*. The next thing I heard was: **"Komo de lugar es este? Es lugar de komer o es lugar ande venden perros y yo nunka tengo oido de perros kalientes. Me da askeyo de komer aki."** ("What kind of place is this? Is it a place to eat or a place to sell dogs? I never heard of a hot dog. It disgusts me to eat here.")

What really ticked my cousin off was, after having dinner in a very fancy restaurant, he noticed that the waiter at the table next to ours was putting the left-over food in tinfoil, and putting it into paper bags. Then he noticed the people got up to leave the restaurant with the bags. He asked what that was all about. We told him about the custom of taking home a 'doggy bag,' either to really give it to their dog or to eat it themselves. He went bananas, and started barking like a dog. He said in Turkey no one ever took food home from a restaurant. It was unheard of and he would consider that only a very low-class person would do such a thing.

On the way home, I asked him if he would like to live here. You guessed what his answer was. **"En Turkiya yo bivo komo un rey. Aki me tienes de meterme en una timarana, o en un haivaneh."** ("In Turkey I live like a king. Here, you would have to put me in an insane asylum, or in a zoo.")

VISIT TO TURKEY

Two years following my cousins' visit to Florida, my wife and I toured Europe. We had a wonderful trip, but the two weeks we spent in Turkey – the land of our roots – were the best of all. Upon our arrival in Istanbul, I phoned another cousin, Eli Baruh, with whom I had corresponded but never met. The reception I received made my head spin. **"En ke otel estas? Salte de ayi agora pishin. Vas a venir y te vas a estar en mi kaza."** ("What hotel are you staying at? Check out now, immediately. You are staying at my house.") My cousin was most accommodating when we expressed a desire to visit LuleBurgaz, Silivria and Salonika, the birthplaces of our parents. Salonika is in Greece, where we went on our own, but all the arrangements were made by Eli.

Istanbul is a fabulous metropolis that ranks with New York, Paris, London and any other major city in the world. It is a city of mosques, minarets, parks, theaters, fantastic restaurants and unbelievable traffic, and perhaps the largest indoor mall in the world, the Grand Bazaar, covering more than fifty acres.

My cousins live a wonderful life there. They belong to synagogues, clubs, philanthropic organizations, and cultural groups, much the same as we do here. I was very much impressed with the cordiality shown to one another, reminding me of my childhood when our folks greeted each other with the old world courtesies. Another thing that made a deep impression on me was the given names of the children. Many were still the traditional names the Sephardim used in the generations before ours. I became especially aware that the female names were mostly beautiful, gracious names, and the names of the males were mostly biblical names.

The sun, the moon, the stars, faith, hope, jewels. Here they are: **Alegra** (Happy), **Bella** (Beautiful), **Diamante** (Diamond), **Esperansa** (Hope), **Estreya** (Star), **Flora** (Flower), **Fe** (Faith), **Fortuneh** (Fortune), **Gracia** (Grace), **Joya** (Jewel), **Luna** (Moon), **Mazalto** (High Luck) **Palomba** (Dove), **Regina** (Queen), **Rosa** (Rose), **Sol** (Sun), **Victoria** (Victory), **Vida** (Life), **Violeta** (Violet).

With all due respect to the present generation of Sephardim in America, moving along with the times, we don't hear names of boys today like Moish, Ike, Izzy, Hymie, Abie, etc. My cousins in Turkey still had such names: Aaron, Avram, Adam, Binyamin, David, Haim, Eliahu, Eliezer, Izak, Israel, Moise, Shalom, Salamon, Yakov, Yusef, Yuda.

One of my cousins named his son Irving (pronounced in Turkey, ***Earving***). I questioned him, and his answer was, **"El Tio Israel, ke se yama Earving en la Amerika, mos echo taled a mi y a mi mujer kuando mos kazimos, y yo le prometi, si kierre el Dyo, kuando me nase el primer ijo, le va meter el nombre suyo."** ("Uncle Israel, who is called Irving in America, draped the **taled** around me and my wife when we got married, and I promised him, God willing, when my first son is born, I will name him Irving, in his honor.") **Echar taled** is usually reserved for parents or grandparents. In their absence, it is given to someone revered.

An interesting custom that is practiced in Turkey to this day is one that is called **fashadura**. It is a sort of baby shower that is held during the fifth month of the pregnancy. The baby's first garment is sewn by friends and family of the mother-to-be. When the **fasha** (the swaddling cloth) is finished, Jordan almonds are tossed on the **fasha**, a gesture to wish the baby a long and sweet life. To go a step further, in Turkey today it is the custom for the new parents to publicly thank the doctor who delivered the baby by placing an advertisement in the local newspaper.

The surnames I came across in Turkey were much the same as those we have here. During a discussion of **alkunyas** (surnames), it was brought out that they have a special relationship with Hebrew, the Bible, cities or regions in Spain such as Castile, Aragon, Andalucia, Toledo, Toledano, Saragossi, Tarragano, Murciano, Cordova, and others as well as Arabic, prefixed with **Bar, Ben, Al**, and **Abu**. I did notice a trend in Turkey, where some are changing their surnames to conform more with the tone of Turkish names, very much like what has happened here in America.

DJOHA Y LOS MOKOSOS

Las kriaturas de la male ke bevia djoha lo insultavan, le azian pizmaz, y lo maldezian. Djoha se disho de si para si, "Yo los va azer tirbiye a estos animalikos." La proximo vez ke vinyeron les disho, "Mira mokosos, yo kierro ver si vosotros tenesh meyoyos. Si venesh a lunes y azesh esto, vos va dar dos liras a kada uno." Los mokosos lo izieron kon muncho gusto, y rekojeron las dos liras. "Agora, kierro ke vengash mierkoles y vos va dar una lira si azesh lo mismo." Kuando vinieron mierkoles y los mokosos otra vez lo molestaron, les dio una lira a kada uno. "Agora," disho Djoha, "Si venesh viernes vos va dar un metalik a kada uno." "Loko estas?" Disheron, "Olvidate, por un metalik piojento no venimos mas." Y nunka mas lo molestaron.

DJOHA AND THE SNOTNOSE BRATS

The children of the town where Djoha lived used to insult him, tease him and curse him. Djoha said to himself, I will tame those little animals. The next time they came he said, "Look, you Snotnose Brats, I want to see if you have any brains. If you come here on Monday and do what you are doing now, I'll give you two liras each." The Snotnose Brats did it with great pleasure and collected their two liras. "Now, I want you to come on Wednesday and I'll give each of you one lira if you do the same thing." When they came on Wednesday and the Snotnose Brats bothered him again, he gave each of them one lira. "Now, If you come on Friday I'll give each of you a penny." "Are you crazy?" they said. "Forget it, we're not coming anymore for a lousy penny." And they never bothered him again.

* * *

NAMES / PHRASES

The Sephardic system of naming the children caused some internal problems within the family groups. In my mother's family there were five brothers and three sisters. I don't know how many brothers and sisters were still in Turkey, but those did not have any effect on the problems that we had here in America.

My grandfather's name was Aaron and my grandmother's name was Sol (pronounced *Soul*). Each of the five brothers and the three sisters fondest wish was to have children they could name for their parents. Somehow, the names Aaron and Sol were changed to Henry and Shirley. I have no explanation for the reasoning concerning the change.

The aforementioned minor problem came to light as we (the grandchildren) were growing up. When we referred to cousin Henry or cousin Shirley, we had to qualify each one by saying which Henry or which Shirley we meant. That problem was partially resolved by calling the eldest, Big Henry and Big Shirley, and the youngest ones Little Henry and Little Shirley. As more came along, we identified them by their parents' names, such as **Aaron del Tio David** (Uncle David's Henry), and **Sol de la Tante Ester** (Aunt Esther's Shirley), and so on. As for those in Turkey, we had no problems, because we had no occasion to refer to them.

I had several cousins named Henry and Shirley. My cousin Henry Benedict, was Big Henry and I was Little Henry until our teens when our friends started to call us Hank. Tante Esther's Shirley was Big Shirley and Uncle David's Shirley was Little Shirley. One of the in-between Shirleys changed her name to Lee, and the youngest of all, to Shelley.

Ike Amira, who has been most prolific in sharing his gems with me, reminded me of **Kippur**, when I would have flowers delivered to me at the synagogue (which, of course, were paid for before the holiday). I would wait outside until my father and mother came out, and I would present them to my Mom. Her smile was worth a million bucks. **Se le kayiva las bavas de alegria.** Once a year my father would go to *City Hull*. Actually, it was during **Selihoth**. **Selihoth** is the period before **Roshana** when a special ritual is performed. It always sounded like City Hall to me.

Ike writes that every summer, his father took him to the barber shop to get a 'baldy.' Everyone called the kids with 'baldies,' **eskalavrados**. How about when your mother sent you to the **shastre para dar ootee al vestido muevo de tu papa** (tailor to press your father's new suit). He mentions going to birthday parties and remembers the sponge cake and the cream soda. Not like today's elaborate birthday parties.

Some more of Ike's memories: **Asta ke le viene la gana del riko, se le kita la alma del prove** (By the time the rich man gets the desire to help, he takes the heart out of the poor man). When one of the kids acted up, it was said that **se estava azneyando** (he was acting like a jack-ass). **Vamos a merkarte un par de *shoozes*.** (Let's go and buy you a pair of shoes.) **Me vino al tino.** (It came to my mind.) **Se estan komportando komo zinganos.** (They are behaving like gypsies.) **Ke no me manke.** (May I never miss it.) **Me ize pishman.** (I regretted it.) **Es muy arezvalado.** (He is very vain, or very smooth.) **Troka el lakerdi.** (Change the subject.) **Otra vez!! Ya abasto!!** (What again!! That's enough!!) **La vida es para el ke la save bivir.** (Life is for the one who knows how to live it.) **Me kedee kon la boka avierta.** (I stood there with my mouth open.)

* * *

DJOHA – BUEN NEGOSIO

Un dia Djoha merko una kantidad de guevos por dies sentavos la dosena, los estava vendiendo por nueve sentavos por la dosena. Memet, el amigo de Djoha le demando, "Porke estas vendiendo los guevos a perdida?" Djoha le disho a Memet ke keriya ke sepan los amigos ke el no estava bushkanda a ganar paras de eyos, solo keriya amostrar les ke el era ombre de buen negosio.

GOOD BUSINESS

One day Djoha bought a certain amount of eggs for ten cents a dozen, and was selling them for nine cents a dozen. Memet, his friend, asked him, "Why are you selling the eggs at a loss?" Djoha told Memet that he wanted them to see that he wasn't out to make money on them, he only wanted his friends to see that he was a good business man.

* * *

SORROW AND HUMOR

My wife Phyllis and I had the sorrowful duty of paying a condolence call to our esteemed friend, Pauline Hasday, on the loss of her dear sister, Claire. After paying respects to the bereaved family, it is customary for everyone to make small talk on a solemn occasion such as this one. Yet it is impossible to suppress humor. One couple had to leave early in order to baby-sit for their granddaughters. Pauline could not resist telling us about her mother's baby-sitting for her. When her husband Levi came home from military service, she and Levi moved in with her mother, Neama Telvi. Grandma Neama loved listening to the radio. She especially liked the narration of "Cinderella." Her little granddaughter, Irene, loved hearing it. Grandma Neama called it **La konseja de *Gingerella* kon la madrasta negra y las tres ermanastras gursuzas.** (The story of *'Gingerella'* with her bad stepmother, and her three miserable stepsisters.)

After coming to America in 1929, my father-in-law's aunt and her son lived in his house until they were able to have a place of their own. She was a frail sweet thing whom everyone loved, and called **Tia**.

The only one who could speak Spanish and English was my father-in-law, and when he wasn't home to act as interpreter it was a comedy of errors. The family resorted to unstudied sign language, and it was a fantastic learning process for all. For instance, if you wanted a pair of scissors, you moved the first two fingers of your hand apart and together until you got the idea across. I'm sure many of you can recall this happening in your own homes.

Many years later, lamentably, **Tia's** son predeceased her. She carried on so at the funeral, that I was afraid she was going to have a heart attack. I picked her up to carry her away from the gravesite in order to calm her, but in a very strong and authoritative voice, she said to me, **"Mete me enbasho, y desha me. Yo kale ke aga lo ke esto aziendo. Es mi ijo ke se murio."** ("Put me down, and let me go. I must do what I am doing. It is my son who has died.") My father-in-law explained that it was traditional for **Tia** to act in that manner, even if it killed her. Had it happened in Salonica where she was born, it would have been expected of her.

Therein may lie a reason that Sephardic women were discouraged from going to the cemetery. The Sephardic men cared so much for their womenfolk that they wanted to spare them this trauma of seeing a loved one buried.

* * *

DJUDIO BOVO NO AY
EL MEYOYOUDO

En Espanya, durante la Inquisition, vino el tiempo para el papaz ke pase djuzgo a un dezmazalado. En akel tiempo ningunos se salvavan la vida kuando aparesian delantre de este papaz. El era muy kurnas. Metiya en un chapeo dos pedasos de papel ke tenia eskrito 'Kulpavle' en los dos papeles. Siempre el papaz les dezia a los desmazalados, "Kita uno de los papeles de el chapeo. Si el papel ke kitas dize, 'Kulpavle' te mueres. Si dize 'Sin kulpa,' bives."

Este Djudio no era bovo. Tomo uno de los papeles de el chapeo se lo metyo en la boka, y lo mashko y se lo engluto. El papaz le demando, "Por ke izites esto?" El Djudio le disho, "Si el papel ke keda dize "Kulpavle," es seguro ke el papel ke me engluti, dize, "Sin kulpa."

THERE ARE NO DUMB JEWS
THE BRAINY ONE

In Spain, during the Inquisition, the time came for a priest to pass judgement on an unfortunate. At that time, no one was ever saved when they appeared before this priest. He was very shrewd. He used to put two pieces of paper in a hat that had 'guilty' written on both pieces. He always told the unfortunates, "Take one of the pieces of paper out of the hat, if it says, 'Guilty' you will die. If it says, 'Not Guilty' you will live."

This Jew was no dope. He took one of the papers, put it in his mouth, chewed it and swallowed it. The priest asked him, "Why did you do that?" The Jew said, "If the paper that remains says, 'Guilty,' then surely the one I swallowed said, 'Not Guilty.'

* * *

MOM'S CITIZENSHIP

There can't be many first-generation Americans of Sephardic origin who don't know their birthdates. But how many of our parents and grandparents who were born in Turkey could say they knew the day, month and year they were born?

I remember very clearly asking my parents about their birthdays, and I am willing to wager that many of you received the same answer I did. My father said, **"Mi padre me disho ke yo nasi en el segundo dia de Pesah, en el anyo ke Turkiya y Bulgaria estavan en guerra."** ("My father told me that I was born on the second day of Passover, in the year that Turkey and Bulgaria were at war.") Some research revealed the date to be April 10, 1876.

My mother maintained that she was born **"En Las Frutas y so dos anyos mas grande de mi ermano Israel ke nasio en el anyo del fuego ke destrouyo muestro kal."** ("I was born during the holiday **Tu BeShevat,** and I am two years older than my brother, Israel, who was born in the year that the fire destroyed our **shul** [synagogue].") My uncle told me that the year of the fire was 1889. **Las Frutas** falls on the 15th of **Shevat**, making her birthday February 5, 1887.

As the need for citizenship papers, driver's licenses, passports, and so forth arose, our people were faced with a problem. Many who were born on days that were not historically significant would figure out approximate dates by speaking to friends and relatives they grew up with to establish a date they could live with. Once decided upon, it was theirs forever.

Around 1939 my mother was attending reading and writing classes in an adult education program at Taft High School in the Bronx. The war in Europe had begun, and of course our sympathy was with the Allies. A separate class was formed to prepare adults for citizenship. Mom told me about it and I suggested she drop out of the reading and writing class, as she only took it as a refresher, and enroll in the citizenship class. Mom had always been under the impression that she was a U.S. citizen by virtue of my father's naturalization in 1924. She protested, **"Porke ke me vaya a esta klasa kuando yo so sitizen de este pais?"** ("Why do

I have to go to that class if I am a citizen of this country?") Up to that date, marriage to a U.S. citizen granted citizenship to an alien wife and children under 21 years of age. I told her that the law had been changed on October 22, 1922. She said, **"Si esto es el kavzo, va azer lo ke me dizes."** ("If that is the case, I will do as you say.") She accepted and agreed to switch.

Mom enjoyed tripping me up by asking questions about our government that I had forgotten. She would say, **"Estas viendo,yo se mas de ti komo kamina muestro governo, y tu sos nasido de aki."** ("You see, I know more than you do about our government, and you were born here.") At one of the gab sessions with her classmates, someone suggested that those who didn't have birth certificates add a few years to their ages so that they could collect social security pensions earlier. Mom became very angry. She said, **"No es onesto, y ke mujer desente se aze mas vieja por paras?"** ("It's dishonest, and what decent woman makes herself older for money?")

The day of the examination for citizenship finally arrived. Prior to her appearance before the judge, Mom was a nervous wreck. **"Kuando me avla el *george* me va olvidar todo lo ke me embezaron en la eskola. Ke me van azer si me desmayo? Guayas de mi se esto me akontese. Si no reusho, se me va echar la kara en lodo."** ("When the judge speaks to me, I am going to forget everything they taught me in school. What will they do to me if I faint? Woe is me if I don't succeed, my face will be in the mud.") When her turn came she was shaking all over. I said to her, **"Ma, no te espantes, yo va estar a tu lado todo el tiempo."** ("Don't be afraid, I will be at your side all the time.") Mom said, **"Ya se, ijo mio, ama es a <u>mi</u> ke el *george* va azer las demandas."** ("I know, my son, but I am the one the judge is going to question.") Here's how it went:

First question: Who is the president of the United States?
Answer: *Meester Franklee Roosevel* (Mr. Franklin Roosevelt).

Second question: How many congressmen are there?
Answer: *Four hunded thuty fi* (435).

Third question: How many states are there in America?
Answer: *Foree et* (48).

Fourth question: How many senators are there?
Answer: *Nanedy-six* (96).

Fifth question: What are the three branches of government?
Answer: *Judisha, executee y leches leche* (Judicial, executive and legislative).

Sixth question: Which president freed the slaves?
Answer: *Meester Abrahahm Lin Ko-hen.*

Judge: I see that you were born in Turkey. Is that correct?
Mom: Yes, *george* (Mom's version of 'judge').

Seventh question: If the United States goes to war with Turkey will you do everything in your power to help this country?
Answer: Why not?

Judge: Answer yes or no.
Mom: (ready to faint) Yes, *george.*

* * *

Needless to say, Mom was awarded her citizenship papers, and it was one of the happiest days of her life.

CONEY ISLAND

En boka serrada no entra moshka. Literally translated, it means 'Into a closed mouth a fly cannot enter.' The American version would be 'Silence is golden.'

I learned that lesson early in life, when I came home with a black eye. My father said to me, **"Estavas avlando kuando devias de estar oyendo."** ("You were talking when you should have been listening.") How else does one get a black eye if not by provoking a fight?

Kids got into fights mostly during the summer months, when we were out of school and too young to go to work. The heat, the mosquitoes, and the lack of something constructive to do made us irritable. Summers in the early twenties and thirties were brutal for us city kids. We depended on the good graces of the local firemen to close off some streets and set up make-shift showers so we could cool off, physically and mentally. Sometimes one of the bigger fellows would get hold of a wrench and open the fire hydrant on our street. It didn't take long for the cops to come, and we took off like thieves. We wore those ugly woolen bathing suits that itched when they dried, so we stayed under the shower until our lips were blue. Many of us got sick, and our folks would hide our bathing suits on hot days.

None of us ever went away for the summer. Who ever heard of the 'mountains'? Who could afford it even if we knew about it? Sometimes we would hear, **"Lo embiaron al *cawntree.*"** ("He was sent to the country.") Those kids were generally charity cases, and critically ill, mostly with some kind of respiratory disease. They were said to have **tikiya** (tuberculosis). It wasn't unusual for them never to be seen or heard of again.

The streets of the Lower East Side were our 'country.' The East River was our 'seaside resort,' and if you weren't brave enough for that, you went to *'Tar Beach,'* the roof. When it got too hot to sleep at night, we often would spread some blankets on the fire escape and sleep out there. That was our 'air conditioning.'

Some of the more enterprising kids would find jobs running errands or making deliveries for the local grocer or butcher at no pay, just for whatever tips they could scrounge up. The smart kids saved their pennies and took a trip to Coney Island, commonly known to our folks as ***Koonee Eyela***. For the kids living in the Bronx or Harlem, it was an expensive proposition to go to Coney Island. They had to pay two fares of five cents each way, making for a total of twenty cents round trip. That was a lot of money.

They took the IRT to the Times Square Station, and changed for the BMT to the last stop on the Sea Beach Line. Some of the braver kids would sneak under the turnstile in order to save a nickel. I never knew of anyone who got caught. It's hard to believe that at one point in our lives, pennies and nickels meant so much to us.

Once we got to Coney Island, we were in a different world. Walking down the long ramp in the Surf Avenue station, seeing the side shows, hearing the brassy voices of the barkers, the wonderful smells of popcorn, french fries, cotton candy, the whole character of the area was exhilarating. Everything cost a nickel. We gorged ourselves on small budgets and still had enough left to go on a few rides. Nathan's had the biggest and best hot dogs. Our parents called the hot dogs ***franfooreez***, and the drinks, ***ohrahnge y pineahp dring***. How about 'Gabila's knishes' (by the way, Mr. Gabay, a Sephardic, was 'Gabila'), the French fries, the fried onions, the Turkish taffy, (Joe Bonomo, one of ours, was the manufacturer), and the cotton candy? I don't know about the other guys, but one counter I never went near was the clam and oyster counter. That was strictly taboo: **Solo para los kristianos** (Only for the gentiles).

PROVERBS

El ke mira lo muncho, piedre lo poko.
The one who looks for much, loses the little.
Don't be greedy

Mas vale pasharo en mano ke dos bolando.
A bird in hand is worth two in the bush.
Better to be safe than sorry.

Mas vale dulsor de boka de paras en aldikerra.
A sweet mouth is worth more than money in the pocket.
One catches more flies with honey than with vinegar.

MOOM PITCH

"I've got three, who's got two?" Only septuagenarians who lived on the Lower East Side of New York will have heard that expression. Admission to the movies in those days was two for five cents. Nickels were hard to come by; when a youngster had amassed the great sum of three cents, he stood in front of the movie house announcing, "I've got three, who's got two?" When the one with the 'two' came forward, an alliance was formed, and they enjoyed the movie. Many a life-long friendship was shaped that way, even some courtships.

Everyone loved the movies! Do you remember your folks saying. **"Oy mos vamos a ir al *moom pitch.* Vamos a ver a *Cholly Chop* y *Jaki Coogy, Fahti Abooky*, el sashooto, y al peltek, komo se yaman?** ("Today we are going to the moving pictures. We are going to see Charlie Chaplin, and Jackie Coogan, Fatty Arbuckle, the cross-eyed one and the stutterer, what are their names?") They referred to Ben Turpin and Roscoe Ates.

It was a real outing. They brought sandwiches, fruit and other **bavajadas**, such as **pipitas, fistookes, *joozy froo* y *spirmin choonga*, shiftilis**, and more (pumpkin seeds, peanuts, Juicy Fruit and spearmint chewing gum, peaches, etc.). Remember the vendors who used to walk around while the movie was playing, selling cigars, popcorn, cigarettes, candy, sugar-coated peanuts? How about the prices in those days compared to today?

Coming back to **pipitas**, the question always asked was, **"Kon kashkas o sin kashkas?"** With shells or without? It was an art to separate the shell from the seed. You had to crack the point of the shell with your front teeth just hard enough for the shell to divide into two parts and then work the meat out of the shell with your tongue. **Pipitas** eaters were placed in two categories: The ones that could separate the shell from the seed, **sin kashkas**, and those that ate the whole thing, **kon kashkas**. You just couldn't eat one **pipita,** you had to finish every last one. They were a **hazinoora** (a sickness).

After eating a couple of hundred **pipitas**, you could taste the salt for a week. What a mess the shells made, in the street or wherever you ate them. Mom would say, **"Te kito los ojos si me ensusyas la kaza."**

("I'll take your eyes out if you mess up my house.") At home, of course, we usually used ashtrays for the shells!

When we were kids, we looked up to and tried to emulate our parents. The boys would put on acts depicting their fathers; the girls, their mothers. Many of the boys started smoking because of that. We tried not to let on that we were smoking, but who were we kidding? Our folks knew from day one. Finally, my father, after dinner one night, offered me a cigarette. I refused. He said, **"Es *awrai*, ijo. Yo se ke estas fumando del dia ke empesates. Si kierres fumar, puedes fumar en frente de mi. Ya sos de edad."** ("It's all right son. I've known you have been smoking from the day you started. If you want to smoke, you may smoke in front of me. You're old enough.") Too bad they didn't know about the risk of smoking in those days.

The girls fared better. One day my mother and my aunts announced that they were going to the **Kal (Shul)** for a sisterhood meeting. Of course, the men used to poke good-natured fun at them and call them, *'society leddeez.'* The girls figured out that they would be away for at least three hours, giving them enough time to make a batch of **biskochos** (cookies). Well, they really worked hard manipulating flour, water and whatever other ingredients they could remember went into making an acceptable **massa** (dough). You can imagine what the kitchen looked like. Pans all over the place. Flour on the floor, the ceiling, the walls, in their hair and on their faces. All one could see was a pair of dark eyes staring out of a white face.

What happened next? You guessed it. Our moms came home sooner than expected, and the mess was there for all to see. God bless those beautiful, understanding, unforgettable souls. They pitched in, helped put the finishing touches to what was left to do, and instead of **gritando** (yelling), and threatening the girls with a good **haftona** (beating), made them clean up so that everything was **parlak** (shining) like **espejos** (mirrors). **Si no te puedes ver la kara en el tifsin, no esta limpyo** (If you can't see your face in the pan, it isn't clean).

That evening I heard my mother talking with her sisters, saying, **"Vos akodrash kuando mosotros eramos chikas y aziamos lo mismo?"** ("Do you remember when we were small and we did the same thing?")

Yo me akodro kuando (I remember when), for a penny, you bought a cream-filled piece of chocolate. You took a small bite out of it and, if it had a pink filling, you got another one free. We could get a small glass of seltzer for a penny. If you wanted a larger glass, you asked for a 'two cents plain.' For the handsome sum of a 'buffalo nickel,' you got an 'egg cream.' I hate to think how much I would have to pay for an egg cream today. The last I heard was that it cost a buck and a quarter – that is, if you can find a store that even knows what it is. How long has it been since you had one? What is this world coming to? Things may be better now than they were when we were growing up, but somehow I long for those good old, care-free days. **Onde se fueron akeyos dias?** (Where did those days go?)

* * *

DJOHA – AMOR PERDIDA

La mujer de Djoha se muriyo, y el estava muy triste. "Era tan buena, tan ermosa, me aziya komidas tan buenas, la kaza siempre era limpya. Ke yo va azer sin eya?"

El amigo, Memet, trato a konsolarlo, y le disho, "Mira Djoha, no yorres tanto te vas a azer hazino. En sesh mezez topas una mujer ke es mijor, mas ermosa, y mijor guizandera."

Djoha disho, "Sesh mezez!!! Ma, esta noche ke ke aga yo?" *

LOST LOVE

Djoha's wife passed away, and he was very sad. "She was so good, so beautiful, she made me such good meals, the house was always clean. What am I going to do without her?"

His friend, Memet, tried to console him, and said, "Look Djoha, don't cry so much, you're going to get sick. In six months you will find a better woman, prettier and a better cook."

Djoha said, "Six months!!! What am I going to do tonight?"

* * *

*__"Esta noche ke ke aga yo?"__ was a widely used expression in Salonika, signifying "But what do I do now?"

The Halio family. New York City, circa 1920. Joe (Yusef), Susie (Sultana) and 3 year old Hank (Aaroniko). Note my Pop's fancy shoes and my Mom's gold watch and chain.

Corner of Orchard and Rivington Streets, on the Lower East Side, New York City, during the early twentieth century. The Sephardic community resided mainly between the Bowery, Houston, Clinton and Division Streets, with the greatest concentration between Chrystie and Allen Streets, from Houston to Grand. *Collection of the New-York Historical Society.*

Hester Street on the Lower East Side, at the turn of the century, though looking pretty much the way I remembered it when I was a kid. By the time I was seven years old, the entire Halio clan moved ***Ahptahn*** to Harlem. *Collection of the New-York Historical Society.*

Bronx River Avenue in the East Bronx, having moved up from Harlem. This picture was taken in 1930, just 6 months before my **Bar-Misvah**. From left to right: cousin Betty Halio, myself, my pop, and cousin Esther Hattem on Pop's lap.

Hank on guard duty, Camp Stewart, Georgia, 1942. Mom was relieved when she saw this picture of me. She said, **"Me paresyo ke se iva azer hazino en la armada, ama aki parese muy sano y reziyo. Mashala."** ("I thought he was going to get sick in the army, but he looks hale and hearty, may the Lord protect.")
Inset: Upon graduation from Officer Candidate School, 1943.

The *Sun Ray Social Club,* circa 1930's. Left to right, seated: Charles Catarevas, Solly (Brown) Jacobs, Moe Cohen, Charley Rousso, Max Cassiola. Standing, left to right: Al Levy, Dr. Abie Castro, Al Torres, Lou Miones, Sam Cohen, Jack Levy, Dan Eskenazi. *Courtesy of June Rousso.*

'The Turks' with ILGWU president David Dubinski. *Unity House,* circa 1941. Located at Bushkill Falls in the Poconos, the summer resort was open only to ILGWU members. Seated: David Dubinsky. Clockwise, left to right: Joe Camhi, Morris Calderon, Abie Elias, Charlie Rousso and Danny Eskenazis. *Courtesy of June Rousso.*

A July 4, 1940 tribute at the New Lots Branch of ***Hesed Ve Emet Kastorialis*,** (Malta Street and Hegemon Streets) which supported three synagogues and Hebrew schools in Brooklyn and downtown Manhattan. *Courtesy of Marilyn Mayo and Phyllis Modiano.*

Bar-Misvah of Salamon (Sol) Elias, 1930. First person to **Bar-Misvah** at the newly built synagogue on Malta Street ***(Hesed Ve Emet Kastorialis)***, New Lots, Brooklyn. Rabbi Solomon Behar officiated. *Courtesy of Sol Elias.*

Wedding ceremony of Hank Halio and Phyllis Torres, New York City, 1947. Note the ***taled*** draped over the bride and groom, which in the Sephardic custom is used as a ***hupa***.

Another picture of the happy bride and groom, showing who's the boss!!

A typical Sephardic **Ketuba**, or marriage contract, for use in the United States. Printed by the *Sephardic Publishing Company* (publishers of ***La Vara***). See chapter **Mesa Franka** for translation of the text.

My father-in-law, Albert J. Torres. He was the owner and publisher of the Ladino newspaper, ***La Vara***, published from 1922 to 1948.

Uncle Joe and family at a picnic in Bronx Park, 1937. Left to right: daughter Rose, son-in-law Morris Bello, granddaughter Susie, my Aunt Esther, and Uncle Joe Fintz.

קומפלוטו פור אוקופאר סאלוניקו

LA VARA

לה באֿרה

FRIDAY, September 19 1924

פריסיו די סליחות

5 סינטימוס

Address: 7 RIVINGTON ST., N. Y.

Tels. Orchard 8940 — Dry Dock 7591

VOL. III No. 108

PRICE 5 Cents

Early edition of ***La Vara*** from September 19, 1924, reporting the local and world news events. Note the satirical graphics in the masthead.

אימבארגו די ארמאס פארה ציון טרוקארה

LA VARA

לה באֿרה

אחד

Friday, February 20, 1948

7 RIVINGTON STREET

NEW YORK 2, N. Y.

PRICE 5 CENTS

פריסיו 5 סינטאבוס

VOL. XXVI, No. 25

The last edition of ***La Vara***, dated February 20, 1948. When the newspaper folded, it was the last Judeo-Spanish newspaper in the world.

The *Sephardic Home for the Aged,* on Cropsey Avenue, Brooklyn, New York. Established May 20, 1951. Originally the *Harbor Hospital*, the building was purchased from the City of New York when it was closed in 1950. *Courtesy of the Sephardic Home.*

Dedication of the new facade and Lasha Pavillion of the *Sephardic Home for the Aged,* Brooklyn, September 8, 1968. *Courtesy of the Sephardic Home.*

EL ERMANADO

איל אירמאנאדו

אוג״ינה ריב״יסטה אנואלה די לה

אירמאנדאד ספרדית די אמיריקה, אינק.

סומאריין

PUBLICITY COMMITTEE LEON SAADY EDWARD BESSO DANIEL BOTTON	5689 1928	קומיטי די פוב״ליקאסיון ליאון סעדי אידואורד ביסו דניאל בוטון

אימפרימידיאה דיל ז׳ורנאל ״לה ב״ארה,״ 7 ריב״ינגטון סטריט, נוייורק.

El Ermanado *(The United)* – the original newsletter of the *Sephardic Brotherhood* **(La Ermandad).** Now published in English, it is called *The Brother.*

BROOME AND ALLEN BOYS ASSOCIATION, Inc.

THE BABA

GIVE TO
THE
CAMP FUND!
GIVE
GENEROUSLY

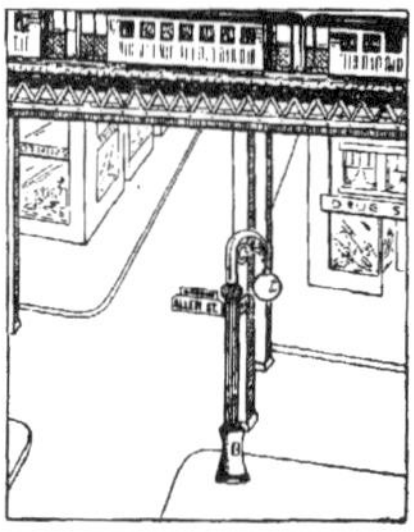

THE RICH AND
THE POOR MEET
TOGETHER.
THE LORD IS THE
MAKER OF THEM
ALL.

VOL. II — JUNE, 1951 — NO. 11

NOTICE OF MEETING

Dear Member:

You are cordially invited to attend the next R E G U L A R M E E T I N G of the BROOME AND ALLEN BOYS ASSOCIATION, Inc. to be held at the

PARK SHERATON HOTEL
55th Street and Seventh Ave.
New York City
ON
Tuesday Eve., June 19th, 1951
at 8:00 P. M. PROMPTLY

Matters of great importance to the Association will come up for discussion and voting, including the Annual Affair to take place next fall, the report on the Camp Fund Drive for 1951, the President's Annual Report on the state of affairs of the organization and finally, but of importance to you as a member, will be a discussion of social events and activities to be planned for the summer among the members and their families.

Please come to this meeting and bring a friend and prospective member.

Fraternally yours,

JACK MEVORAH, Secretary — EDWARD A. DAVID, President

Cover page from *The Broome and Allen Boys Association* newsletter, dated 1951. *The 'BABA'* was organized in 1938 by combining some of the smaller clubs from the Lower East Side. The *Association* still exists today, supporting their original Camp and Scholarship funds.

Immigration-Language class at Taft High School, Bronx, NY, circa 1939. It was in such classes that many Sephardic immigrants learned English and prepared for naturalization exams. Standing by the blackboard, in a dark dress, is my mother, Susie Halio.

Hank and Dr. Albert Menache, a Holocaust survivor from Salonica. Dr. Menache was the physician at the Sephardic Home and author of the first book published about the Holocaust in Greece. This photo was taken in 1990, shortly before Dr. Menache's death. *Courtesy of Stuart Fishelson.*

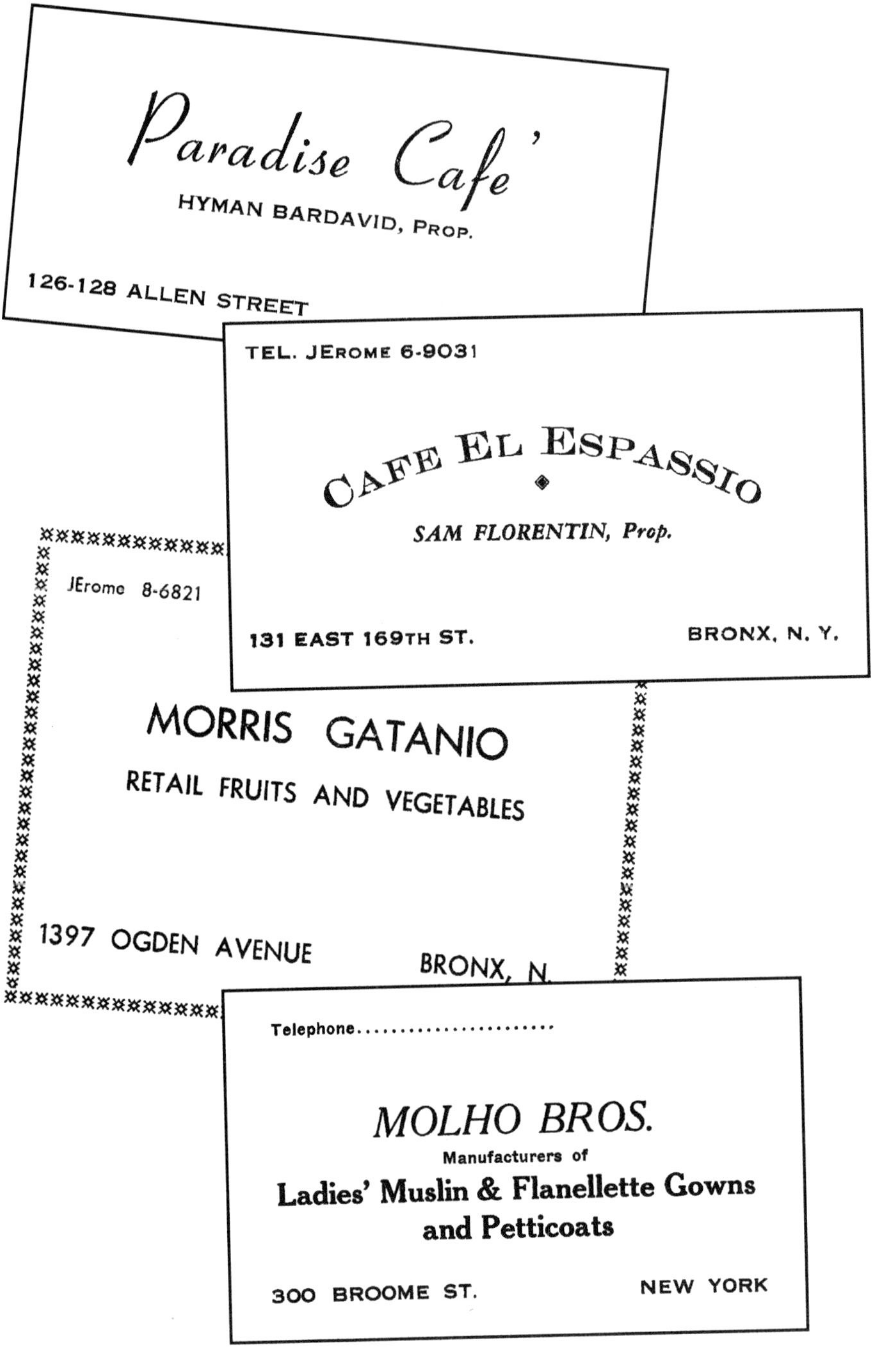

Business cards of some Sephardic merchants from the Bronx and the Lower East Side. Some may be familiar to you.

MADAM DOODOO

I received this gem of a story in the mail. The writer is a gentleman whom I have known for many years and wishes to remain anonymous. It is being presented here exactly as it was sent to me in order to preserve its original flavor.

"As you know most of us live on east side especially old time. It was real bad but life must go on. One tenement building Rivinton-Houston, I live in 12, 2 room aparments most of the tenants they are Sephardi. In the bad times 3 person die in one week. All of them are in bad mood. So this woman by the name of **Madam Doodoo** deside to make **kaparah**. She wen around to collek a few nickless **i** dimes and bought a chicken alive. She wants **Shohet Rabbay** to do the job, so she pick on me a 13 year ole boy to go around. I got a **Haham Shohet**. I tole him to come with me, so he follow me to the house. I went up to **Madam Doodoo** and bring the **Rabbay** to her. The **Rabbay** cut the chicken and give it to me. I went up to **Madam Doodoo** and give to her the chicken. She give a quarter to give to the **Rabbay**. I went down to him and give the 25 cents piece to him. He say, "No, and give back to me the 25 cent piece and he say, "Is half dollar, 50 cents." I wen up istess to **Madam Doodoo** and say, "He want 50 cents." She get mad take the ***kawreh*** (quarter) from me run down estess say to **Rabbay, "No tienes verguensa, por una gayina kierres medio dolar?"** ("Aren't you ashamed, for one chicken you want a half dollar?") The **Rabbay** look on her and he say, **"No era gayina, era un gayo."** ("It wasn't a chicken, it was a rooster.")"

The term **kaparah** means forgiveness or pardon in Hebrew. When something broke my father would say, **"Kaparah."** ("Forgiven.") It is more commonly recognized as ritual used to ward off evil, or as a last resort to cure a malady. My interpretation is that they believed the malady was the result of a sinful act by the afflicted one, and a plea was made for forgiveness. As a child I heard someone say, **"Ke pekado ize yo para mereser esto?"** ("What sin did I commit to deserve this?")

The ritual of offering a slaughtered fowl as sacrifice for this purpose probably had its origin in medieval times. A chicken or a rooster, depending on the sex of the individual, was slaughtered by a **Shohet** (an authorized slaughterer). He would pass the fowl over the subject's head three times, intone his/her name, and plead that the malady be transferred to the fowl, by saying, **"Agora esta hazinoora pasara a este animal."** (Now this sickness shall pass to this animal.) It was permissible for the family to eat the fowl, but it almost always was donated as a **Mizvah** (a good deed) to a poor family. The English used in the story by that gentleman is typical of the Sephardim who came to this country at the turn of the century in their teens. They learned English as adults and never had the opportunity to go to school to study the language. Times were hard then, and people like him had no choice but to find work to earn a living to survive. The beneficiaries were their children, who were in danger of incurring the extreme wrath of their parents if they even dreamed of dropping out of school. Happily, it paid off.

* * *

DJOHA – MUY KARO

Djoha tenia de menester un moso para su kaza. El vezino, Memet, le disho a Djoha ke konosiya un ombre ke estava eyelak y ke era buen lavorante. Djoha le disho al amigo ke lo embiye. Despues de unas semanas, Memet le demando a Djoha komo estava lavorando el moso ke le embiyo. Djoha le disho ke el ombre era buen lavorante, ama ke era muy karo, y ke le demandava por paras kada dia. Memet le demando a Djoha, "Ke aze este ombre kon todas las paras?" Djoha respondiyo, "No te puedo dezir porke no le pagi dainda."

VERY EXPENSIVE

Djoha was in need of a servant for his house. His neighbor, Memet, told Djoha that he knew a man who was out of work and was a good worker. Djoha asked his friend to send him. After a few weeks, Memet asked Djoha how the servant was working out. Djoha told him he was a good worker, but that he was too expensive, he asked for money everyday. Memet asked, "What does he do with all that money?" Djoha said, "I can't tell you, because I have not paid him yet."

* * *

HOME CURES

Richina!! Castor oil!! Everybody hated it. That was a patent medicine our mothers made us take when we got sick. I don't know about anyone else, but I know how it affected me. The favorite chaser for that dreaded medicine was to suck on a **portokal** (an orange). The result was that for many years the very thought of eating an orange or drinking orange juice was nauseating. It brought **boulanteez** (nausea). **Richina** was not administered for every ailment, though. If someone complained of not feeling well, and nothing seemed seriously wrong, the diagnosis was **"Tiene el koulo en dos."** ("His ass is in two parts.") Some **keshas** (complaints) I remember were: **Dolor de tripa** (a stomach ache), **Dolor de kavesa** (a headache), **Esta gomitando** (He's throwing up), **Esta chapeteado, puede ser ke tiene kayentura** (His face is flushed, maybe he has fever), **El garon esta kolorado, seriya agayas?** (His throat is red, could it be tonsils)? **No te espantes, solo es abashada** (Don't be afraid, it's only a cold).

Shakeka!! I heard of two versions of the meaning of this word, and I must assume that both are right, depending on which part of Turkey one came from. My understanding of **Shakeka** was a kerchief that contained thin slices of potatoes sprinkled with fresh ground coffee and was wrapped around the head, concentrating on the temples. The other version I heard was that the word **Shakeka** meant headache. In Salonika it referred specifically to a migraine headache. The remedy for that was to dip two pieces lemon in powdered coffee, and apply one piece to each temple.

Being an only child and a nosy one at that, I often had nothing better to do than hang around the adults and listen in on their conversations. Home cures was one of the topics that intrigued me. Although I did not get to witness many of these 'cures,' I did manage to see and experience some. For a stomach ache, a mixture of **raki y pimienta** (raki and pepper) was rubbed on the stomach. Hopefully, it really was just a belly ache and not a case of appendicitis. For a chest cold, **ventozas** was the way to go. It was a relatively simple process. A small piece of absorbent cotton, lightly moistened, was placed in the bottom of a small specially designed glass. The cotton was lighted with a match and the glass was then instantly inverted and placed on the chest or upper back. When the oxygen in the glass was used up, it created a vacuum sucking the skin up under it. As many as a dozen would be applied. The result was a puffing and reddening of the skin. The redder and puffier it got, the worse the cold was believed to be. **Mira tanto ke esta sufriendo, zavali** (Look at how she's suffering, poor thing). Upon removal of the **ventozas** the 'patient' was rubbed with *Musterole*, a patent medicine, and a piece of flannel was placed on the treated area. Some amazing cures were achieved by this process.

For a head cold, a mustard plaster was concocted. A couple of teaspoons of powdered English mustard was mixed with some water and made into a thick paste, a little **raki** and pepper added, put into a thin cotton cloth, and placed on the top of the head. It couldn't stay there too long. Your brains felt like they were on fire. It must have worked. I saw it done year after year.

Bleeding, the removal of 'so-called' bad blood, was another age-old method of 'curing' many ailments. For this treatment **sandjurwelas** (leeches) were used. In the old days leeches were prominently displayed in the windows of local pharmacies. One of the ailments this was used for was the removal of 'bad blood' from varicose veins. The leeches would remain in place until it was believed all the 'bad blood' was removed. This one, I am happy to say, I never witnessed.

A more humane 'cure' was the one used to repair a sprain. A large onion, minced, was placed in a piece of gauze-like material and wrapped around the afflicted part, be it an ankle, a wrist or what have you. Another 'cure' for a sprained ankle or wrist was to bandage the afflicted limb and apply a beaten egg white on the bandage to form a sort of cast. After a few days it was removed, and more often than not, it worked.

One thing that has remained a mystery to me is the phrase, **El ombligo esta desatado** (the navel is untied), which referred to a herniated navel. The afflicted one was never taken to a doctor to correct this malady. The only person who could fix this was a 'specialist.' I saw this done when a cousin of mine was suffering from it. This 'specialist' cut an onion in half, placed it on my cousin's navel, applied a certain kind of pressure, did some maneuvering with his hands around the area, and after some time would say, **"Ya esta atado."** ("It's tied.") It had a success rate of 100%. I never heard it to fail.

When an ailment was diagnosed as not being physiological, and if the affected one developed uncharacteristic symptoms, such as becoming moody, withdrawn, or inordinately cranky, the family held a pow-wow and concluded that he/she was suffering from **espanto** (a scare or a fright). The folks from the old country had many ways to combat this malady. In a mild case it was customary to sprinkle sugar around the window sills and in front of the building. The sugar was used in order to influence only good things and allow only good thoughts to enter the house. If that didn't work, then a person known in the community as a **savida** (knowledgeable one) would be called. This person was also referred to as an **Ichizera** (a witch doctor), but never to her face. I had seen two instances where the **Ichizera** was called in for a consultation. The symptoms were discussed, the possible cures or approaches were proposed, and a price was established. Of the methods that were proposed, I witnessed two. One was called **brazikos** and the other **livianos**.

Brazikos are embers of hot charcoal. It was a relatively simple procedure. The subject sat in a chair, a large towel was placed over his head and the **Ichizera** placed a **tava** (a pot) under the towel, dropping hot embers into the pot one at a time. This caused an outpouring of steam up into the subject's face and each time the **Ichizera** would intone some unintelligible words. After several repetitions the **Ichizera** would declare the person cured, and ask to be left alone with him. The **Ichizera** remained silent, as if in a trance, for several minutes and then left to collect her fee.

Livianos was a more complicated technique. Several people were required for the process to work without anyone getting hurt. A large chunk of **kourshoum** (lead) was melted down and kept molten throughout the procedure. The afflicted one was made to lie on a table; four people, one at each corner, held a large white sheet over him, one person held a large pot half-filled with water over the sheet, and the **Ichizera** poured the molten **kourshoum** into the water. The result of this action was frightening. The hot lead hitting the cold water caused a sort of an explosion, spraying hot water and stray pieces of lead all over the sheet. The cooled lead formed a spectacular array of hills, valleys, sharp jagged points and symbols. This conglomeration formed a hodgepodge that was 'read' by the **Ichizera**. The process was repeated three times for verification and effect. Each time the inspection was going on, the **Ichizera** performed a dramatic incantation of some kind of mumbo-jumbo. The only words I did understand were, **"Komo esta maldad te vino, esta maldad se va desaparaser al dip de la mar, nunka para retornar."** ("As this malady came to you, so it shall disappear in bottom of the sea never to return.")

The **Ichizera** would show the afflicted one what she thought was the cause of the problem, from her interpretation upon looking at the chunk of lead that had been dropped into the water. It might have been a person, an animal, a vehicle or anything the **Ichizera** wanted the family to believe, and who was to dispute the decision? Once the cause of the problem was established, certain precautions were prescribed to eliminate the problem, all for a hefty fee: two bucks.

I assume that these practices had been used for generations – and must have had some kind of a success rate, but the odds are that there must have also have been some disastrous results.

* * *

DJOHA – DIVINO O MORTAL DISTRIBUSION

Un dia kuatro ijikos se aserkaron a Djoha y le dieron un sako yeno de liras de oro. "Djoha, no savemos komo de distribuir estas liras ke topimos. Mos puedes ayudarmos?" Djoha les demando, "Keresh la manera del Dyo para distribuir, or la manera de mortal?" "Manera del Dyo!" Los ijikos dishieron. Djoha avriyo el sako y le dio al primer ijiko dos punyados de liras, un punyado al segundo, al treser le dio las tres liras ke kedavan y nada al kuatren. "Ke modo de distribuision es esto?" Los ijikos demandaron. "Esta es la menera del Dyo," respondyo Djoha. El Dyo da muncho a unos de la djente, a otros un poko, y a otros nada. Si me demandavas por la manera mortal, vos dava lo mismo a todos.

DIVINE OR MORTAL DISTRIBUTION

One day four boys approached Djoha and gave him a sack full of gold liras. "Djoha, we don't know how to distribute these liras that we found. Can you help us?" Djoha asked them, "Do you want me to distribute them in God's way or in a mortal's way?" "God's way!" The boys said. Djoha opened the sack and gave the first boy two handsful, one handful to the second boy, to the third boy he gave the three liras that were left, and to the fourth, he gave none. The boys asked, "What kind of distribution is this?" "Well, this is God's way," He answered. "He gives some people a lot, some people a little and nothing to others. If you had asked for the mortal's way, I would have given you all the same amount.

* * *

EL PASHA ESTA GUIZANDO

My wife had an attack of vertigo, and **y este pasha estava en grande trouble** (and this prince was in big trouble). Aside from the fact that vertigo is a very debilitating malady for the one that has it, it is no picnic for someone who has never had to lift a finger to do anything in the house. **Barminan y leshos!** (Heaven forbid and faraway!) No one should ever have to go through such an ordeal as vertigo, nor the ordeal of tending to one who is afflicted, especially if the attendant is a spoiled only son, **pasha por ijo** (prince of a son).

Vertigo affects a person in such a manner that you just want to die and get it over with. You can't do anything for yourself, or anyone else. Consequently, this **pasha** was constantly on call. "Hank, get me this and get me that." "Where is it? I can't find it." My mother used to say about my father: **"Si lo embiyas a la mar no topa agua."** ("If you send him to the ocean, he won't find water.") **La mansana no kaye lejos del arvole** (The apple doesn't fall far from the tree).

Being a compassionate and loving husband, I tried to ease the situation by helping in every way that I could. At one point when Phyllis finally fell asleep, I felt that she would be hungry when she woke up. I ran out and bought chicken soup, a broiled chicken, and some bread. When Phyllis awoke and asked for some food, I gave her the chicken soup. Wouldn't you know it, she asked for dessert: Jello. Anyone can make Jello, right? Not I. "How do you make Jello," I asked. Her answer was, "You don't know how to make Jello!!! Everyone knows how to make Jello. Read the directions on the box." "No," I said, "Tell me how." We got over that hurdle, but new ones arose.

What was I going to do for dinner? I figured we would have the broiled chicken that I bought at the kosher butcher. You just don't eat chicken by itself. No self-respecting Sephardic would eat chicken without rice. "Phyllis, how do you make rice?" Rather than go through that conversation I'll just give the recipe Phyllis dictated to me as I remember it.

1 cup of rice (8 oz.), 1 can of tomato sauce (8 oz.), 1 cup of water (8 oz.), bring the 2 cups of liquid to a boil. Add 1 teaspoon of chicken flavoring, stir, add the cup of rice and cover. Bring to a boil again. Stir, cover again. Reduce the heat and allow to simmer until all the liquid is absorbed (approximately 16 minutes).

The sink was piling up with dishes. "Use the dishwasher." "I don't know how! Besides, I do a better job by hand." Lucky for me that I had taken a job at my uncle's luncheonette when I was a kid, and my primary duty was to wash the dishes. That, of course, was BDW – Before Dish Washers. I think I'll skip the ordeal of the clothes washer and dryer. Never having handled those two appliances, it was **koza mueva para mi** (a new thing for me).

A few days later, when Phyllis was feeling a little better, I tried to impress her by enumerating my accomplishments during her period of incapacitation. Her response was, **"Koza grande!"** ("Big deal!") Nevertheless, I knew that she really appreciated it all when she said, **"Para bueno ke te topes siempre."** ("May you always be here when I need you.")

* * *

Jenny Cohen sent the following **Djoha** story.

DJOHA – ME VA ENFORKAR

Djoha estava kaminando en el charshi kon una sesta de guevos en la kavesa. Una persona paso en muncha adjile, le dio un golpe, kavsando los guevos ke le kaygan enbasho, y se rompieron todos los guevos. Djoha empeso a yorrar, diziendo, "Todo esta pedrido. Agora me va a enforkarme." Un amigo le demando, "Djoha, te vas a enforkar por la garganta?" Djoha disho, "No, por los guevos." *

I'M GOING TO HANG MYSELF

Djoha was walking in the market with a basket of eggs on his head. A person in a hurry bumped him, causing the basket of eggs to fall from his head. All the eggs broke. Djoha started to cry, saying, "All is lost. Now I am going to hang myself." A friend asked him "Djoha, are you going to hang yourself by the neck?" Djoha said, "No, by the eggs."

* * *

* In some Spanish dialects, the word for eggs – **guevos** or **huevos** – is a euphemism for testicles.

HANANEL EN PAPEL

I had just started high school when the depression caught up with my father's business. He closed the factory; and my mother decided to go to work in order to maintain our standard of living.

Since I had lots of time on my hands, I used to run errands for my aunts who lived on my block. The first time I ran those errands for my aunts, they tried to tip me. I refused because I felt that it wasn't right to take money from them. They liked what I did for them and didn't want to lose a good thing, so they made me an offer I couldn't refuse. **"Tu madre se va a lavorar kada dia y viene a kasa kansada, no tiene tiempo ni fuersa para azerte desayuno komo aziya kuando no estava lavorando, te daremos kada viernes un poko de desayuno para ti. Esto sera tu *'tip.' Okay?"*** ("Your mother goes to work everyday and comes home tired every night, she hasn't the time nor the energy to bake, as she did when she wasn't working. Every Friday we will give you some of what we bake as your 'tip.' Okay?") I liked the idea, and a deal was made.

One evening I was running late, and it was just about supper time when I finished my deliveries, and I arrived at my aunt's. Everyone was home, waiting for dinner to be served. My uncle asked, **"Ke ay para komer, mujer?"** ("What's for supper, woman?") My aunt, tired and frazzled from a hard day's work of cooking, baking and cleaning, replied, **"La de Hananel en papel."** ("Hananel's on paper – on a plate.") They all had a big laugh at that remark, except yours truly. I had no idea what was so funny or what it was all about. I gathered my **desayuno**, ran for home, and promptly forgot the incident.

Many years later, I heard that expression again. This time I made an effort to find out. A friend of mine sent me some material which provided the answer. It seems that in Salonica, Turkey, many jokes and stories circulated about a man named Hananel, who had an organ so large that everyone knew about it. But the most famous story was the one about a tired, harried housewife who offered a sandwich to her impatient husband for supper: **La de Hananel en papel.**

YANYOTS

The culture of the Greek Jews, the **Romaniotes,** is very closely related to that of the Spanish Jews. Even though our languages are dif ferent, our ritual in the synagogue is pretty much the same. We enjoy much the same foods, and practice the same old world courtesies.

Almost all their customs are very much like ours, for example, the way they greet **musafires / imsifer** (visitors) in their homes, the food, **dulses / glika** (sweets), the **kave / kafe** (coffee), and so forth. We co-mingle with them much more comfortably than we do with our Ashkenazi brethren. Other than the difference in the languages, we are as one. And there have been many instances of intermarriage between us.

Many of the **Yanyots** (Greek Jews from Yannina) who migrated to the United States in the early 1900's spoke Ladino, and many of the Sephardim spoke Greek. We all know that most of that generation were multilingual, owing to the network of schools that France established in the Ottoman Empire through the *Alliance Israelite Universelle.*

The Sephardic Social Club of Florida has many **Yanyot / Romaniote** members who enrich our meetings with their Greek singing and dancing. I was approached by several of them and asked if I could include some Greek anecdotes, proverbs, vocabulary and possibly a recipe or two in my column. Not being Greek, I really didn't have the material at my fingertips, but since the request was made, I felt an obligation to satisfy my readers. People like Anna and Jesse Asser, Jesse Besso, Joe Ezra Cohen, Nat Negrin, Julia Mathios, Rose Citron and many others offered their assistance, and I thank them. This is what I learned:

The ancient Jews in Israel were blessed with a sea-faring nation as a neighbor: the intrepid Phoenicians. Oftentimes, Jews accompanied the Phoenicians in their voyages around the Mediterranean. Thus Jews found their way to Spain, Italy, Greece and other Mediterranean sites centuries before the Common Era. As early as 400 BCE, Jews had migrated to Greece, where they were known as **Romaniotes** – Greek-speaking Jews. They settled in such cities as Arta, Chalkis, Patras, and Yannina, as well as on the Islands of Rhodes and Crete. Yannina, in particular, had the largest Jewish population and was the most representative of the Greek Jews.

History tells us that during the 1500's and 1600's Yannina had a **Romaniote** population of 7,000 Jews, and that by the 1900's the numbers were reduced to about 3,500. The development of wars in the Balkans and throughout Europe during the early part of this century, and diminishing economic opportunities, prompted many of those Greek Jews to leave their homes for such places as Athens, Palestine, Paris and the New World. In New York, the **Yanyots** formed synagogues in various parts of the city. The first, *Kehila Kedosha Yannina,* is still in service at 280 Broome Street in Manhattan.

Visitors to the Jewish Museum in Athens can see an impressive collection of ancient Jewish artifacts, literature, and domestic articles dating back to the time of Alexander the Great. For over two millennia the Jewish communities in Greece survived, withstanding wars, changes in governments and other catastrophes – that is, until the Nazi invasion of Greece in 1941. By the end of the war the **Romaniote** communities were decimated, so that today a bare shadow of their grandeur remains, with less than 50 souls in Chalkis, and less than 100 in Yannina.

An observation: I have noticed in speaking to several **Yanyot** people that there are differences in the way some of them pronounce certain words. I wonder if they have the same problem that we Sephardim have with the regional differences in Ladino.

SOME YANYOT SAYINGS

Efto leep itee.
This is the only thing missing in my life.

Aloss api thau.
Here's another wise guy.

Heide stou drumoo.
Hit the road, scram, beat it.

Me gapas?
Do you love me?

SOME YANYOT VOCABULARY

Agapi mou	- My love	**Nehro**	- Water
Andeeo	- Goodbye	**Okhee**	- No
Beerah	- Beer	**Pahgoto**	- Ice cream
Boufous	- Stupid	**Parakalo**	- Please
Efharesto Polee	- Thank you	**Peeronee**	- Fork
Frouta	- Fruit	**Polee kala**	- Fine
Greeghora	- Hurry up	**Poss**	- When
Hasou	- Get lost	**Poteeree**	- Glass
Kaleemera	- Good morning	**Poteh**	- When
Kaleeneehta	- Good night	**Pringipesa mou**	- My dear, and only
Kaleespera	- Good afternoon	**Psaree**	- Fish
Koukla	- Doll	**Psomee**	- Bread
Koutalee	- Spoon	**Sakatziz**	- Joker
Makeree	- Knife	**Tee kanete**	- How are you?
Monakpiva	- My princess	**Teepota**	- It's all right
Neh	- Yes	**Vouteero**	- Butter

This seems like an appropriate time to relate an anecdote that had happened to me.

When I was a teenager, a mutual attraction arose between me and a very pretty **Yanyot** girl, who was in one of my classes. I was very shy and we were getting nowhere. She took the initiative and whispered to me, **"Me gapas?"** and ran away. When my father, who was fluent in Greek, came home from work that evening, I asked him what it meant. He didn't answer immediately, but smiled, and asked me if she was **ermozika** (pretty). When I said, "Yes," he said, "Tell her **sagapo**." ("I love you.") I did, and we got along famously!

One last note: The **Yanyot** people referred to our Ashkenazi co-religionists in an affectionate way as ***Ziggy Zooks*** (from a Yiddish phrase, *sie gesunt,* meaning 'be healthy').

AHPTAHN/DAHNTAHN

We used to move quite often in the old days, since every time we moved, we got two or three months 'concession' (no rent), which amounted to a savings of about twenty or thirty dollars. That was a fortune of money then. Sometimes when we moved, we got lucky and found a player piano in the new apartment. It cost a lot of money to transport pianos, and more often than not, people just abandoned them. When I say that it cost a lot of money to transport a piano, I meant it cost five or ten bucks, and make no mistake about it, five or ten bucks was a lot of money in those days. Some of the kids even acquired a desire to study music. Sometimes we even got luckier and the apartment wasn't on the top floor, where the rent was cheapest. Everyone I ever knew lived on the top floor.

When we moved from ***Dahntahn***, the Lower East Side, to ***Ahptahn***, Harlem, we really upgraded our standard of living. We had a bathroom in our own apartment, albeit adjoining the kitchen, not **en el hull komo los proves** (in the hall like the poor people).

The kitchens were marvelous. We did most everything there. We did our homework, we listened to our crystal sets (radios), played games, and so on. Pop would read ***La Vara*** every Friday night. Mom loved hearing Pop read the love stories that were serialized and translated into Ladino – the story of *Ramona, The Count of Monte Cristo,* etc.

Mom did her sewing on the portable Singer sewing machine. Remember them? One had to move the foot pedals constantly in order to get any sewing done. I still have my mother's machine, only now it is electrified, and it still works beautifully. It had four **kashones** (drawers) – two on each side. Each drawer served a purpose: one contained **las agujas y el ilo** (the needles and the thread), another would have **la tijerra y las navajikas** (the scissors and the razor blades), another **los botenes** (the buttons) **y los ferme jupes** (French for: metal closures or snaps). The last one would hold all kinds of trimmings. I can't recall what my mother called them. Maybe she referred to them as ***los treemees***.

Being the only child had its advantages and disadvantages. Since most of my mother's time was devoted to me, she taught me how to sew on that machine. I couldn't reach the peddle to make the machine work, so she had my father rig it so I could reach it. Can you believe that I could sew before I could read? (I drew the line when she tried to teach me how to knit. Even as a pre-schooler, I had enough street sense not to want to be classified as a 'sissy' by my peers.)

Sam Zalma of California, contributed this gem of a memory: "We lived on the corner of Stanton and Orchard Streets, and we went to the nearest movie which was on Rivington Street. My mother used to pronounce it ***Revento***, which in Ladino means to expire. Well, it happened that a certain lady went to the movies one day and fell asleep. When she awoke, she realized that the show was over and that the theater was closed. She didn't know what to do until she saw a telephone on the wall. She picked up the receiver and almost panicked when the operator asked, "Number please." She did not speak English very well, but she pulled herself together enough to say, ***Me eslip*** (sleep), ***Me no eslip. Me go home, me no go home. Me it*** (eat), ***Me no it***. She kept repeating this over and over again. The operator, who sensed something was wrong, had the call traced, and notified the police, who rescued her.

Sam Samarel told me about the time he was growing up on the East Side where he ran around trying to hustle up a few cents on his time off from school. When his father found out about it, he said to Sam, **"Mira, Shomueliko, lo ke estas aziendo es bueno, y me alegro de verlo, ama si azes una favor por paryentes, kierro ke esperes asta ke te lo dan tres veses antes de tomar lo ke te ofresen. Si te lo ofresen tres vezes lo puedes tomarlo.** ("Look, Sammy, what you are doing is good, and I am glad to see it, but if you do a favor for a relative, I want you to wait until the tip is offered three times before accepting it. After the third time, it's all right to take it.")

That was all well and good, but his relatives would play games with Sam once they caught on to what was happening. They started by offering the tip twice while Sam kept refusing waiting for the third offer. Can't you just see Sam squirming and sweating it out, waiting for that third offer to come?

My friend Ike Amira wrote me recently, reminiscing about the snowfalls he remembers ***Ahptahn*** as a kid. "The mounds of ice and snow on 117th Street from Park Avenue to Fifth Avenue were so high that the firemen came with their hoses and literally 'lifted' the ice from the gutters in the early spring to clear the streets because the Carnival would be coming in a short time with their clowns, acrobats, and animals, giving us a preview of the upcoming circus." He says this year in New York is even worse than those years he remembers as a kid.

When we lived ***Dahntahn***, we used expressions that appear to have been forgotten. Let's see if you remember some of these.

Azete del bovo (Make believe you're the dope). **Va trava la araba** (Go pull a wagon), the true meaning: Get lost, scram, beat it. **Azelo liviano** (Make it light). The intent being "Get to the point, cut it short." **Komo un guevo partido** (Like an egg divided), equivalent to 'two peas in a pod.' **Meter ojo** (To put an eye on), meaning to put a 'whammy' on, to jinx. **Echa ojo** (Throw an eye) has a different meaning: Take a look, keep an eye on. **Nunka ni no** has several meanings, such as: take it or leave it, so don't, drop dead, etc. **Bivir y ver** (To live and to see). This phrase is often used when something unusual or incredible occurs. It is akin to 'As I live and breathe.' **El Dyo es grande** (literally: God is great). Our intent is that, in saying that, God will look out for us. **Kitar el kueshko** (To remove the pit) actually refers to resolving something or putting an end to it. **Ke azno se murio?** (Which donkey died)? Sephardic meaning: "Now you tell me?" "It's about time." **Ya me lo paso** (I'll get by). **Me estas kitando la alma** (You are taking out my soul, you are killing me). **Para bueno ke te topes** (May you be here for good). **Es un shavdo** (an insipid, boring person). **Manyana es otro dia** (Tomorrow is another day).

PROVERBS

Antes ke te kazes, mira lo ke azes.
Before you marry, look at what you are doing.
Careful guys, it's telling you to beware. Look before you leap. Okay, girls too!

Azno no se trata komo benadam.
A jackass is not to be treated as a human being.
Unfortunately there are too many ***aznos*** *around.*

El oro fino arelumbra.
Fine gold shines. *A fine person reveals himself as such.*

THE AUTOMAT

I recently read a nostalgic article about the demise of the *Horn and Hardart Automats.* It was a beautifully written article that brought to mind the first time I took my mother to Times Square, and we visited the Automat. What a marvelous experience it was for her to see the automation of that era. She marvelled at how the cashier at the front of the store slid out the nickels in groups of five at a time. I had given the cashier a one-dollar bill, and he tossed the nickels back at me five at a time without missing once. Mom stayed there for a few minutes watching him in amazement as he made change for several customers before moving into the store.

"Este hombre parese komo una *mashina.* Mira komo esta aziendo *chench.* Nunka espera para kontar los *niklehs.* Este lugar es maraviyoso! Mira lo ke akontese kuando metes paras en la pared, te sale kave kon leche. Komo fue ke salyo sin asukar? Y si kierres un *sahnwich* de kezo o otro modo de *sahnwich,* o un biskocho, solo kale de meter unos kuantos *niklehs* en el bourako en la pared y te sale lo ke deseyas." ("This man looks like a machine. Look at how he's making change. He never stops to count the nickels. This place is miraculous! Look at what happens when you put money into the wall, out comes coffee with milk. How come it didn't come with sugar? And if you want a cheese sandwich, or another kind of sandwich or a piece of cake, all you have to do is put a nickel in the hole on the wall, and out comes whatever you desire.")

That same article also brought me back to the days of the elevated trains that we used to take to go from ***Dahntahn***, the Lower East Side, to ***Ahptahn,*** Harlem. It became particularly dangerous in the summer time because in those days one could open the windows on the trains. One hot Sunday afternoon we got on the train to visit some relatives in Harlem. The windows were open and a few seconds after the train started to pull out of the Houston Street station, a few men standing on the platform reached inside the windows and pulled the hats off the heads of the men who were seated on the platform side of the car.

One of the men who lost a hat was my Uncle Joe Fintz. He was furious. Knowing my Uncle Joe, if he had been able to get his hands on any of those guys, he would have torn them to pieces. As it was, he was very fast, and still seated, almost caught the man's hand, but he only got a hold of his sleeve. His grip tore the man's shirt, leaving my uncle holding the flapping sleeve. Waving it like anything but a white flag, he got up and turned to the window screaming, looked the guy in the eye and said, **"Ijo de un azno, yo me akodro komo tu pareses. Si yo te veygo algun dia, te va a matar, *san a ma betch*!"** ("You son of a jackass, I remember what you look like. If I ever see you some day, I'll kill you, *san a ma betch!")*

My folks used to eat out a lot when I was small. The one restaurant I remember well, because we ate there most of the time, was owned by a man called Ishuwa Penso. There was another restaurant, the name of which I can't recall, that was unique. This place had a great big sign in the window stating it used only **guevos freskos** (fresh eggs). To prove it, the owner kept a chicken roosting in a sort of a coop in his front window. He always made a big show of taking the eggs from the coop when an order called for eggs to be used. From my juvenile point of view, he did a good business. One evening we went there and saw that the chicken was no longer in the window. It turned out that a city ordinance prohibited the exploitation of live animals and a restaurant was not permitted to have pets.

TOPLESS OKAY – SMOKING NOT OKAY

Things certainly have changed since the old days. I recently read an article describing the so-called 'quality of life' issues that New Yorkers are now facing. It was an update for tourists. Apparently, Transit Authority attorneys have declared that it's OK for women to ride the subways topless, so long as they don't smoke. The attorneys had, of course, consulted with the Manhattan District Attorney's Office before deciding that bare-chested women on subways can be arrested only if they create a "disruptive situation." A police spokesman is reported to have said that if the women were violating any other rules, like sitting on a subway bench topless and smoking a cigarette, then the police would surely take action!

The first thing that came to my mind when I saw that item in the newspaper was, "What would my Uncle Joe say if he were here with us today and he had read or heard about that same article?" Throughout his lifetime the goings-on in this country never ceased to amaze my Uncle Joe. "God Bless America," he would say. He was an inveterate smoker and I'm sure his reaction would have been something like this: **"La djente en esta sivdad son lokos, yo vide una mujer en el *suboowe* asentada kon las tetas enkolgando, y no le izieron nada. Esto, me dishieron es lo ke se yama *'woomen's lib.'* Kuando yo fumee un sigaro en el *suboowe,* me dieron una djeza de diez dolares."** ("The people in this city are crazy. I saw a woman in the subway sitting with her ____ hanging out and they didn't do anything to her. This, they told me, is called 'women's lib.' When I smoked a cigarette on the subway, I was given a fine of ten dollars.")

Dr. Jack Crespin told me this story about his father: "My father and I always spoke to each other in Spanish. One day he came to me and said, **"Mira, ijo, oy yo kompri un estok ke se yama Dr. Pepper. Kreyes ke es buena *idea?"*** ("Look son, today I bought a stock called Dr. Pepper. Do you think it is a good idea?") This was back in 1946. Dr. Pepper was a very popular soft drink in the South, but practically unknown in the North. When Dr. Pepper was first introduced up North, it was a big hit, making it fairly attractive for investment. Jack had never heard of the company and could not understand how his father could buy a stock named for a doctor. He questioned his father, **"Komo puede ser ke un doktor se izo un korporasion y estava en el Estok Market?"** ("How can a doctor incorporate himself and go on the stock market?")

One evening after dinner, a group of us sat around shooting the breeze. As happens very often, we mixed a little Ladino in our dialogue. During the course of the evening, the conversation drifted to divorce. Different reasons were given, but most agreed that the biggest bone of contention in most cases is custody of the children. Lily Cohen said, **"Yo y mi marido Harry, despues de mas de sinkuenta anyos no mos estamos pasando bueno mas, y estamos avlando de divorsarmos, ama no lo vamos a azer porke kon mosotros, no es kien va a tomar a las kriaturas, es kual de las kriaturas se va enkashar kon Harry."** ("My husband Harry and I, after more than fifty years, are not getting along, and we are talking about getting a divorce, but we're not going to go through with it because with us it isn't a matter of who is going to get the kids, but which of the kids is going to get stuck with Harry.")

* * *

DJOHA – KIEN ES EL DUENYO AKI?

Un dia Djoha tomo una sesta de las mijores serezas de su guerta y se fue al charshi. Metyo la sesta yena de serezas ensima de su azniko y se fue. Kuando yego al charshi, se fue al mijor lugar y empeso a yamar a la djente diziendo, "Ermosas serezas aki, ermosas serezas aki." Al azniko le gusto el grito de Djoha, y empeso a gritar, "Hee har, hee har." Djoha se inyervo kon el azniko, ama no izo nada. Por la segunda vez Djoha empeso a avlar a la djente, "Ermosas serezas aki, ermosas serezas aki." Otra vez, el azniko grito, "Hee har, hee har." Esta ves, muncha djente se arekojeron a ver komo Djoha lo iva kayar al azniko. Djoha estava muy inyervoso ama ni esta vez no izo nada. Por la tresera ves Djoha empeso a avlar a la djente, "Serezas aki, ermosas serezas aki, serezas aki." Una vez mas el azniko grito, "Hee har, hee har." Mas djente vinyeron. Agora, Djoha estava muy bien inyervado y

abolto al azniko y le disho, "Mira azno, ijo de un azno, kien vende estas serezas aki, yo o tu?"

WHO IS BOSS HERE?

One day Djoha took a basket of his best cherries from his garden. He put the basket on his donkey and went to the market. When he got there, he picked the best spot and started to call to the people, "Cherries here, beautiful cherries here, cherries here." The donkey, who liked hearing Djoha yell, brayed, "Hee Har, Hee Har." Djoha got angry with the donkey, but he didn't do anything. For the second time he started to yell, "Cherries here, beautiful cherries here, cherries here." Once again the donkey brayed, "Hee Har, Hee Har." Lots of people gathered around to see how Djoha was going to quiet the donkey. Djoha was very angry, but not even this time did he do anything. For the third time, Djoha started to talk to the people, "Cherries here, beautiful cherries here, cherries here." Once again the donkey brayed, "Hee Har, Hee Har." More people gathered around. By this time Djoha was really mad, he turned to the donkey and said, "Look you jackass, son of a jackass, who sells these cherries here, you or I."

* * *

MAMA! TU SOS?

LA MADRE Y EL IJO KE KIERRE VENIR A VISHITAR

Un mansevo desho la kaza de su madre y padre munchos anyos antes. Se kazo y la mujer le paryo dos ijos, y agora el kierre venir a pasar el verano en la kaza de su parientes. Los yama al telefon, y la konversasion sige en esta manera:

Ijo: Mama! Tu sos?

Mama: Si ijo de la madre. Komo estas? Y tu mujer, y los chikitikos?

Ijo: Todos estamos muy bien, grasias al Dyo. Mama, yo kierro venir este verano y pasar un mezeziko en tu kaza.

Mama: Seguramente, presiado. Ven en la buena ora. Te espero ojos a ojos.

Ijo: Va venir kon mi mujer. Onde mos vas a echar?

Mama: Vos va dar mi kamareta. No tengas kudyado. Tu padre y yo mos pasaremos bien.

Ijo: Onde vos vash a echar?

Mama: Mos echamos en el *"livin ruhm."* No te mirikeyes.

Ijo: Keremos venir kon los ijos. Onde los vas a echar?

Mama: Traelos, los echamos en el *"livin ruhm."*

Ijo: Tu y el papa, onde vos vash a echar?

Mama: Mos echamos en la kamareta chika.

Ijo: Ama mi suegra, no tenemos onde desharla.

Mama: Bueno ijo, traela.

Ijo: Onde la vas a echar?

Mama: Le daremos la kamareta chika.

Ijo: Y vosotros, onde vos vash a echar?

Mama: Yo me echo de la ventana, y tu padre ke aga lo ke kierre.

MAMA! IS THAT YOU?

THE MOTHER AND SON WHO WANTS TO VISIT

A young man left the home of his parents many years ago. He is married and his wife has given birth to two children. Now he wants to come to spend the summer in his parents' house. He calls on the telephone and this conversation follows:

Son: Mama! Is that you?
Mama: Yes my dear son. How are you and your wife and the little ones?
Mama: We are all well, thank God.
Son: Mama, I would like to come this summer and spend a month in your house.
Mama: Of course, precious. I await you with all eyes.
Son: I am coming with my wife. Where will we sleep?
Mama: I will give you my room. Don't worry, your father and I will manage.
Son: Where are you going to sleep?
Mama: We will sleep in the living room. Don't fret.
Son: We want to come with the children. Where will you put them?
Mama: We will give them the living room.
Son: You and Papa, where will you sleep?
Mama: We will sleep in the small room.
Son: But my mother-in-law, I have no place to leave her.
Mama: Very well son, bring her.
Son: Where will you put her?
Mama: We'll give her the small room.
Son: And you two, what will you do?
Mama: Me, I am going to jump out of the window. Your father, he can do whatever he wants.

Written by Beki Bardavid, Istanbul, and submitted by Hillel J. Franco.

ME AND MY MOM

The older I get the more I miss my parents. I remember more and more that they were always there for me. I also remember the difficult times I gave my folks because I didn't understand the reasoning behind many of their actions toward me. One phrase sticks in my mind and never goes away. **"Yo kierro bivir a ver kuando tu vas a tener ijos tuyos, y mos vas kreer."** ("I want to live to see you have children of your own, and then you will believe us.") I find myself echoing their very words to my children, and they reacting exactly as I did. Too bad that our hindsight is 20/20, and our foresight zero. After I was married and moved out of the house, I used to call my Mom about once a week. That wasn't enough for Mom. She hoped that I would call every day. Generally that was done by the girls in the family, and they seemed to enjoy doing it. As a rule, the girls got jobs as secretaries or bookkeepers, and it was easy for them to call. Since I was an only child, it was my job.

After a very short while it really got to be a chore. I couldn't very well do it while I was working, and to call every evening from Brooklyn to the Bronx got to be kind of expensive. If you remember, in those days, it was a toll call between those two boroughs. After a few minutes of small talk, I couldn't wait to say 'goodbye.'

Here's how a typical conversation with my mother went:

Me: Hello, Ma, Komo estas? Me alegro ke estas buena.

Mom: Aroniko, tu sos? Antes de darte keshas, digame, komo estan Phyllis y los chikos? Ya te akodrates ke tienes madre? Porke no me yamates ayer? Yo esto aki sola y seka, yo no se ke te esta pasando a ti. Si estas komiendo bueno, si estas hazino. Estas avlando komo tienes yelor. La boz esta ronka. Te fuites al doktor? Mira no te la deshes la yelor ke se aga mas mala. Si no te miras, te se enreyna, y nunka se sale del puerpo.

Me: Kalma te. Phyllis y los chikos estan buenos. Yo no tengo abashada. Y no esto ronko. Es la koneksion de el telefon ke esta negro. Yo esto bueno.

Mom: No mires de enganyarme. Yo so tu madre y yo te konosko mejor ke te konoses a ti. Dime, komo esta el *beeznez?* Komo te estas pasando kon el *Union,* y kon tu haver? No tienes trouble kon eyos? Tienes *orders?* Tu haver, esta vendiendo? Estas kortando la ropa? Komo de lavoro estan aziendo los kontraktores? Estan saliendo las fustas sin *demidj?*

Me: Ma, kreye me, yo esto bueno. Mi mujer esta buena, y los chikos se estan aziendo guerkitos. Mira, ma, no puedo avlar mas, tengo otra yamada.

Mom: Siempre me das esta bamya ke tienes otra yamada kuando no me kierres avlar mas. *Awri,* beza a Phyllis y a los chikos. Akavidate. No te agas hazino, y ayde *goobye.* No te olvides de yamarme a manyana.

Me: Hello, Ma, how are you? I am happy that you are well.

Mom: Is that you Aaron? Before I start complaining, how are Phyllis and the children. Did you remember that you have a mother? Why didn't you call me yesterday? Here I am all alone, and I don't know what is happening to you. If you are eating, if you are sick. You're talking like you have a cold. Your voice is hoarse. Did you go to the doctor? Look, don't let it get worse. If you don't look after it, it will become critical and you will never get it out of your system.

Me: Take it easy. Phyllis and kids are fine. I don't have a cold and my voice is not hoarse. We have a bad telephone connection. I'm all right.

Mom: Don't try to fool me. I'm your mother, and I know you better than you know yourself. Tell me, how is the business? How are you getting along with the Union and your partner? You aren't having any trouble with them? Do you have orders? Your partner, is he selling? Are you cutting the goods? What kind of work is coming out of the contractors. Are the skirts coming out undamaged? (My mom and pop ran their own shop for many years; she knew about those things.)

Me: Ma believe me, I am well. Phyllis is well, and the kids are growing up to be little devils. Look, I can't talk to you anymore, I have to make another call.

Mom: You always give me the same baloney that you have to make another call when you don't want to talk to me anymore. All right, kiss Phyllis and the kids. Take care. Don't get sick. Goodbye. Don't forget to call me tomorrow.

In retrospect, I wish I hadn't been so abrupt. I'm sure she was hurt by it!

PROVERBS

A buen konpanyo, buena kompanya.
A good husband, a good wife.

De el dia ke me kazi, buen kadena me ati.
Since the day of my marriage, a wondrous chain I tied.

El ombre en la plaza, la mujer en la kaza.
The man on the town, the woman in the house.

La buena mujer yena la kaza.
The good woman fills the house.

No ay en el mundo amiga komo la madre.
There is no friend in the world like your mother.

Oya y mujer tienes bien ke eskojer.
A stewpot and a wife must be well chosen.

LUNA Y IZAK

Izak: Allo, Luna, es tu marido, Izak. Oyeme mi amor, te esto yamando para desirte ke va a venir a kaza mas tadre esta noche, y ke no te mirikeyes. (Hello, Luna, this is your husband, Izak. Listen my love, I am calling to tell you that I will be home late tonight and that you shouldn't worry.)

Luna: Ke te parese, ke yo so bova? Topates otra mujer para esta noche? (What do you think, that I am dumb? Did you find another woman for tonight?)

Izak: Mi vida, ke estas avlando? Tu sos mi unika amor. Me vino agora mismo un mushteri muy grande del estor ke se yama *Messy*. (My life, what are you talking about? You are my only love. A big customer from the store called Macy just came in.)

Luna: Ah kien te parese ke estas enkashando esta bamya? (Whom do you think you are sticking this bull to?)

Izak: Mira kerida, no es bamyas ke te esto enkashando. Este mushteri es muy grande y puedemos azer muncho beezenez kon el. (Look my dear, it is no bull that I am sticking to you. He is a big customer, and we can do a lot of business with him.)

Luna: La komida se va kemar en la estofa, y si no vienes a kaza, kale ke la eche a la kaye. (The meal will burn in the stove, and if you don't come home, I will have to throw it into the street.)

Izak: No bijou, no la eches a la kaye. La puedemos komer manyana. (No my jewel, don't throw it into the street. We can eat it tomorrow.)

Luna: Traelo a kaza, y komemos los tres aki. (Bring him home, and the three of us can eat here.)

Izak: No puede ser. Vamos a lavorar tadre in la fakturia amostrando los *semplees* y despues lo va a yevar al restoran de Ishuwa Penso en *Rivinton Estrit*. Mira, si dainda no me kreyes, ven al restoran y kome kon mosotros. Ya me se tomo el suluk de avlar tanto. *Goobye*. (It can't be. We're going to work late in the factory showing the samples and afterwards I am going to take him to Ishuwa Penso's restaurant on Rivington Street. Look, if you still don't believe me, come to the restaurant and eat with us. I am getting short of breath talking so much. Goodbye.)

DJOHA – DOURME RESPOSADO

Una noche Djoha se echo a la kama, y la noche entera no pudo dormir. Se abolto por aki y se abolto por aya. La mujer le demando, "Djoha, por ke no estas dormiendo? La noche entera te estas aboltando."

Djoha le disho a la mujer, "Me empresti sien mil liras de Rofat, muestro vezino. Le di mi palabra ke se lo iva pagar a manyana. Malarozamente, no tengo las paras, y no se ke vo azer."

"Espera," le disho la mujer, "Yo se lo ke yo va azer." Eya levanto la ventana, y empeso a gritar, "Rofat, Rofat." El vezino, Rofat avrio la ventana, y demando, "Ke kierres de mi, por ke me estas yamando en medio de la noche?"

"Mira Rofat, mi marido no te va pagar las sien mil liras ke te deve a manyana." Y serro la ventana. Djoha le demando a la mujer, "Porke izitez esto?" Eya le disho, "Dormete reposado. Agora el ke se lo pense, y el ke no pueda dormir."

SLEEP RESTFULLY

One night Djoha went to bed, and the whole night he couldn't sleep. He turned this way and he turned that way. His wife asked him, "Why aren't you sleeping? You have been tossing and turning the whole night."

Djoha told his wife, "I borrowed one hundred thousand liras from Rofat, our neighbor. I gave him my word that I would pay him tomorrow. Unfortunately, I don't have the money, and I don't know what I am going to do."

"Wait," his wife said, "I know what I am going to do." She opened the window and started to yell, "Rofat, Rofat." The neighbor, Rofat opened the window, and asked, "What do you want from me. Why are you calling me in the middle of the night?"

"Look Rofat, my husband is not going to pay you the hundred thousand liras he owes you tomorrow." And she closed the window. Djoha asked her, "Why did you do that?" She said, "You sleep restfully. Now let him think about it, and he won't be able to sleep."

* * *

TELEPHONES AND KAVANES

Don't tell your kids or grandkids; they won't believe you. When we were kids there was no radio, no TV, no telephone, and to own a car was just a dream. We were living in the dark ages, right? Today it is impossible to comprehend having to get along without these *expensive* necessities. Let's talk about them.

Before telephones were installed in our homes, we depended on the local candy store for our calls. In those days a telephone call almost always meant that something was wrong. When a call came in, one of the kids hanging around was sent to summon the person who was called. Invariably, that person lived on the fifth floor. That trip usually yielded a two-cent tip. Some of the kids made it their business to hang around all day in the hope of running an errand or two. If more than one kid was around at the time of a call, the biggest and toughest kid got to run the errand and got the two-cent tip. It took a long time before the telephone became the indispensable part of the household that it is today. It was the first status symbol that I can remember.

Anyone who had a telephone had to be 'rich.' If I recall correctly, the telephone bill was four dollars a month for forty local calls. (Who ever heard of long distance calls?) There was a surcharge for all over-calls. The calls were very closely monitored, and you can bet there were very few over-calls. Just like today!

Each call from the house cost ten cents as opposed to five cents for a call made from a pay phone. If one had to make a call from someone's house, it was common courtesy to offer to pay the ten cents for the call. The dime was hardly ever accepted, but the offer was always made.

In those days calls were placed directly through the operator. When dial phones were invented and you got a wrong number, did some wise guy ever say to you, "You must have put your finger in the wrong hole"?

Getting back to placing a call directly with the operator, do you remember the frustrations our folks used to go through? The procedure was to give the operator the exchange and the number. Reception was nothing like it is today, and the operators weren't especially helpful toward foreigners trying to make calls. Some of the exchanges were pretty tough to pronounce; Susquehanna, Lackawanna, University, Gramercy, Tivoli, Esplanade, to name a few. Some of the folks even had trouble with the numbers. They went something like this: *wan, tu, tree, fo, fie,* for 1, 2, 3, 4, 5.

A typical phone call:

Operator: Number please.
Izak: *Oporetta, please geeve to me Sooskoohana-fo, tu, tree, wan.*
Operator: Please repeat the exchange and the number.
Izak: **Moshon, ke kierre dezir, *repee*?** (Moishe, what does *repee* mean?)
Moshon: **Kierre ke se lo digas otra vez.** (It means say it again.)
Izak: *Sooskoohana-fo, tu, tree, wan.*
Operator: How do you spell the exchange?
Izak: *Har you spell? Wassa mata fo you, you no go to eskool?*

When the call finally went through, here's how it went:

Izak: ***Allo?***
Jack: ***Allo.***
Izak: **Jeck es?** (Is this Jack?)
Jack: **Si Jeck es.** (Yes, this is Jack.)
Izak: **En kaza estas?** (Are you home?)
Jack: **Seguro ke esto en kaza. Si no estava en kaza, te puedia reponder?** (Of course I'm home. If I were not home, would I be able to answer you?)
Izak: **Porke estas gritando?** (Why are you yelling?)
Jack: **Porke estas leshos. Si no grito, komo me vas a oyirme?** (Because you are far away. If I don't yell, how are you going to hear me?)
Izak: **Mira, me va ir a la kavane. Me kierres enkontrarme?** (Look, I'm going to the coffee house. Do you want to meet me?)
Jack: ***Okay,* ande Nessim Mazliah, en las sien y diez y sesh, en *fif avenoo*.** (Okay, at Nessim Mazliah, on 116th and 5th Avenue.)

Now to the **kavane,** the old coffee house. We'll never see them again. The **kavane** was a throwback to the old days in Turkey. There, **los borachones** (drunkards), **los kumardjis** (gamblers), **los ke estavan eyelahk** (the unemployed), and those who just wanted to get away from their wives and kids for a little while, went there **para echar lashon y pasar el tiempo** (to shoot the breeze and pass the time).

The **kavane** served a useful purpose for the newly arrived immigrants in New York. They were able to find jobs, a place to live, locate relatives and friends, hear the local gossip, get something to eat or drink, play a little cards or **tavli** (backgammon), place a little bet, or just while away the time. The disadvantages were that it promoted laziness and caused some discord within the families. **Raki** was served there, as well as **kave turko, baklava, kadayif, bourekas, filas, salep, malebee, sutlach, lekoom** and other traditional Turkish delicacies.

Playing cards were supplied for **pokeriko** (poker), **pastra** (casino), **pinaka** (pinochle); also a backgammon set for **tavli** was supplied. Every now and then the police raided the **kavanes**. The owners would **untar** (pay off) and all was well until the next time. The wives gave their husbands a rough time for spending much of their time and money there, but with all of that, the **kavanes** flourished. I don't doubt that bookmaking and heavy gambling took place in the back rooms. Of course, as the Sephardim moved from one neighborhood to another, so did the **kavane**.

The **kavanes** downtown were on Broome, Orchard, Rivington, Allen and Delancey Streets. The ones uptown were on 110th, 116th, and 125th Streets, on Park, Madison and Fifth Avenues. And of course, in New Lots (Brooklyn) – on Malta Street and New Lots Avenue. When it was supper time or if the men were needed at home for some reason, the Moms sent their kids to fetch them. Girls were only sent when a boy was not available. The boy was allowed in just long enough to tell the owner that his father was wanted at home.

Ike Amira tells us of the time, when he was six or seven, when his mother said to him, **"Vate a las kavanes y bushka a tu padre, dile ke venga a kaza ke es ora de komer."** ("Go to the coffee houses and look for your father. Tell him it's time to eat.") Ike never knew in which **kavane** he would find him. When he finally found him, his father was feeling 'pretty good,' and 'the old man' persuaded the owner to let Ike in for a few minutes. Ike was thoroughly embarrassed when his dad kissed him and introduced Ike as his **bohoriko** (his beloved eldest).

KAVANES

Below is a list of **kavanes** and their owners, some Sephardic grocery stores and their owners, and a few Sephardic musicians and singers, mostly from the New York area. How many do you remember?

Cafe El Espasio
Sam Florentin
131 E. 169th Street
JErome 6 - 8582

Cafe El Successo
Joseph Namir & Nessim Crespin
136 Allen Street

Jack Hane
64 Rivington Street

Cafe de Amigos
18 Malta Street

Paradise Cafe
Eli Massod
128 Allen Street

Oriental Garden
Fins & Bendicha
158 Allen Street

Benny Cohen Cafe
158 Allen Street

Samuel Telvi
154 Allen Street

Nessim Masliah
116th Street & 5th Avenue

Cuban Casino
Sabeby Benruby
300 W 45th Street

Isaac Cohen (Cafe)
143 New Lots Avenue

Kings Cafe,
Morris Cohen
1491 Brook Avenue
JErome 6 - 8915

Paradise Cafe
Herman Bardavid
126-128 Allen Street
GRamercy 5 - 8914

SEPHARDIC GROCERIES

Manhattan

Ezratti & Cohen
168 Orchard Street

Mair Eskenasi & Sons
Essex Market

Nathan Aldoroty
147 Allen Street

L. Habib
65 Rivington Street

Louis Aldoroty
45 Spring Street

Elia Cohen
97 Stanton Street

East New York

S. Candiotti
242 New Lots Avenue

Max Nahmias
302 New Lots Avenue

Isaac Motola
274 New Lots Avenue

Williamsburgh

Abraham Passy
274 South 2nd Street

Sea Beach

Albert Fis
1975 60th Street

Joe Aldoroti
6211 20th Avenue

David Candiotti
1932 63rd Street

Hy Food Store
6320 20th Avenue

Sheepshead Bay

D. Comerchero
1012 Woorbass Avenue

Isaac Cohen
1421 19th Street
Coney Island

Marco Varon
29-79 Coney Island Avenue

Cohen
Mermaid Ave. & 23rd Street

Bronx

Eliezer Mahmoiram
1505 Brook Avenue

I. Levy
1491 Brook Avenue

Saragossi
1526 Brook Avenue

Taragano
131 East 169th Street
near Grand Concourse

S. Gomerobero
1566 Washington Avenue

N. Alcana
1382 Grant Avenue

Taragano & Matarasso
221 East 170th Street

New Brunswick, NJ

Sam & Hasday Arouh
89 Morris Street

Salomon & Simon Ayash
44 North 4th Avenue

Albert Naar
14 Hiram Street

Jacob Saltiel
37 Hiram Street

A. Salteil
New York Grocery
31 Hiram Street

Atlanta, GA

Mr. Franco
Roxy's Delicatessen & Grocery
1011 Peachtree Street, NE
(also Liquors)

Musicians

Morris Gannon
(Violin, Oud)

Rebecca Levy (Oud)
1400 Grand Concourse
Bronx

Abraham Gabay (Cannon)
65 Sackett Street
Brooklyn

David Crespi (Pellie Rep)

Leon Matalon, Nathan Matalon
1378 College Avenue
Brooklyn

Joseph Israel (Oud)
1900 Surf Avenue
Coney Island

Singers

Mentech Amira
Victoria Hazan
Moise Levy
Miss Ruth Emanuel
(Montediz' niece)
Joseph Levy
Samuel Henen (from Paris)
Maximo Mallelel
1159 E. 165th Street
Robert E. Shilton, Baritone
Sunnyside, Long Island

NEW LOTS

A contingent of former residents of New Lots, a neighborhood in Brooklyn that I'm sure you all are familiar with, has formed a sort of informal organization in South Florida that meets every Thursday around noon time at the Coral Springs Plaza. I was invited by Simon Calderon to attend, and I was happy to attend. Even though I did not live in New Lots, I was surprised at the many faces I recognized, faces I had seen at the many affairs I have attended which the Sephardim have sponsored over the years. Many of the faces were also familiar because of our mutual connection in the garment center in New York. Most of them were **Monastirlis.** Since most of them know that I am not one of them, they labeled me **el ajeno** (the stranger). Sam Testa asked me where my parents came from. I said to him, **"Mi madre era Estanbolia y mi padre era Silivrili."** Sam said, "Look at him, he's an another **li**." In Turkey, you were a **Chanakaleli, Churluli, Izmirli, Selanikli, Ankarali, Rhodesli, Yeriboli, Kastoriali**, etc., etc., but if you were from **Galipoli**, they would say, **"Es de Galipoli,"** not **Galipolili**.

As one would expect, stories were flying fast and furious. It's too bad many of the stories cannot be printed. A few, those that were on a higher plane, follow.

Some of the names those guys gave each other were: Sleepy Sam, Texas Lou, Poopsie, Cue Ball, Joe Pop, Beezie, Smiley, Big Chick and Little Chick from Chicago, and Papou. Papou lost all his teeth when he was about 12. In those days only **Papous** (old men) lost their teeth, hence the nickname.

Simon Elias told of a young lady who visited the *Sephardic Home* and spotted an elderly resident there whom she recognized as an old friend of her mother's. After talking to her for a while, she realized that the lady was reacting as though she didn't know her, so she asked the lady, **"No sabes kien yo so?"** ("Don't you know who I am?") The lady turned to her and said, **"Si tu no sabes kien tu sos komo kierres ke yo sepa?"** ("If you don't know who you are, how do you expect me to know?")

Jenny Cohen's mother used to sing a couple of songs when she was rocking the cradle that went like this: ***Tsi lon gwe Titsi Pareri, tsi lon gwe to go.*** (It's a long way to Tipperary, it's a long way to go.) Remember that one? She also loved to sing: ***Harelooya aribam*** (Hallelujah, I'm a bum).

Al (Romano) Roberts commented on the idea someone had about starting a **kavane** in these parts. He said, "Can you imagine if they do something like that here, and if the women knew how to speak Ladino, what they would say? **Esto es lo ke van a dezir: "Ke, otra vez te vaz a ir a la kavane? Vaz a azer kumar y vaz a pedrer tu semanada, o te vaz a emborachar, y vaz a mirar para darme haftona kuando vienes a kaza. Yo me va kedar en kaza el dia entero sola y seka kuando tu estas repotreando kon otra mujer. Mi madre y tu madre tuvieron bastante de estas boverias, ama yo no te va deshar ke me lo agas a mi. Si esto es lo ke kierres, toma te la mashinika de arapar y la furcha de dientes y vate de esta kaza."**

(This is what they are going to say: "What, again you are going to go to the **kavane**? You're going to gamble away your salary, or you're going to get drunk, and you're going to take it out on me when you get home? I am going to stay home all day alone, high and dry, while you are enjoying yourself with another woman. My mother and yours had enough of that nonsense, but I am not going to let you do that to me. If that is what you want, take your razor and blades and your toothbrush and leave this house.")

Esther Benezra came up with this knock, knock joke. "Knock, knock." "Who's there?" "Dolly." "Dolly who?" **"Dolly (Dale) un beziko por mi."** ("Give her a little kiss for me.") Belle Paparo told us about her grandson visiting her mother-in-law who was a marvelous cook. Grandma Paparo asked the little boy what he would like to eat. The little boy said, "A frankfurter." Mrs. Paparo threw a fit. **"Yo esklavo el dia entero guizando y aziendo desayuno y este pishaloniko me demanda por un *franfooree*."** ("I slave away the whole day cooking and baking, and this little pisspot asks me for a frankfurter.") Lou Hasson was asked if he knew a Joe Fresco, (**Fresko,** meaning fresh) he said, "No, but I know a Joe Bayat." (**Bayat,** meaning stale.) Someone said, "Did you ever hear the proverb, **El ke no tiene meyoyos ke tenga pachas** (He who has no brains needs legs)." We all said, "Of course." This same fellow said, "Boy, I sure did a lot of walking in my day."

Sammy (Sleepy Sam) Cohen told of the time he entered a Sephardic owned **bakal** (grocery store). The owner asked him, "What I do for you? I de boss here." Sam said, **"Yo kierro fustoukes, pipitas y pitagra."** ("I want peanuts, sunflower seeds and shoe leather.") The owner said to him, **"*Sana ma gahn*, porke no me dishites ke sos uno de los muestros?"** ("Son of a gun, why didn't you tell me you were one of us.")

FEEJONEEZ

When we migrated to Florida some years ago, we had a lot of redecorating to do. We shopped around for a few weeks, and everywhere we went, we saw pretty much the same type of furniture and accessories. The white sectional couches and love seats, the glass-topped brass tables, the large paintings, and so on.

We finally decided on a white brocade sectional sofa and other customary Florida-type pieces to fill out the rest of the decor. The only thing that wasn't 'Florida' was our cherry mahogany formal dining room set that we just couldn't part with. One day I came home after a round of golf and plopped down on the sofa to relax for a minute before showering. My wife screamed, "Get off the couch with your messy golf clothes." I jumped up and burst out laughing. My wife, obviously upset, asked, "What's so damn funny?"

It reminded me of my mother when we moved to the Grand Concourse in the Bronx. Before moving to the Concourse we used to hang out in the kitchen. In those days the kitchens were always large, and most of our time was spent sitting around the kitchen table. At one end was the usual kitchen paraphernalia, at the other end, a radio, a phonograph, and other knickknacks. Papa was the 'Chairman of the Board.' He counseled us, read ***La Vara*** to us, and played **tavli** (backgammon) and **kartikas** (cards) with us. Now that we were living ***haya kless***, on **de *Gren Konkoss*** (Grand Concourse), Mom decided to buy new furniture for the 'parlor.' She bought a **kanape** (couch) that was decorated with beautiful **mavi katife** (sky blue velvet) and two easy chairs of the same material in **kolor de vino** (burgundy). It really was pretty. I don't think I have to tell you what came next, but I will. Mom made slip covers for the three pieces, and on top of that, she placed a sheet of clear plastic on each piece, **para ke no se ensuziye el *sleep cawver*** (so that the slip cover shouldn't get dirty). The only time that room was used and those covers removed, was when **musafires** (guests) came.

My thanks to Pearl Esformes for this beauty:

A relative of hers married a lovely Ashkenazi girl who was born and raised in Atlanta. Let's call her Scarlett. She loved her husband and got along beautifully with her in-laws. After sampling a good deal of Sephardic cooking and seeing how much her husband enjoyed the meals and how much he looked forward to the weekly visits to his parents' home, she decided to learn how to make his favorite dishes. She made a list and asked her mother-in-law for the recipes. Her husband was elated.

On a visit the couple paid to Pearl in New York, Scarlett was bubbling over and couldn't wait to tell Pearl of her culinary skill. "Pearl, mah marriage always was great, but now, it's FAN-TAS-TIC. Ahm cooking and baking mah husband's favorite things, and he just don't know what to do for me. Pearl asked, "What are you making?" "My Mama-in-law is teaching me to cook Sephardic, and Ahm making him ***pee pee tas, bee sko chose, yahp rakees, bahm yahs, boo rek ahs***, and ***fee joh neez*** with ***karnee.***

SOME EVERYDAY SAYINGS

No por sedaka. Literally: Not for charity. Don't you dare.
Figuratively: under no circumstances, no way.

Chapetas pretas, chapeteada. Literally: Black cheeks, flushed face.
Figuratively: To be flushed with excitement, embarrassment.

Esto no me inche. Literally: This doesn't fill me.
Figuratively: I couldn't care less, don't bother me, get lost.

No es mi etcho. Literally: It is not my business.
Figuratively: I can't be bothered, it is no concern of mine.

Mushteri yagli. Literally: An oily customer.
Figuratively: A shrewd cookie, watch out for this one.

DJOHA EL MAESTRO

El rey ande biviya Djoha kerriya saver kien eran la djente en su reynado ke estan azyendo lo mas para el bienestar de la sosyedad. Izo una yamada por representantes de todos los ofisyos, y profesiones ke le presentaran informasion sovre la kondision del buenestado de la popoulasion. Kada representante avló kon ardor en la kondision superior de la djente en su propyo ofisyo and profesion. Al fin de la linya estava un ombre muy viejo oyendo atantivamente a todos los ke avlavan. "Y tu, mi buen ombre, ke tu kontribuites por la buendad de la sosyedad?" Siendo muy viejo, Djoha avlo muy avagar, "Mi senyor, kuando todos de estos ombres y mujeres ke avlaron oy, eran kriaturas, yo era sus ensenyador."

DJOHA THE TEACHER

The king of Djoha's province wanted to know which of the people in his kingdom were doing the most for the welfare of the society. He called for the representatives of all the trades and professions to present him with information about the welfare of the population. Each representative spoke with ardor of the condition of the people in his or her particular trade or profession. At the end of the line stood a very old man listening attentively to all who spoke. "And you, my good man, what have you contributed to the welfare of the society?" Being very old, Djoha spoke very slowly, "Sire, when all these men and women who spoke here today were children, I was their teacher."

* * *

KUMARDJI

When I was a little kid, on Friday nights, my father would read to us from ***La Vara***. My mother, afraid that the newspaper stand on Allen Street would run out of the paper before my father came home from work, would send me out to buy the paper. She would say to me, **"Aroniko, na sinko sentavos y vate ande venden las gazetas y merka *La Vara* antes ke se eskapen."** ("Aaron, here's five cents and go where they sell the newspapers and buy ***La Vara*** before they are sold out.") We would wait for my father to come home from work and read it to us. There were many steady features that people looked forward to reading every week.

More often than not, I got to the newsstand much too early. So did a few of the other Sephardic kids. To pass the time away we used to pitch pennies or match pennies under our shoes, a game we called *'underlegs.'* Our fingers used to get filthy from sliding the pennies under our shoes on the dirty streets of New York.

One time, instead of giving me a nickel, my mother gave me five pennies. Having become a compulsive gambler by the ripe old age of seven, and after losing the few cents that were my **ashlik** (allowance), without thinking I played the pennies Mom had given me for the newspaper. You guessed it – I lost those too. No one would lend me a nickel, and the newsstand operator decided to teach me a lesson by not 'trusting' me. I was scared to death to go home, as I was sure to get the **haftona** (beating) of my life. But God looks out for drunks and young gamblers. That night, my father brought home a paper he intended to send to his brother in Mexico. From that day forward, this little **kumardji** (gambler) vowed never again to gamble for the rest of his life. If you believe that, I'll sell you the Brooklyn Bridge!

KUMBARA

El Dyo ke la bendiga a mi muy estimada media Sefardi y media Yiddisha mujer, Phyllis (God Bless my esteemed half-Sephardic and half-Ashkenazi wife, Phyllis). She inspired the start of my original column by asking me if I ever had a piggy bank when I was a kid. I said, "I certainly did."

I had a silver-looking cylinder that held five dollars' worth of dimes when it was full. Once you put a dime into it, there was no way you could get it out without breaking it. It was a very attractive object, and no one would want to break it. The design was such that it had to be filled with dimes before it could be emptied. I used to change all the nickels and pennies I could save into dimes. It took forever to accumulate five dollars in dimes. If I remember right, one had to turn a screw at the top of the cylinder when it was full in order for the dimes to be forced out of the bottom. I cannot recall if these little banks were purchased or if a particular bank gave them away as a promotional item. Do any of you remember what we called that little bank? That's right! We called it a **kumbara**. Dr. Jack Crespin tells me that in some parts of Turkey, the small boxes that were in most households for **sedaka** (charity) were called **kumbaras**.

Here are a few more words that may ring a bell or inspire a discussion: A backyard is called a **kortijo**. **Manyana** is tomorrow and it can also mean in the morning. **Por la manyana**. How about **endurmeser**? To become numb. How does one say, 'I'm sorry' in Ladino? Does **'Me embarasa'** sound okay? I always thought that a **kazika** was a small house. When the late Dr. Menache retired as medical director of the *Sephardic Home For the Aged,* my son, Dr. Joe Halio, visited him in his retirement home in Florida. Dr. Menache asked my son where I lived, and my son told him, **"Mi padre bive en una kazika en Delray Beach."** ("My father lives in a **kazika,** a 'small house,' in Delray Beach.") Dr. Menache laughingly told him that he must mean a **kazetika,** not a **kazika.** He explained that in Salonica, a small house was referred to as **una kazetika; una kazika** meant an out-house.

After writing about my **kumbara,** I received some interesting mail. Emilie Levy wrote that in her town in Turkey, a bank was called **kamizia**, and **kazika** was a small house. That only in Salonika, **kazetika** was a small house. Sophie Passo did some baking and brought some over to my house. She said, "I thought you might like some **taralikos**." I love them, but what she brought was what we call **biskochos**. The **Monastirlis** and the **Kastoriyalis** use many words that are different from those used by most Sephardim. That's why they call the rest of us **los de afuera** (the outsiders).

Dan and Ethel Matarasso invited my wife and myself to a dinner party at the *High Ridge Country Club* in Hypoluxo, Florida. Phyllis and I also had the pleasure of meeting the gracious Julia Rousso for the first time that evening. During the course of the evening, Ethel handed me a poem in Ladino. She said a dear friend of hers, Lillie Reader, had sent it to her, and Lillie later told me that she got it from her cousin Esther Candioty. It is reprinted here, exactly as it was given to me, and my daughter, Susan, has translated it into English. I hope you like it as much as I did.

EL PRANSO
by Isahar Avzardel

Grande pleto en la kuzina
De la senyora Perla mi vezina
Un grande pranso tenia ke aparejar
Y ayinda no savia kualo gizar
Ensima de la meza, en la kuzina
De la senyora Perla, mi vizina
Tomates, pimentones, berendjenas,
Patatas, pipinos, sevoyas y kalavasikas...
Salto la berendjena:
-Yo so ermosa, grande y morena
Y en la meza yo so la reyna
Me komen en salata o me gizan-
Salto el tomat, kolorido y pulpozo
-A mi me komen gizado o krudo
Me meten en kada komida
Y ansi se aze mas savorida-

**-Bueno, bueno, disho la kalavasika
Gizandome kon ajiko y tomat
Yo tambien so muy savorida-
Saltaron la sevoya, la patata y el pipino
-Porke a mozotros no metes tino?-
Entonses la sinyora Perla, mi vezina
Mareada se fuyo de la kuzina
Se asento en el salon
En la mano un papel y un kreyon
Y en el papel ansi eskrivyo:
Salata de tomat, sevoya, pipino
Azeyte, prishil y limon
Por seguro le agradara a mi marido Shimon
Berendjena frita kon tomat, vinagre y ajiko
Es la salata preferida de mi ijiko
La kalavasika bien kavakada
Sera kon arroz, karne y preshil bien inchida
Y muncha savor le va dar
Mizmo al mas difisil paladar
Una gayina al orno, kon patatikas y bezelya
Por seguro se chuparan los dedos la famiya
Un buen arroz, kon salsika de tomat y garvanso
Kompletara este ermozo pranso
Y ansi es ke la senyora Perla, mi vezina
Metio a orden la kuzina.**

The following translation, while not literal, attempts to preserve the levity and flavor (if you will forgive the pun) of the original.

THE FEAST

by Isahar Avzardel

Madame Pearl, my neighbor, a cook of distinction,
Was planning a sumptuous meal
When the vegetables on her kitchen table
Began to bark and squeal.

Tomatoes, potatoes, eggplant and onions,
Cucumbers, peppers and squash
At once had begun to bicker about
Who had the most panache.

The eggplant arose, resplendent and shapely.
"I'm succulent, purple sateen!
Roasted or fried or prepared in a salad
On the table, I am Queen!"

The tomato puffed up. "Look at me! Cooked or raw,
I am plump, luscious and bright.
I'm delicious – savored at every meal,
Morning, noon and night!"

"All right," said the squash. "Try me sautéed in garlic,
I'm exquisite as well with tomato."
"Why don't you, Madame, consider us also?"
Urged the onion, cuke and potato.

Madame Pearl dizzily ran from the kitchen
With pen and paper in hand.
In the parlor, determined to quiet the quibbling,
She sat down, and a menu she planned.

"A salad of onions, tomatoes and cukes,
Parsley, lemon and oil
Will surely delight my dear husband Simon
And perhaps end all this turmoil!

Eggplant fried with tomato and garlic
And vinegar is preferred by our son.
The most sensitive palate will surely acknowledge
It's a dish that cannot be outdone.

I'll amply pack a scooped out squash
with parsley, rice and meat
And serve chicken roasted with peas and potatoes –
A finger-lickin' treat!

Rice with tomato paste and choice chickpeas
Will top off this delectable feast."
And that is how Madame Pearl, my neighbor,
To her kitchen restored the peace.

PROVERBS

En kaza yena presto se giza la sena.
In a well-stocked house, dinner is quickly prepared.

Ke tengas una kaza yena komo el guevo.
May your house be as full as the egg.

La pasensya ez un arbole, su raiz es amarga, su fruta es dulce.
Patience is like a tree, its roots acerbic, its fruit sweet.

Pan no tenemos, ravanos komemos.
We have no bread, we'll eat radishes.

KAPANDJA/RATONERA

Bonnie Kessler told me of an incident that happened to Charlie Rousso, may he rest in peace, which I wouldn't dare print until I verified it with Charlie's wife, June. Charlie, the prospective groom and a **Kastoriyali**, was invited to June's mother's house for dinner. After a delightful dinner as only a Sephardic cook can serve, June and the guests adjourned to the ***parlor***. After the dishes were washed, everyone overheard this conversation that took place in the kitchen between June's mom and grandmom. **"Mama, asentate, yo va lavar la pila."** ("Mama, sit, I will clean the sink.") Grandma said, **"No ija, vate al *parlor*, yo va lavar la pila."** ("No daughter, go into the parlor, I will clean the sink.") You **Kastoriyalis** can imagine what was going on in Charlie's mind during this conversation. In Kastoriya **pila** is the word for the male organ!

Kapandja is the word we used at home for a rat-trap. Others have used **ratonera**. **Kapandja** is one of the many Turkish words the Sephardim use every day in their Ladino, but **ratonera** is the word used in conventional Spanish. My first encounter with those pesky animals came when we moved to Harlem sometime around 1925. The first time my mother saw one of those creatures, she yelled to my father, **"Yusef, ay un raton en kaza, prepara la kapandja."** ("Joe, there's a rat in the house, prepare the rat-trap.")

In the old days, as well as today, electricity was expensive. The people in those days were a lot more cost-conscious than we are now. As the men got older and started having prostate problems, they very often got up during the night to urinate. They made damn sure to lift the toilet seats or their wives would raise holy hell, but they hardly ever put them back down. The trouble was that on a rare occasion **Mrs. Fulano de Tal** (Mrs. So and So) would also have to get up during the night for the same purpose. Of course **Mrs. Fulano de Tal** got up <u>after</u> **Mr. Fulano de Tal**, and not wanting to use the electricity, would set herself down in the dark without checking to see if the toilet seat was up or down. **"Ijo de un #$@^&!*%^*. No tienes meyoyos? Alevantas la siya de toalet y no la abashas."** ("You son of a 'so and so.' Have you no brains? You raise the toilet seat, but you don't put it back down.")

The first thing a macho guy who had three daughters did when he got into his house, was to go into the bathroom to see if the toilet seat was up or down. What could he have been thinking?

Another problem in those days was with some of the women who were domineering enough to make their husbands do what no self-respecting 'Turk' of a husband would do – wash the dishes after dinner. As the men got older, that same old prostate problem arose and in all cases caused big **pletos** (battles) in the house. A typical conversation would go something like this:

Husband: **No puedo lavar los chinis mas. Ke kierres de mi vida? Siempre ke korre la agua, me da ganas de pishar y munchas veses me lo ago in en el pantalon.** (I can't wash the dishes anymore. What do you want from my life? When the water runs, I have the urge to relieve myself, and very often I do it in my pants.)

Wife: **No me dez estas bamyas. Lo mas viejo ke te estas aziendo lo mas ke estas mirando para azer me lavorar mas duro.** (Don't give me that bull. The older you get, the more you look to make me work harder.)

AZETUNAS

Some of you may have had a similar experience as the one I am about to describe. Our 'house,' a tenement apartment usually on the top floor, was the first stop for all our relatives after Ellis Island. They stayed with us until they were able to get settled and move on.

One incident I remember very vividly was a story told by one of our more affluent relatives: His ship had had a stopover in Spain. Having a little time off ship, he walked around the city and spotted a grocery store: **Teniya gana por azetunas** (He had a yen for some olives). He walked into the store and asked the clerk **"Dame una papelera de azetunas."** ("Let me have a bag of olives.") The clerk asked, **"Kierres negras?"** ("Do you want black ones?") [In Ladino, **preto** means black and, **negro** means bad.] My uncle's answer was, **"No kierro negras, kierro buenas."** ("I don't want bad ones, I want good ones.") You can imagine the clerk's reaction.

It wasn't until much later that I became aware of the differences between our Spanish and the conventional Spanish. When I entered high school, I chose Spanish for the required foreign language, expecting that it would be a snap course. It wasn't all that tough, but there was a difference.

I did very well, since my Uncle David Benedict had come to the United States via Cuba and I became exposed somewhat to Spanish as it is spoken in Latin America. Nevertheless, early in the course we came to the days of the week. The teacher called on me to recite them. My answer was, **"Lunes, Martes, Miercoles, Djueves, Viernes, Shabat, y Alhad."** You can picture her reaction. That same day, I was supposed to have a composition ready. When I was called on, my answer was, **"No esto *ready* dainda."** ("I'm not ready yet.") The answer should have been, **"No estoy preparado todavia."** I really was in a rut. It was obvious that she was curious to know where these words were coming from.

That afternoon she asked to see me after class. I didn't mind that at all, as she was very pretty. Since I used the words so glibly, she asked me for an explanation. She said my accent was the best in the class and that she knew that I could speak Spanish, but there were times I used words that she knew were definitely not Spanish. She, being Jewish, knew where **Shabat** came from, but where did **Djueves** and **Alhad** come from? I told her that was the way we said it at home. Now she was really confused. Where did my parents come from? When I told her Turkey and that we spoke Spanish at home, she understood, because she knew about the expulsion of the Jews from Spain.

I often wonder what her reaction would have been if I asked her to answer these two questions? **Kuantas revanadas ay en un karpooz?** (How many slices are there in a watermelon?) And **Kuantos fildjanes ay en un librik?** (How many cups are there in a Turkish coffee pot?)

Incidentally, I must mention the fact that I won a prize in a Spanish competition while in high school. The last question asked that the other students couldn't answer was, "What are the three definitions of **Lima**?" The few students that were left knew that **Lima** was a city – Lima, Peru, and a bean (lima). I was the only one who knew that it also was a file (as in nail file).

I have received some proverbs from the venerable Albert Amateau that I must share with you:

PROVERBS

El reposo y la pasensya se puede ganar kon la sensya.
Peace and patience can be gained with knowledge.

Kien no aze kuando puede, no va azer kuando kierre.
He who doesn't produce when he can, won't when he desires.

No desdenyes konsejo, sea mansevo o viejo.
Do not scorn counsel, be you young or old.

Penseryos negros siegan los ojos.
Bad thoughts blind the eyes.

SHANE FERGESSEN

This is the story of how a Jewish man got a name like Sean (Shawn) Ferguson. I will relate it here for those of you who may be unfamiliar with it. An immigrant from Poland was carefully coached by his mentor on what to say when he arrived in Ellis Island. The first question he was asked was, "What is your name?" The poor man became so flustered that all he could say was, **"Shane Fergessen, Shane Fergessen."** Which, of course was interpreted as Sean (Shawn) Ferguson. In Yiddish, **shane fergessen**, means, I forget, or I forgot.

I recently spoke at an Ashkenazi synagogue on the customs and folklore of the Sephardim. The name of the spiritual leader of that synagogue is Samuel Silver. I kiddingly suggested that it was possible that Rabbi Silver could be Sephardic, and that his name had probably been mutilated by some unknowing INS man *(Immigration and Naturalization Service)* when Rabbi Silver's antecedents arrived in the United States. **Silva** is a Sephardic name, and it seems reasonable to expect that when that person said, "Silva" that it was interpreted as Silver.

But how a nice Sephardic man like Hy Schmill got his name intrigued me. Hy is a longtime member of the *Sephardic Social Club of Florida,* and I finally got around to asking him, who was Sephardic, he or his wife? He laughed, and said that they were both Sephardic. He explained that his father's name was Israel Shemuel, and that the family name has been Schmill ever since his father entered this country. I can only assume that Hy's father was interviewed by the same INS man who interviewed Sean Ferguson and Rabbi Silver's antecedent.

Eli Cohen's family had always been in the garment industry in New York City. The boys in the family were urged to go into the trade upon graduation from high school. Eli's brother, Albert, was a very bright student. Eli's father, Izak Cohen, wanted Albert to become a cutter, a patternmaker, or a salesman – anything in the garment industry. But Albert persevered and went on to higher education. He eventually became a nuclear physicist working for RCA. One of the projects Al was involved in wound up on the moon in one of the Apollo moon flights. Papa

Cohen was not too impressed. Had Al been a salesman and landed a big account like Macy's or J.C. Penney, that would have been something Papa could be proud of!

* * *

DJOHA – LA ORA

Djoha tenia de menester una ora para su kaza. Le demando al amigo, Memet, una persona muy savido, en kien Djoha tuvo muncha confiansa, ke le topé una. Ama kalia ke ser buena y barata y muy ermosa. Despues de unos dias de bushkando, Memet le disho a Djoha ke topo una ora muy espesial, ke kamina ocho dias sin kuriyar. Djoha estava tresalido, y riyendose, le demando a Memet, "Y kuantos dias puede kaminar esta ora si la kureyas?"

THE CLOCK

Djoha was in need of a clock for his house. He asked his friend, Memet, a very knowledgeable person, whose judgement he trusted, to find him one, but it had to be a good one, inexpensive, and it had to be very beautiful. After several days of searching, Memet told Djoha that he had found a clock that was good, inexpensive, very beautiful, and that it had a special feature. It would run for eight days without winding. Djoha was elated, and he laughingly asked Memet, "And how many days will it run if you do wind it?"

* * *

MESA FRANKA

My son paid a visit to the 'Club' at the *Sephardic Jewish Center of Forest Hills* where a group of Sephardic men, and these days women also, go in the evening to play cards. I remember having heard about lots of Sephardic Clubs as I was growing up.

The older generation went to the **kavanes**. The 'boys' had their clubs: *The Sun Ray Club, The Neo Club, The Alba Club, The Progressive Club, The Filo Club, The Bronx Social Club, The Classic Club*, and the *Broome and Allen Boys.*

The Broome and Allen Boys, active to this day, still deserve our support for their Camp and Scholarship Fund. How many of the younger kids got a week or two off the streets during the summer to go to the country while the older folks were collecting money, a few cents at a time, at the card games? How many of our kids have gotten college scholarships from funds left over after the card games stopped? How much could you win or lose in a few hands of **pastra** or **chinikos** which the **Saloniklis** played, each player taking out his money from the little **chini** (plate) he kept it in. Remember what the face cards were called? **El Fant** (the Jack), **La Mosa** (the Queen), **El Pappaz** or **El Rey** (the King), **El Azo** or **El Aziko** (the Ace), **El Dos Bueno** (the Good Deuce), **El Diez Bueno** (the Good Ten).

Conversation at the card games has not changed much. One of the men asked my son if he was married. Would he, my son, like him to arrange something, a marriage, for instance? In the old days and especially in the old country, the custom was to arrange marriages between two good families, settle the dowry (**dote-kontante** or **ishuar**) and make marriage plans. Once agreed upon, there was absolutely no backing out!!

Sometimes there was the addition of a condition called **mesa franka** (free table). The bride's family, **la famiya de la novia**, paid the dowry directly to the groom, **el novio**. This was done in order to give the newlyweds a head start to buy a house, go into business, and so forth. In order to save more money after **la boda** (the wedding), there was **la mesa franka**, usually for a period of one year, never more than three. During that time the bride and groom would live rent free and their food would be provided as well. All of this, unheard of today, was still practiced in our time, even here in the United States.

My wife Phyllis and I were introduced through my uncle, Irving (aka Ben) Benedict, and her father, two good friends who belonged to the same Masonic Lodge. The wedding served as the dowry without calling it as such. There was a **mesa franka**. We signed a **ketuba**, a marriage contract, and moved in with Phyllis' parents in Sea Beach (Bensonhurst) Brooklyn, then later with mine in the Bronx. Here is the **ketuba** we signed:

> **Oy el dia trenta del mes de nisan del anyo 5707 de la kriasion del mundo sigun la kuenta ke kontamos aki en New York, Amerika, yo el novio, Aron, ijo de Yusef y Sultana, digo a la novia, Fina, ija de Avraam y Sara, kualmente la tomo por kompanyera de mi vida sigun la ley de Moshe y Israel y me ovligo a apresiarla, mantenerla, vistirla, y akordarle todos los gastes menesterozos mientres todos los dias de su vida. Tambien deklaro a ver resivido de parte de eya en moneda kontante ansi ke valor de sus vestimientos suma totala de tanto.**
>
> **Yo el novio envelunto y pujo a mi novia un presente de la suma de tanto y me ovligo de respektar los ovligamientos notados en este sertifikado matrimonial, ketuba, mientres todos los dias de mi vida y mizmo en kavzo de mi muerte h"v eya tiene el dirito de kovrar el valor de este kontrato de los bienes y averes ke restarian a mis eredores.**
>
> **Yo el novio, me ovligo tambien a konformarme sigun las leyes de muestros antiguos savios en todo lo ke konserna los usos de las ijas de Israel.**
>
> **Nosotros el novio y la novia despues de aver meldado todo lo ke esta eskrito en esta ketuba, mos deklaramos de akordo y de buena veluntad a respektar todo su kontenido. Por ser verdad, mos afirmamos.**
>
> **El novio** — **La novia**
>
> **testemonios (2)** — **kidushin**

On this 30th day of the month of Nisan (April 19, 1947), in the year of the creation of the world 5707 according to our accounting here in New York, America, I, the Groom, Henry, son of Joe and Susie, say to my Bride, Phyllis, daughter of Albert and Sara, that I take her for my lifelong companion according to the laws of Moses and Israel, and I obligate myself to appreciate her, maintain her, clothe her, and provide for all the necessary expenses all the days of her life.

I also declare that I have received from her the certain sum of money and value of her vestments totaling a certain amount, and I the Groom, voluntarily present to my Bride a certain sum, and obligate myself to respect the obligations noted in this matrimonial certificate, **ketuba**, all the days of my life, and in case of my death, God forbid, she has the right to claim the value of this contract and goods that remain to my inheritors.

I, the Groom, obligate myself to conform to the laws of our ancient wise men regarding all that concern the customs of the daughters of Israel.

We, the Groom and the Bride, having read everything written in this **ketuba** declare ourselves in agreement willing to respect its content. In truth we sign:

The Groom	The Bride
Two witnesses	The Rabbi

MONASTERLIS

What you are about to read is a piece of history. There may be more fiction than truth to it, but I'll let you be the judge.

The Ottoman Empire grew to the proportions that it did by design, not by accident. The Sultans ruled from the 14th century until the early 20th century (the Ottoman Empire was finally broken up at the end of World War I when it became the Republic of Turkey). The Empire stretched from the Danube to the Euphrates, which included Albania, Bosnia, Bulgaria, Greece, Hungary, Iraq, Macedonia, and Yugoslavia, making it one of the great powers of Europe. Much of this was accomplished by exploiting the resources of the Empire, specifically by the ruthless maneuvering of the population of a town or village to another area whenever the need for a group of people with a particular area of expertise arose. Farmers, munitions workers, doctors or nurses, or workers with skills in sewing to make uniforms for it soldiers, were all relocated whenever development of the Empire called for it. I mentioned this at a dinner party, and Milton Herscher, an Ashkenazi who is married to Adele Cohen, **una de las muestras** (one of ours), said, "So that's why there were so many Monasterlis in the garment industry in New York City!"

On a visit to Fran and Eli Cohen, we reminisced, as Sephardim do when we get together, about our folks' early days in America. Eli told this story: "Shortly after my mother (Becky Cohen) entered the *Sephardic Home,* I asked her how she was going to vote in the upcoming presidential election. My mother looked at me and explained how she and my father voted while he was alive. She said that my father always voted for the candidate of the Democratic Party, and that she always voted for the Republican Party. Her reasoning was logical. Evidently she had some feeling for the oppression the Jews had gone through. Afraid that the authorities would deport them if they voted for the wrong party and wanting to be on the safe side, she made sure that both parties were represented by someone in the family."

DJOHA – INSENSITIVO

Djoha torno a su kaza despues de munchos dias en el kamino. Antes de yegar a su kaza Djoha enkontro al el ombre ke tomava kargo de la kaza kuando Djoha se iva en kamino. El momento ke el moso lo vido a Djoha le disho, "Djoha, tu aziniko se murio!!" Le vino una ravia a Djoha porke el ombre fue tan insensitivo para desirle una kosa tan grava en supito, y empeso a gritar, "No tienes meyoyos, este mo de haberes kale ke des a poko a poko. No kierro ke lavores por mi mas. Va bushka otro lavoro." Kontinuo a kaminar para su kaza, y penso, este ombre lavoro por mi por munchos anyos, no lo puedo echar a la kaye ansina. Lo yamo al moso y le disho, "Me puedias desir ke avia una tempesta kon lamparos y truernos y el azniko se izo hazino, yamimos al doktor, ama no pudo venir en tiempo. Mozotros izimos todo ke pudimos, y se murio. Agora dime, komo esta mi mujer?" El moso le respondyo, "avia una tempesta muy fuerte kon lamparos y truernos y yamimos al doktor..."

INSENSITIVE

Djoha returned home after many days on the road. Before arriving at his house, Djoha met the man who took care of things at the house while Djoha was away. The moment the man saw Djoha he said, "Djoha, your donkey died!!" Djoha became very angry because the man was so insensitive as to give him such terrible news all of a sudden, and started to yell, "Have you no brains, this kind of news you must give a little at a time. I don't want you to work for me anymore. Go look for other work." Djoha continued on the way to his house and thought, "That man worked for me for many years. I can't throw out into the street just like that." He called the servant and told him, "You could have told me that there was a terrible storm with thunder and lightning, that the donkey had gotten sick, you called the doctor, but he couldn't come in time, you did all you could, and that the donkey died. Now, tell me, how is my wife? His servant answered, "Well, there was a terrible storm with thunder and lightning, we called the doctor..."

* * *

KIEFSIZ

Since the advent of my column, I have been very fortunate in the many friends I have made. Israel Cohen, of Boynton Beach and New York City among them, prodded me with, **"Hank, ke kierre dezir, kiefsiz?"** ("Hank, do you know what **kiefsiz** means?") I told him that it meant an incongenial person, to say the least. But like many things that come up, I wasn't quite satisfied with the answer I gave him.

I went to my trusty Turkish-English dictionary and found that the definition for **kief** was: inclination, whim, pleasure, merry, and for the state of being happy, **kiefli**. I knew that, because I often heard my father say, **"El kief mio es komer, bever raki, y ser alegre."** ("My pleasure is to eat, drink and be merry.")

The dictionary went a step further and also added **siz**, to the word which gives it a negative connotation. The dictionary says: indisposed, depressed, out of sorts and beastly.

My mother was deathly afraid of catching a cold and always avoided open windows and fans. On her first airplane trip, she was a little apprehensive and looked the plane over very carefully when she boarded it. She sat down, fastened her seat belt as instructed, and noticed that the temperature in the plane was to her liking. She turned to me and said, **"Esta *verrry nize* aki en el avion. Digale al ombre ke lo draveya ke no avra las ventanas en el kamino, porke no me gusta tomar *dreft*."** ("It is very nice here in the plane. Tell the man who drives it not to open any windows on the trip because I don't like to get a draft.")

My friend, Joe Oziel, had a **patriote** from Turkey working for him. Joe is positive that this man was a direct descendant of our famous Djoha. One day, Joe said to him, **"Es ora de ir a kaza. Amata la luz y serra las ventanas."** ("It's time to go home. Shut the lights and close the windows.") The **patriote** asked Joe, **"Ke kierres ke aga enprimero? Si amato luz, no va pueder ver las ventanas."** ("What do you want me to do first? If I shut the lights, I won't be able to see the windows.")

DJOHA – PEDRIDOS Y TOPADOS

Djoha se merko un vestido muevo, y desidiyo a echar el viejo afuerra. En bushkando las aldikerras de el vestido viejo, topo un bilyete del koundouryadji ke era de mas de vente anyos antes. Se disho de para si, "Agora se ke le akontesyeron a akeyos chismes!"

Djoha penso, "Puede ser ke el koundouryadji los tiene los chismes dainda." Se fue al lugar del koundouryadji, le presento el bilyete. El koundouryadji le disho, "Este bilyete es de mas de vente anyos antes." Djoha disho, "Yo se ke es mas de vente anyos, ama no puedes mirar si los tienes?" El koundouryradji los bushko y los topo. Le demando a Djoha, "Estos son los chismes tuyos?" Djoha estava tresalido, "Seguramente, estos son los miyos, kuando me los puedes dar?" Disho el koundouryadji, "Te los puedo aremender en una semana."

LOST AND FOUND

Djoha bought himself a new suit, and decided to throw his old one out. On looking through the pockets of the old suit, he found a ticket from the shoemaker that was more than twenty years old. He said to himself, "Now I know what happened to those boots!"

Djoha thought, "Maybe the shoemaker still has my boots." He went to the shoemaker and presented his ticket. The shoemaker said, "This ticket is more than twenty years old." Djoha said, "I know it is more than twenty years old, but can't you look to see if you still have them?" The shoemaker looked for the boots and found them. He asked Djoha, "Are these your boots?" Djoha was delighted, "Of course these are mine. When can you give them to me?" The shoemaker said, "I can fix them in one week."

* * *

YADES

I get letters!!! My good friend Murray Tarragano writes asking if I am familiar with a game that was very popular in our Sephardic homes. The name of the game? **Yades.** To refresh some memories, here is the letter as Murray sent it in, with a few refinements from Ike Beresid and myself.

The traditional Friday night ritual was for Mama to light the candles and Papa to recite the prayers. The customary Friday night meal was **gayina kon arroz y avikas** (chicken with rice and navy beans). Mama always cautioned the butcher not to break the wishbone when he chopped the chicken into separate parts. When the meal was over and the chicken was picked clean, leaving only the bones, someone always managed to find the wishbone. That was the signal for someone to say, **"Kien kierre djugar Yades?"** ("Who wants to play **Yades**?")

The term Yades is the *'Ladino-ized'* plural of **Yad** (Hebrew for hand), since the game dictates the use of the hands. Two players were required, and usually it was a young man and a young lady. Each participant would take hold of one end of the wishbone and break it. I don't think there was any significance attached as to which one of the two got the larger piece. Now a coveted item was wagered: a pair of silk stockings (there were no nylons in those days), a silk necktie, a pin, whatever. The rules of the game were as follows: Each participant was required to carry his part of the wishbone at all times. If, when challenged, it could not be produced, that person lost, but the asking party had to say **"Yades."** If both parties had the bone in their possession, no one won, and the game continued.

The other requirement was for one participant to offer an article to the other. If the article was accepted without the recipient saying, **"Sin Yades"** ("No hands"), the game was over, the loser being the person who failed to recite the required **"Sin Yades."** Of course, the offering party had to then say, **"Yades."** However, if the accepting party dropped the object, that person would win, even if the donor had said **"Yades."** Since this could be dangerous and messy, the use of liquid in any type of container was a no-no. The game would sometimes go on for weeks, each time the two participants saw each other, until one of them won. At other times it was over in a matter of hours. At any rate it kept us on our toes, and we all had fun.

* * *

DJOHA – PAPA EL ZAMPARA

El ijo de Djoha era edad de kazar. Topo una ijika y le disho a Djoha, "Papa esto enamorado kon la ija del kunduryadji y me kierro kazar." Djoha le disho, "No te puedes kazar kon eya porke es tu media ermana." Paso una semana y el ijo se fue a Djoha y le disho, "Papa, topi el amor de mi vida, es la ija del boyadji." Djoha le disho, "no te puedes kazar kon eya porke es tu media ermana." Mas tiempo paso y esta vez el ijo estava tresalido. Se fue a Djoha y le disho, "Papa esto enamorado kon la mujer de mi suenyos. Es la ija del tenekedji." Otra vez Djoha le disho, "No te puedes kazar kon eya, porke es tu media ermana." El ijo, en desperasion, se fue a su madre y le disho lo ke paso kon Djoha. La madre lo abraso y le disho, "Tu te puedes kazar kon kien kierres – Djoha no es tu padre."

PAPA THE PHILANDERER

Djoha's son was of marriageable age. He found a girl and told Djoha, "Papa I am in love with the shoemaker's daughter, and I want to marry her." Djoha said, "You can't marry her, she's your half-sister." A week went by, and Djoha's son again went to him and said, "Papa, I have found the love of my life. She is the painter's daughter. Djoha said, "You can't marry her, she's your half-sister." More time passed, and Djoha's son, again was delighted. He went to Djoha and said, "I am in love with the woman of my dreams. She is the tinsmith's daughter. Once more Djoha said, "You can't marry her, she's your half-sister." The son, in desperation, went to his mother and told her what Djoha said. She hugged him and said, "You can marry whomever you wish – he's not your father."

* * *

ECHAMOS LASHON – WE CONVERSE

Sometime ago I received a phone call that went something like this: **"Allo, esta es la kaza de Hank Halio?"** ("Is this the house of Hank Halio?") **"Si, kien esta yamando?"** ("Yes, who is calling?") **"Yo me yamo Benardo Nifoussi, y so miembro de un klub en New York ke se yama *Echamos Lashon* y *Klub Ladino*.** ("My name is Bernard Nifoussi, and I am a member of a club in New York called *We Converse* or *Club Ladino*.") **"Me alegro muncho de oir ke estas sano y rezyo despues de tu hazinoora."** ("I am happy to hear that you are well after your illness.") **"El Dyo respondyo a muestras orasiones."** ("The Lord answered our prayers.") (Author's note: I am deeply touched and thankful. I strongly believe in the power of prayer.)

The club, *Echamos Lashon*, that Mr. Nifoussi refers to was the brainchild of Esther Varon Weiss. Below is an excerpt of her letter to me of October 1987, recounting her idea of starting the club:

"...I have been reading your column since it started. The sweet, sad, and happy memories brought to mind the beautiful language I yearn to hear. ***Ladino Reveries*** inspired me to reach out to a few other Sephardim and form a club named ***Echamos Lashon***. The birth of this club is the best thing that happened to us..."

I attended a meeting of the club in the summer of 1991. The reception I received was wonderful. Since this club was initiated in Little Neck, New York, two other clubs that I know of have been formed. One is exclusively (not out of choice) for residents of the condominium complex, Huntington Lakes, in Delray Beach, Florida, and was founded by Lisa Gattegno Weiss and Matilda Cohen Simons. The other club, in West Palm Beach, Florida, was launched by Betty Yshoel Goldstein and Rosina Karako, and is open to all.

Echar Lashon - *Club Ladino* was the first small club that I know of started with *the exclusive purpose of speaking Ladino* as the main format of the club. There is another group, not a formal club, that meets in the Coral Springs Plaza, Florida, started by former residents of New Lots, Brooklyn. I am not aware of who is responsible for starting this group.

Strangely enough, all of the clubs were formed by Sephardic ladies who married Ashkenazim. Maybe it isn't so strange.

Although it has been five hundred years since our people were forced to leave Spain, the Sephardic spirit, albeit somewhat diminishing, still exerts a strong pull upon our Sephardic descendants. With education being secularized, with radio and television invading the home, with intermarriages, the Sephardic language and traditions passed down by our ancestors are being diluted to such a degree that today, even in Turkey, our Ladino language and customs are slowly disappearing. These clubs are doing much to perpetuate our beautiful Ladino. They provide hope that we will prolong for a little longer the rich Sephardic heritage that is ours.

DJOHA – NO KORTES MAS
STOP CUTTING

Mehmet: Djoha!! Stop cutting, you're going to fall.
Djoha: *!*¢*)@+* Go home. You don't know anything!

MISCONCEPTIONS

Of course, misconsceptions regarding the Sephardic Jews and our history and customs abound. One grand misconception, even among our own people, is that our ancestors were expelled from Spain because of the Inquisition. The Roman Catholic Church first instituted inquisitions during the Middle Ages. In 1233, Pope Gregory IX formally established the Papal Inquisition. The Spanish Inquisition did not come into being until 1480 and was not officially terminated until 1834. By the time the Jews were expelled from Spain, they had already been expelled by decree from both England (1290) and France (1392). Furthermore, far greater numbers of Christians were persecuted and died at the hands of the Inquisition than Jews.

One famous case is the great astronomer, Galileo. He became a victim of the Inquisition in Italy, and was threatened with burning at the stake if he continued expounding his theory that the earth rotated around the sun. In February of 1616, the consulting theologians of the Holy Office characterized the proposition that the sun is the center of the world, and that the earth rotates around it as heretical. Nevertheless, Galileo chose to live by his beliefs, accepting the sentence to recite once a week for three years the Seven Penitential Psalms.

Joan of Arc, another Christian denounced for her beliefs, was tried on charges of heresy and witchcraft in France, where her visions were declared diabolical. After being tricked into confessing, she retracted her confession, to no avail. She was sentenced and burned at the stake. After her death Joan was rehabilitated in a formal trial called for by Charles VII, who had been complacent during her lifetime. She was ultimately canonized.

The fact of the matter is that in Spain, the Inquisition was not directed at Jews themselves, but at the *Conversos*, or *Marranos* (converted Jews). The Spanish Inquisition read in part: "With regard to the Jews, they may profess their religion and observe its rites without being in a state of heresy. They will only be judged heretics when they attack the Christian faith, attempt to proselytize, or return to Judaism after converting." The idea was to see that the *Conversos (Marranos)* did not practice Judaism in secret, which was considered heresy by the Inquisitors.

Misconceptions about the Sephardim as a people are also prevalent. Because we are Spanish-speaking, many people mistakenly identify the Sephardim with the Latinos, or Hispanics, that have migrated to the United States from Cuba, Puerto Rico, and Central and South America, many of whom are of Indian origin and most of whom are Christian. Louis N. Levy, the founder of the *Foundation for the Advancement of Sephardic Studies and Culture,* once told this story: As a little boy on the lower East Side, his mother took him with her to the tailor. She was illiterate, but she recognized Hebrew letters when she saw them. Of course, she had no way of knowing that the words were in Yiddish! She began speaking to the tailor, in Spanish of course, saying that she was also Jewish. When he finally figured out what she was saying, he accused her of being a liar. Unable to believe that a Jew would speak Spanish rather than Yiddish, he chased them out of his shop!

Further, many who are only superficially familiar with the Sephardic community do not distinguish among the many different non-Ashkenazi groups that the word Sephardic has come to encompass. Following the Israeli Six-Day War of 1967, the term *'Sephardic'* began to be applied to all Jews not of eastern European descent for the purposes of consolidating political power.

To bring the subject closer to home, I must say that I am appalled at the misconceptions that some of our co-religionists among the Ashkenazim have of the Sephardim. During a lecture on Sephardic history at an Ashkenazi synagogue, the speaker mentioned that the Sephardim are *'Mediterranean types.'* What did he mean by that? That they are of swarthy complexion? Along the Mediterranean, one can find *'Nordic types'* as well. In my mother's family there are blue eyes, blonde hair, and very fair skin. I didn't have an opportunity to question this fellow about it, as he left immediately after his talk, but it often appears to me that they are patronizing us. "Oh, you're Sephardic. Some of my best friends are Sephardic. You Sephardics don't speak the real Spanish. I have a Sephardic sister-in-law who flunked Spanish in high school." My answer to that one is, "I know some Americans who flunked English in high school. I guess they don't speak English." **Apurados konklusiones trayen pensamientos malentendidos** (Hasty conclusions bring misunderstandings).

On other occasions, the uninformed have remarked, "You people don't speak Spanish. The real Spanish is Castillian." As those of us who have traveled to the many Spanish-speaking countries of the world know, we get along remarkably well. True, our accent is different, and very often, we use Turkish words like **paras** (money), **kira** (rent). However, in very short order, we learn the appropriate words to use. A lawyer I met in Mexico, knowing my background, commented, **"Usted se defiende muy bien en Espanyol."** (You handle yourself very well in Spanish.) I laughed!

Almost every Spanish Jew who speaks the language of his ancestors speaks it somewhat differently, reflecting diverse communities and disparate influences in the lands in which they resided. Yet it is fundamentally Spanish, albeit with outside influences. Ladino, as it was spoken in Spain among the Jews, had many Hebrew words in the vernacular, and it retains them today.

During the first half of this century, a strong influence was exerted on the Sephardim in the United States by the Ladino newspapers published here by a few of the many educated and civic-minded individuals of the Sephardic community – men like Moise Gadol, publisher of ***La Amerika***; Albert Covo, ***El Emigrante;*** Albert J. Torres and Albert Levy, ***La Vara***. There were others, but these were the best known. The most influential and longest running periodical was ***La Vara***, which ran from 1922 to 1948. The Sephardim still remember that publication with admiration and affection.

To this day, Ladino has strong traces of medieval Castillian. My good friend, Dr. Jack Crespin, lent me a copy of *Novelas, Don Quijote de la Mancha,* by Miguel de Cervantes Saavedre, written in the original Castillian. I will admit, it is not easy reading, but after studying a few chapters, the meaning started to fall into place, as similarities to our Ladino became apparent. Indeed, those of us who retain a knowledge of Ladino may even have an advantage over Spanish scholars, who are said to have difficulty reading this classic in the original Spanish. If you can obtain a copy, you will recognize many common words and expressions that we Sephardim use today in our everyday conversation. **Kalsas** (my spelling) is a word we use for stockings. Cervantes uses this same word. The present-day Spanish word for stockings is **calcetinas**. I also found the words **lentejas** (lentils), **pantuflas** (slippers), **mancebo** (young man) and others. At one point our hero, Don Quijote, greets his friend with **"Entra en la buena hora"** (literal translation: enter in the good hour). That is an expression one always hears when entering a Sephardic household.

As far as the language is concerned, it is true that the Spanish we speak is antiquated, but it definitely is Spanish. Some call it Ladino,

Djudeo-Espanyol, Judezmo; *Webster's Universal Dictionary of the English Language*, by Noah Webster, (the World Syndicate Publishing Co. 1936) says: "Ladino, the old language of Spain; the ancient Castillian language." Yet, Prof. Mair Benardette wrote: "We never called our **Judeo-Espanyol** dialect Ladino. We used the word LADINO for certain kinds of liturgical Spanish which forms a language that goes back to the 13th and 14th centuries." Another description comes from the *Encyclopedia Britannica:* "The Sephardim still speak the Spanish current in Castille at the time of their expulsion." Dr. Isaac Jerushalmi in his translation of an Ottoman Turkish text, writes: "The aim of this official translation is to bring together a nineteenth century Ottoman Turkish text with its free translation into Ladino." Here we have several versions of what our language is called. I opt for Ladino.

That the Sephardic culture has been able to endure into the present time is truly a miracle. However, with the secularization of education and the external influences of the modern world, the old ways are being eroded. We are aware of a lot of apathy toward our culture and heritage. Spanish is no longer the language of the house; it has been replaced by the national language. There is no doubt that the Spanish-Jewish dialect – **Djudeo-Espanyol** or Ladino – has been undergoing a steady decline and is literally on the verge of total extinction as a spoken language.

In the United States, only the older generation of mostly non-American-born Sephardim still speak Ladino regularly among themselves. Of the first-generation Americans of Sephardic ancestry, many still are conversant and use it on special occasions. While one or two publications in Ladino exist, the language is rarely seen in current print and even more rarely heard. However, lately we have seen a strong revival of interest due to the recent celebration of the 500th anniversary of the migration from Spain to Turkey and the publicity commemorating it.

The year 1992 marked the 500th anniversary of the acceptance of the Jews in Turkey. *The American Association of Jewish Friends of Turkey* (AAJFT) with branches in New York, Los Angeles, Dallas and South Florida made plans for the celebration of that historic year. In those 500 years our people found refuge and had been able to practice their religion openly and freely in this Muslem country.

The Sephardic influence will continue to survive as long as there are Jews. Such noted authors as Joseph Caro, who wrote the ***Schulhan Aruh***, Shelomo Halevi Alcabes, who composed ***Leha Dodi***, Moses Ben

Maimon, better known as Maimonedes, known and revered by the entire Jewish world and philosophers of all persuasions, are all Sephardim.

For those of us who were fortunate enough to have been participants in the saga, I hope that these pages engender many warm and rich memories. For those who were not so fortunate, it is hoped that they will serve as a testament to that which once was. In any event, the Sephardic story will always be a meaningful part of cultural history.

Nasreddin Hodja, more commonly known as ***Djoha.***
(Likeness taken from an old Turkish journal.)

KONSEJAS (FABLES)

Prior to my writing ***Ladino Reveries,*** my use of Ladino was confined to an occasional family gathering where we would reminisce about our dear departed relatives. We would ask questions. We would talk about our favorite uncles, aunts, cousins, etc. We would mention names that we don't hear today: **Tante Sultana, Tante Booka, La Tia Doodoo, Tio Nisimachi, Tia Zafiroocha, Tio Moshon, Tio Bohor, Izakucho, Yusefachi, Yusefiko,** and so on. We had a great time remembering the things they used to say and do. Unfortunately, those gatherings were too few and far between.

In the old days, families were the brothers and sisters of our parents and their children, our cousins. It wasn't unusual to have as many as twenty or thirty of us gathered together in a three room railroad flat in Harlem. On a Sunday, our parents would chip in and hire a truck to take us to Bronx Park for a picnic.

Every family had its official **konsejero** (story teller). Mine was no exception. Uncle Joe Fintz was ours. Anytime the family got together for a holiday, or on any festive occasion, there were always a few **konsejas** (stories) told. Almost always, the stories started with these words: **"Aviya der ser..."** (equivalent to: Once upon a time...).

Uncle Joe would get the kids together, and ask, **"Keresh oir una konsejika?"** ("Would you like to hear a little story?") The answer always was a resounding, **"Si, Tio Yusef."** ("Yes, Uncle Joe.") He may not have known it, but those stories had a terrific impact on us kids. The stories were told for two reasons: One, because the folks looked back fondly on their days in the old country; the other, to give the children a little flavor of the folklore which was impossible to find in this country. I can still see my uncle hamming it up. He told those stories with such feeling, that we actually shivered, particularly when he told a scary story.

Our favorite character was Nasreddin Hodja, more popularly known as **Djoha**. Everyone has heard of **Djoha** and many **Djoha** stories have appeared in this collection; but what do we know about his origin and the numerous yarns about his buffoonery and shenanigans? The name **Djoha** is derived from the legendary figure named Nasreddin Hodja who lived in Turkey around the 13th century. Nasreddin was his proper name given by his parents, meaning "Victor of the Faith," and Hodja, meaning master or teacher, was a title which he acquired later in life. Legend has it that he was an **Imam** (leader of prayer), a **Kadi** (a judge), and a **Bildjin** (a scholar). The stories the Sephardim circulated about him very often had a moral attached to them, but were presented in a tongue-in-cheek manner. They also referred to someone doing something or acting in an outlandish manner as **Djoha**, which is an anagram for **Hodja**. Uncle Joe related the following story at one of our family get-togethers:

DJOHA – EL AZNIKO SE MURIO

Djoha tenia un azniko y le dava a komer kada dia kon mesura, una livrika de sevada. Un dia Djoha se fue al charshi para merkar sevada y vido ke estava mas karo oy de ayer. Se disho de si para si, "Esto no es bueno. Kale ke le embeze al azniko ke koma mas poko." Kada dia Djoha le dio al azniko mas poko a komer. Despues de un tiempo Djoha vido ke el azniko estava muy flako y atemado. A la tadre fue a verlo otra vez y vido ke el azniko se murio. Djoha se travo los kaveyos de la kavesa y grito a la hema, "Agora ke te embezi a komer mas poko, te murites.

THE DONKEY DIED

Djoha had a donkey and he fed him every day with a measured weight of grain. One day Djoha went to the market to buy grain and saw that it was more expensive than the day before. He said to himself, "This is no good. I must teach the donkey to eat less." Everyday Djoha gave the donkey a little less to eat. Some time went by, and Djoha noticed that the donkey was very thin and weak. That evening he went to see the donkey again and saw that the animal had died. Djoha pulled the hair out of his head and said, "Now that I have taught you to eat less, you had to die on me."

* * *

My father was no slouch when it came to telling stories. One I remember him telling was about a young man who loved his father very much. This young man had made moderate success of his life and wanted to show his appreciation. He said to his father, **"Papa, te kierro pagar por todo ke izites por mi kuando me estava engrandesiendo. Sin tu ayuda, y sin tu buendad, yo nunka podia alkansar mi dover."** ("Papa, I want to repay you for all you did for me when I was growing up. Without your help and your kindness, I would never have reached my goal.")

His father replied, **"Lo bueno ke veyo en ti es pagamiento bastante para mi."** ("The good that I see in you is payment enough for me.") The son insisted on reciprocating, and would not take "No" for an answer. The father finally brought the discussion to an end by saying, **"Si esto es lo ke kierres, me puedes pagar en esta manera; kuando tu eras chiko, yo te yevava en brasos a todos los lugares ke yo me iva. Agora me puedes azer lo mismo."** ("If that is what you want, you may repay me in this manner: When you were small, I carried you in my arms everywhere I went. Now, you can do the same for me.")

Every now and then, as my children were growing up, I would tell them some of the stories and folklore I had heard, the story about the father and son among them. Upon graduating from medical school, my own son returned home, and I met him at the airport. As soon as I was close enough to him, he picked me up and started to carry me. I asked him, "What the heck are you doing?" He replied, "I'm trying to show you how grateful I am, and to pay you back for all your help." You can imagine how wonderful that made me feel about my son. But it also made me realize how lucky I was to have been brought up in a Sephardic household and how much more of our heritage I should have imparted to my children.

A HEAVENLY KING'S LIFE

The gift of reverie is heavenly, and the Sephardim are blessed with a wealth of it. An old adage says, "The way to a man's heart is through his stomach." If you want to be happy and live a king's life, make a Sephardic woman your wife. Aside from being great cooks, our Sephardic women are beautiful, intelligent, and sexy. Ask me, I married one.

It seems to me that what we miss the most is the Sephardic cooking we got when we still lived at home with our parents. Mom's cooking. What a rich heritage our ancestors endowed us with!

Throughout the centuries, from Spain to the Ottoman Empire to the United States, our cuisine endured, up to and including, the generation before ours. Now it's hit or miss.

Whenever we get the dishes like **garvansos kon karne** (chick peas and meat), **kyoftes de prasa** (meat patties with leek), **yaprak** (grape leaves stuffed with rice and ground meat), **kodrero y avikas** or **fijones** (lamb and navy beans), **pishkado kon guevo y limon** (fish with egg and lemon sauce), we go 'bananas.' I get these dishes at home once in a while, mostly when the children visit. We all love **burekas, bulemas kadayif, baklava, masapan** (also known as **pita de almendra), pipitas, kave turko, meze, atramuz, abudaraho, fruta seka, agristada,** etc.

Today, we go to the **boyero** (pastry-maker) to buy them. They're good, but somehow I am always left with the feeling that something is missing. The ones Mom made always tasted better. When I called to tell her I was coming with the children, she always prepared **desayuno** for us. As Mom got older, she found it difficult to knead the dough to the proper consistency. Arthritis was taking its toll; she called it *"roomatismo."* Not to disappoint us, she would order **desayuno** from the local **boyero**. We always knew it didn't have her touch, but we never let on.

Anytime we see or hear of them, our mouths water and our minds travel back to the time when they were available at all times. We never thought that some day, it would all be a memory. The same is true of our **Djudeo-Espanyol** with a slight difference: Now, when Sephardim gather there is an interjection of our dialect into the conversation.

DJOHA Y EL PASHARO

Un dia, Djoha fue combiado a la kaza de su amigo, Memet, para komer despues del lavoro. La mujer de Memet preparo una komida muy savrosa de igado kon sevoyas, a Djoha le gusto tanto ke se chupo los dedos. Le demando a la mujer de Memet si eya le puedia dar la reseta de esta komida para dar se la a su mujer. La mujer de Memet se la dio a Djoha kon muncho gusto.

En el kamino para su kaza, Djoha se fue al kasap y merko un kilo de igado fresko y en el bakal merko un kilo de arroz y sevoyas. Kon la reseta en la aldikera y las sevoyas y el igado atados kon una kuedra, kontinuo para su kaza.

En supito un pasharo muy grande apanyo lo ke merko Djoha y se bolo arriba. Djoha se empeso a reir, y grito al pasharo, "No te vas aprovechar de esto. Yo tengo la reseta en la aldikera."

DJOHA AND THE BIRD

One day Djoha was invited by his friend, Memet, to have dinner at his house after work. Memet's wife prepared such a delicious meal of liver and onions, which Djoha liked so much, that he licked his fingers. He asked Memet's wife if she would give him the recipe so that he could give it to his wife. Mrs. Memet gave it to him with the greatest of pleasure.

On the way home he stopped at the butcher and bought a kilo of liver and at the grocery store, a kilo of rice and onions. With the recipe safely in his pocket, and the package of food tied with a cord, he continued on home.

Suddenly, a very large bird grabbed the package of food and flew away. Djoha started to laugh, and yelled to the bird, "It won't do you any good. I have the recipe in my pocket."

* * *

EPILOGUE

EL TIEMPO MOS ESTA PASANDO
TIME IS PASSING US BY

Webster's New World Dictionary defines a clan as a group of people with interests in common. *Roget's International Thesaurus* says a clan is a closed, charmed circle. If we aren't that, what are we? Nearly five hundred years in the Ottoman Empire proved that. We maintained our Ladino customs and heritage.

For five centuries our people considered themselves **Djudios Espanyoles** (Spanish Jews) because, although they were welcomed in Turkey, they were not granted subject status. Suppose, though, that they had been accepted as Turkish subjects. Isn't it possible that Ladino would have become extinct in less than a century there, as it will here in the United States? Because our people were to some degree isolated, our culture flourished. In this sense, the Ottoman Empire was truly the 'Land of our Salvation.'

Contrast this with the circumstances our parents faced when they arrived in America at the beginning of this century. Growing up in a Sephardic environment, we spoke Ladino at home and heard it in the synagogue. However, as we grew older, we told our folks, **"Estamos en la Amerika. Si keresh adelantarvos aki, kale ke vos ambezesh a avlar en Inglese."** ("We are in America. If you want to get ahead here, you must learn to speak English.") And we did get ahead, but we also came apart.

The Sephardim of Turkey and Israel today find themselves in a parallel situation. I witnessed this phenomenon first hand during visits to my cousins. (Two of my mother's brothers remained in Turkey; some of their children have gone on to Israel.) In both countries I noticed that my cousins spoke to their children mostly in Turkish or Hebrew. I questioned this and was told, **"Muestras kriaturas kierren ke avlemos la lengua del pais porke se averwensan kuando avlamos en Espanyol. En la kaye nunka avlamos Espanyol."** ("Our children want us to speak the language of the land because they are embarrassed when we speak Spanish. In the street we never speak Spanish.")

My generation will probably be the last to understand and appreciate fully the Ladino culture, heritage, customs, language, and folklore, the last for whom the culture truly lives. A few second-generation Americans, like my son and Bob Bedford, are close enough to it to lament and resist its loss, and to devote themselves to the historical, if not the actual, preservation of our way of life. But to the members of the third generation, like my granddaughter, the treasure of Ladino life is already a ghost that haunts benignly, perhaps in the recognition of a melodious surname or in the familiar flavor of a delectable **dulse**.

El tiempo mos esta pasando!! And we, **los Djudios Espanyoles,** are now scattered all over the world, so far from each other that we must hold conventions to bring us together. At the May, 1993 American Sephardi Federation convention, at the Grand Hyatt Hotel in New York City, Rabbi Marc Angel was asked by a concerned member of the audience what should be done to impart the spirit of the Sephardim to her grandchildren. "It is not enough, Rabbi," she insisted, "to feed them **bourekas**!" She was right. Of course, we must feed them **bourekas** (and everything else too)! But we can feed them our stories as well. We all have a wealth of memories that we don't want to lose. To me, and I hope to you, ***Ladino Reveries*** has been stimulating and rewarding in the sense that I feel that through my past, my life is starting over again.

One of my mother's favorite sayings was **Kuando uno avla, serra la boka y avre los oidos** (When someone speaks, close your mouth and open your ears). You, my readers, know well that stories beget more stories. In other words, memories make more memories, and they are the glue. I hope this collection has brought back sweet, sticky memories to all of you and that it has inspired you to pass on your own stories to those you love.

Rogo ke este kolleksion de anekdotas les a traido atras memorias dulses de tiempos pasados. Ke tengash salud buena y ke bivash por sien y vente anyos.

APPENDIX

SONGS

I have collected a few songs that were always sung at my house, and I hope they will be as appealing to you as they were to me. This first one was sung by my mother to my youngest daughter, to whom we gave the Spanish name of Sara.

BRE SARIKA BRE

Bre Sarika Bre	Bre Sarika Bre
Traeme un poko de agua	Bring me a little water
Bre Sarika Bre	Bre Sarika Bre
Chika y ermosika	Petite and beautiful
Bre Sarika Bre	Bre Sarika Bre
Linda y savrozika	Pretty and delightful
Yo te va merkar	I will buy for you
Sapatos de Unkapan	Shoes from Unkapan
Chismez de Djibarme	And boots from Djibarme
Bre Sarika Bre	Bre Sarika Bre

The next song was a satire on a dumb or foolish girl which I am sure that most of you will remember having heard at home at one time or another. The meaning of **Barminan** is 'heaven forbid.'

UNA IJA BOVA

Una ija bova tengo, Barminan	I have a foolish daughter
Me la yaman tengere, Barminan	She is called a pot
Kuando sale a la plaza, Barminan	When she walks the street
Me la azen kepazel	She is made fun of
Me la azen kepazel	She is made fun of
Me la azen kepazel	She is made fun of
A si biva Ham Liachi, Barminan	For the sake of Mr. Leachi

A si biva yo kon el, Barminan	For both our sakes
Ke me seya novia, Barminan	Find her a husband
Ke me seya mi plazer	It will please me no end
Ke me seya mi plazer	It will please me no end
Ke me seya mi plazer	It will please me no end
Moda mueva mos kitaron, Barminan	A new fad has come out
Las ijas de Rivington, Barminan	By the girls of Rivington
Kuando salen a la plaza, Barminan	When they walk the street
Se les meneya el digidon	They wiggle their butts
Se les meneya el digidon	They wiggle their butts
Se les meneya el digidon	They wiggle their butts
No me veyas chikitika, Barminan	Don't think I'm young
Tengo anyos en kuti, Barminan	I don't look my age
Boy de me estan kazadas, Barminan	Girls my age are married
Tienen ijos en charshi	And have sons at work
Tienen ijos en charshi	And have sons at work
Tienen ijos en charshi	And have sons at work

Moda mueva mos kitaron, Barminan	A new fad has come out
Las ijas de Rivington, Barminan	By the girls of Rivington
Kitan a los ijos lokos, Barminan	They drive the boys wild
Kon la pudra y kolor	With their powder and rouge
Kon la pudra y kolor	With their powder and rouge
Kon la pudra y kolor	With their powder and rouge

This next one was my father's favorite song, **raki** being the national hard liquor of Turkey.

LA VIDA DO POR EL RAKI

La vida do por el raki	I give my life for raki
No puedo yo desharlo	I can't leave it alone
De bever nunka me arti	I never get enough to drink
De tanto amarlo	Because I love it so

Kuando esta en baril	When it's in the barrel

El no avla deltodo	It never says a word
Kuando me ago yo kandil	When I get drunk
Me ago banyos de lodo	I roll in the mud
Chorus: La vida do, etc...	I give my life, etc...
El ya mos aze divorsar	It causes us to divorce
Kazamiento de oro	A marriage of love
La vida mos aze pasar	It makes our lives pass by
Kon risas y kon yorros	With laughter and tears
Chorus: La vida do, etc...	I give my life, etc...
Me siento yo varon	I feel like superman
Me siento yo primario	I feel like number one
Sin tener liras en kashon	Without a penny in my pocket
Me siento milyonaryo	I feel like a millionaire
La vida do por el raki	I give my life for raki
No puedo yo desharlo	I can't leave it alone
De bever nunka me arti	I never get enough to drink
De tanto amarlo	Because I love it so

The following song was composed by Sophie Hazan. Sung by the residents of the *Sephardic Home for the Aged* (To the Tune of "My Darling Clementine.")

ESTA KASA DE LOS VIEJOS

Esta kasa de los viejos	This Old Age Home
La frawimos kon sudor	Was built with sweat
Kon pasensia y dinero	With patience and money
Esta yena de amor	It is filled with love
O keridos y keridas	Oh my loved ones
Saludosos ke estesh	May you stay healthy
Para pasar la vida buena	To live the good life
Y tener buena viejes	And to have a great old age

Mos pensimos y mos adjuntimos	We thought and adjusted
Komo esta se va azer	How this place would be built
Vino un dia se izo klaro	One day it became clear
Kon ayuda y kon kerer	With help and love
Ahora keremos mas ayuda	Now we need more help
Esta kasa grandeser	For this house to grow
Los ermanos esperando	The brothers are waiting
Para la ora de venir	For the time to come
Si mos metemos todo en uno	If we all work together
Muncho y poko para dar	To give a little or a lot
Las puertas se avren mas presto	The doors will open sooner
Munchos ermanos van a entrar	Many brothers will enter
Estamos alegre y kontentas	We are happy and content
En esta kasa bendicha	In this sacred house
Los kien penaron, munchas grasias	To those who toiled, many thanks
Y por eyos la mizvah	And to them the good fortune
O keridos y keridas	Oh my dear ones
Saludosos ke estesh	May you stay well
Para pasar la vida buena	To enjoy the good life
Y tener buena viejes	And to have a great old age

This next song is the national anthem of Israel. I remember hearing it sung when I was a little boy going to Hebrew school and in the synagogue on special occasions. I found it in a booklet that Mr. Moise Gadol had prepared for the newly-arrived Sephardic immigrants to the Lower East Side, where he published the first Ladino newspaper in the United States, ***La Amerika***. It is my transliteration from the Ladino written in Hebrew characters to the Ladino written in Roman characters that we are all familiar with.

"A la boz del imno national Hatikva." ("To the tune of the national anthem Hatikva.")

HATIKVA

**Fiestaremos djuntos gloriosos
A el dia de oy kon gozas
Dia alegre el es nombrado
Kon plazer de Djudio membrado**

**Este dia de alegria
Mos rekorda la manzia
Ke los mas djudios sufrieron
Y fin oy salvasyon no tuvyeron**

**Dos mil anyos de tan desdenyo
Sin poder repozar sin esfuenyo
Arastando en mil y un lugar
Sin tener kanto por olgar**

**Nuestro korason endecha
Nuestra alma se estrecha
De ver los Djudios persigidos
Y tambien kon dolor abatidos**

**Ma las naves prietas se avren
Nuestros sielos kon flamas adren
Flamas fuertes ke van a saltar
Korason del djudio van a kemar**

**Alsaran la bandiera
Por amor de muestra tierra
Sin sudor de muestra arofyada
Kon rozas, kon konchas ensembrada**

**Lavoremos todos ermanos
En Sion y sera az a nos
La esperansa vieja egziste
Mas ninguno de nos se atriste**

**Biva biva Palestina
Nuestra tierra karisima
Kon sudor del Djudio arofyada
Kon rozas y konchas ensembrada**

EL REFRAN

The heart and soul of our folklore is spiced with our **refranes** (proverbs). Unfortunately, this part of our ancestry is slowly coming to an end. Most first-generation Americans of Sephardic ancestry, born from 1910 on, have been negligent in passing down to their children this treasure of knowledge that was at their fingertips as they were growing up. We took it for granted, and we never gave a thought to the possibility of its disappearance. As we look back, we can see how much of our culture has gone astray. Today, the use of Ladino is, at best, sporadic, but when we hear it, our hearts and ears perk up.

Our Ladino **refranes**, or proverbs, are based on the experiences of our forefathers. There are literally thousands of proverbs in our culture, a gold mine of our glorious past that is fading. All are true to life. The phrase, "A picture is worth a thousand words" does not apply when it is used in relation to a proverb. As an example, try to compose a photograph or a painting that would do justice to: **El ke no tiene meyoyos, ke tenga pachas** (He who has no brains, must have legs).

The origins of the **refranes** are unknown. Having been passed down from generation to generation and used spontaneously, they are just as fresh and timely today as they were ages ago. The **refran** knows no racial, religious or national barriers. It can be applied to anything or anyone you choose. They bring back memories of our folks catching us in apropos situations. You will find references to our daily lives covering likes and dislikes, truth and lies, love and hate, wealth and poverty, parents and children, honor and immorality, drunkenness and sobriety, heaven and hell, laziness and enterprise.

The vitality of our heritage was best expressed when our folks used a **refran** to illustrate a point. Liberally used by our parents, these proverbs made a strong impression. They guided us in the proper direction without sounding like a reprimand.

For example, **Muncho dormir es una vida sin bivir** (Much sleeping is a life without living), is a rebuke not to be lazy; it delivers a message in a broad, non-judgmental manner. Another, **Las mintiras tienen piyes** (Lies have feet), means lies spread quickly. There are some

Ladino proverbs that contradict each other, as there are in English, such as: 'Look before you leap,' and 'He who hesitates is lost.' In Ladino we have **En boka serrada no entra moshka.** Literally, 'A fly will not enter a closed mouth,' interpreted as 'think before you speak,' or 'speak up and get hurt.' **La repuesta en su buena ora vale mil liras.** 'A timely reply is worth a thousand liras.' How many times after an argument have you thought, "I should have said _____?" My contemporaries may very well be 'the last of the Mohicans' – the last to be aware of the glory of the **refran**. Hopefully, this publication will encourage a rebirth.

Although you have come across **refranes** sprinkled throughout this book, here is an extensive collection of our **refranes** with literal translations.

REFRANES / PROVERBS

Admitir un pekado sin ser demandado ez kaji ser inosente.
A free admission of guilt, a verdict of your innocence.

Ago mi echo, al diavlo el resto.
I do my thing and to hell with all else.

Aguantate kon buenos y devendras uno de eyos.
Keep good company and you will become one of them.

Aldikera sin paras es komo arbole sin fruta.
A pocket without money is like a tree without fruit.

Alhad ni enprestes, ni fies.
Neither lend nor borrow on Sunday.

Alegrina de la plaza, eskurina de la kasa.
Delightful on the outside, gloomy at home.

Amor de yerno, sol de invierno.
The love of a son-in-law, the sun of midwinter.

Amor kon amor se paga.
Love is reimbursed with love.

Amores muevos olvidan los amores viejos.
New loves forget old loves.

Ande ay amor, ay dolor.
Where there is love, there is pain.

Ashugar y paras te puedo dar, ama el mazal tu lo bushkaras.
A trousseau and money I can give, but you must seek your own luck.

Ay paras, ay kavod.
There's money, there's honor.

Aze bien y no mires a kien.
Do good, and don't look for whom it is done.

Aze mal y aspera otro tal.
Do harm and expect the same in return.

Azer y kayar.
Act and be silent.

Bien ke tengamos toda la vida.
May we be well all of our lives.

Bive y desha bivir.
Live and let live.

Bivir y ver.
To live and to see.

Bushka y toparas.
Seek and you shall find.

Buen korason aze buen karakter.
A good heart forms a good character.

Dame mazal, y echa me a los perros.
Give me luck, and you can throw me to the dogs.

De el ke tuvo y no tiene, adjideate.
Pity the one who once had and no longer has.

De la roza sale el espino, del espino sale la roza.
Every rose has its thorn, every thorn has its rose.

De tu kaza ke no mankes.
May you never be missing from your house.

De tu pan no me arti, de tu palavras me konforti.
Your bread did not fill me, your words comforted me.

De tu patada veremos hayre.
From your footstep may we see goodness.

Dime kon kien pasas, no de kien nasites.
Tell me who you accompany, not your genealogy.

Djuwar y perder todos saven azer.
Anyone can gamble and lose.

Dos amigos kon una chanta, uno konta, el otro yorra.
Two friends with one bankroll, one counts, the other cries.

El boracho y el loko no dizen mentiras.
Neither the drunkard nor the insane tell lies.

El dar es onor, el tomar es dolor.
It is an honor to give, painful to take.

El dia ke no limpias viene el ke no pensas.
The day you don't clean, someone comes you don't expect.

El estudyar es amargo, el saver dulse.
To study is bitter, to know is sweet.

El ke da en la puerta oye una repuesta.
Ask and you shall receive.

El ke da onor, a si se onra.
One who confers honor, honors himself.

El ke desonra, a si se desonra.
He who dishonors, dishonors himself.

El ke espera, resive en su buen tiempo.
The one who waits receives in good time.

El ke espera, se dezezpera.
The one who waits, waits and despairs.

El ke korre se kaye.
He that runs, falls.

El ke mal pensa para si se lo pensa.
He who thinks evil thinks it for himself.

El ke no tiene la ermosa, beza la mokosa.
He who hasn't the beauty will kiss the snot nose.

El ke no mira adelantre, atras se keda.
He who doesn't look ahead remains behind.

El ke se echa kon perros se levanta kon pulgas.
He who sleeps with dogs awakens with fleas.

El ke tiene kaza de vidro, ke no eche piedras al vezino.
He who has a glass house should not throw stones at his neighbor.

El ke tiene kuatro y gasta sinko, no tiene de menester aldikera.
He who has four and spends five has no need for a pocket.

El lavoro de la manseves da repozo en la viejes.
The toil of one's youth gives solace in old age.

El loko lo gasta, el meyoyudo se lo kome.
The insane one spends his; the smart one eats his.

El loko y la kriatura siempre dizen la vedrad.
The crazy one and the child always tell the truth.

El meyoyudo lo pensa, el borrachon lo dize.
The smart one thinks it; the drunkard says it.

El prove piedre tiempo en kontando la rikeza del riko.
The poor man wastes time counting the wealth of the rich man.

El riko esta hazino, al moso le echan la ayuda.
The rich man is sick, the servant gets the enema.

El tiempo todo kuvre, y todo deskuvre.
Time covers all and discovers all.

En aunamiento ay fuersa.
In union there is strength.

En azer bien nada se piedre, muncho se gana.
Nothing is lost in good deeds, much is gained.

En la espalda de otro, el kargo ez liviano.
On another's shoulders, the burden is always lighter.

En Martes, ni te kazes, ni te embarkes.
On Tuesday, neither marry nor step out.

En vida no te kije, en muerte te dezei.
In life I didn't want you; in death I long for you.

Eridas de kuchiyadas pasan, ama no las malas palabras.
Knife wounds heal, but not the evil words.

Ermano para el dia bueno.
A brother for the good day.

Eskapamiento bueno.
A good ending.

Esperar de otros, ofisio de lokos.
To depend on others is the profession of fools.

Esta eskrito en la palma, lo ke va yevar el alma.
It is written on the palm what the soul will endure.

Fiel y miel son de menester.
Bile and honey – both are needed.

Gato eskaldado de agua yelada se fuye.
A scalded cat will flee from cold water.

Guayas de la armada ke tiene munchos kapitanes.
Woe to the army that has too many captains.

Guayas kuando una koza se empesa yerrado.
Woe to something that starts off wrong.

Ijos de mis ijos, dos vezes mis ijos.
Sons of my son, twice my sons.

Kada gayo kanta en su gayinero.
Every rooster sings in his own coop.

Kada uno resive lo ke merese.
Everyone receives what he deserves.

Kada uno paga segun peka.
Everyone pays for his own sins.

Kada uno se araska ande le kome.
Each one scratches where it itches.

Kamina kon alegria, porke si kaminas kon tristeza y ansya, te se apoka la vida.
Travel happily, because if you travel with sadness and worry, your life will dwindle.

Kamina kon un bueno y te azeras uno kon el.
Travel with a good person and you will become like him.

Kien a dos duenyos sirve, a uno kale ke enganye.
He who serves two bosses must deceive one.

Kien apromete, en devda se mete.
The person who makes promises puts himself into debt.

Kien azno nase, azno se muere.
Born a jackass, dies a jackass.

Kien bien te kierre te aze yorrar.
He who cares for you will make you cry.

Kien muncho save, muncho pena.
The more one knows, the more one endures.

Kien no aze kumar, salva su kaza.
He who doesn't gamble saves his home.

Kien es tu enemigo? El de tu ofisio.
Who is your enemy? The one who knows your business.

Kien se kaza kon amor, bive siempre kon dolor.
He who marries for love always lives with pain.

Kien se yama savio? El ke se ambeza de kualkier persona.
Who is considered wise? He who learns from all.

Kien tiene mujer tiene el guerko al lado.
He who has a wife has the devil at his side.

Kien rizga nada, obtiene nada.
Nothing ventured, nothing gained.

Koza mal dicha no se olvida.
Something maliciously said is not forgotten.

Kitar sin meter, el fondo se viene a ver.
By taking and not putting, the bottom is soon seen.

Konsejo no es bien resivido donde no es bien demandado.
Advice is not well received where it is not solicited.

Krese en la guerta lo ke el guertaleno asembra.
As ye sow, so shall ye reap.

Kuando el gato esta afuera, los ratones djuan.
When the cat's away, the mice will play.

Kuando se serra una puerta, mil se avren.
When one door closes, a thousand open.

Kuanto mas tienes, mas kierres.
The more one has, the more one wants.

La haraganut es la yave de la provedad.
Laziness is the key to poverty.

La kaza del riko se vazyara, ama la kaza del prove nunka se inche.
The rich man's home may empty out; the poor man's never fills.

La lampara sin azete no se ensiende.
A lantern without oil will never shine.

La manseves es una ves, ken la goza save lo ke es.
Youth comes only once; he who enjoys it knows what it is.

La mitad, la miyatad.
Six of one, half a dozen of the other.

La muerte viene kuando no se espera.
Death comes when it is least expected.

La provedad es el infierno de la tierra.
Poverty is hell on earth.

La mas noble vengansa es el perdon.
The noblest vengeance is forgiveness.

La muerte no konese la rikeza ni la provedad.
Death recognizes neither wealth nor poverty.

La vedrad va y viene komo la putana, ama dinguno la kierre.
Truth comes and goes like a whore, but no one wants her.

La ventura? Al ke la bushka.
Wealth? To the one who pursues it.

Las mentiras tienen piyes.
Lies have feet. The truth will out.

Las paredes tienen oidos.
The walls have ears.

Lavoro paga las devdas.
Work pays all debts.

Le das una mano, y toma un piye.
Give him a hand, and he takes a foot.

Lenyo tuerto no se enderecha.
Bent lumber can never be straightened.

Los ijos del sapatero no tienen kalsados.
The shoemaker's children have no shoes.

Madrasta? El nombre es bastante.
Stepmother? The name is enough.

Mal yevado, bien asperando.
Through bad times, hope for good times.

Mas vale kayer en rio furiente, y no en boka de la gente.
Better to fall into a raging sea than into the mouths of the people.

Mas vale ke yorre el ijo de el padre.
It is better for the child to cry than the parent.

Mas vale saviduriya ke piedras presyosas.
Knowledge is worth more than precious stones.

Mas vale ser ijo de un prove, de esklavo de un riko.
Better to be the son of a poor man than the slave of a rich man.

Mas vale tadre ke nunka.
Better late than never.

Mas vale 'toma uno,' de 'dos te dare.'
Better 'take one,' than 'I'll give you two later.'

Mazal de la feya, la ermosa deseya.
The beauty desires the luck of the ugly one.

Muncho miel bulaneya.
Too much honey nauseates.

Mira kon ojos en ventikuatro.
Keep your eyes open 24 hours a day.

Mis ijas kazadas, mis ansyas dobladas.
My daughters married, my miseries doubled.

Mujer ermosa sin buendad es komo eskuralicha en nariz de puerko.
A beautiful woman without goodness is like an earring on the nose of a pig.

Mujer sin kriaturas es komo un arvole sin fruta.
A woman without children is like a tree without fruit.

Ningun governo puede egsistir sin grande opozision.
No government can exist without great resistance.

No avles malo del dia asta ke anochese.
Do not speak ill of the day until it ends.

No se kita sangre de una piedra.
You can't get blood out of a stone.

No ay mijor mandado ke el ke azes kon tus manos.
There is no greater appeal than something made by your own hand.

Nunka ke te se tome el tino.
May you never lose your senses (memory).

Ojos ke no ven, el korason no le duele.
The heart does not feel what the eyes don't see.

Otro gayo me kantara.
Another rooster should crow.

Palavras malas matan mas del tosigo.
Harsh words kill more than poison does.

Para todo ay remedio, menos la muerte.
There is a remedy for everything except death.

Pishkado grande englute al chiko.
A big fish will swallow the small one.

Prenyada y paras siempre salen en medyo.
Pregnancy and money always show up.

Refranes mentirozos no aye.
There are no false proverbs.

Si el viejo era torpe en su manseves, los anyos no deshan topar la vedrad.
If a man was stupid in his youth, his years won't help him discover the truth.

Si mas alto me veyo, mas alto dezeyo.
The higher I go, the more I covet.

Si no puedes lo ke kierres, kierre lo ke puedes.
If you can't achieve what you want, want what you can achieve.

Si te dan, toma; si te demandan, fuyete.
If they give you, take; if they hit you, run.

Si te kierres kazar bien, kaza te kon tu igual.
If you wish to marry well, marry one of your own class.

Todo ke azes kon plazer es kolaye.
Everything that is done with pleasure is easy.

Todos los kaminos no son derechos.
All roads are not straight.

Un buen pleto traye una buena paz.
A good battle brings a good peace.

Un padre para sien ijos y no sien hijos para un padre.
One father for a hundred sons, not a hundred sons for one father.

Una mano lava la otra.
One hand washes the other.

Una miaja, una damla.
A tiny bit, a drop.

Uno es prometer, otro es azer.
It is one thing to promise. It is another to give.

Unos asembran, otros arrekojen.
There are those that sow, those that reap.

Vida sin penas no ay.
There is no life without problems.

Ya le amanesyo.
It finally dawned on him.

HEBREW WORDS COMMONLY USED IN DJUDEO-ESPANYOL

The origin of our people dates back a few thousand years, when Hebrew was our common language. After the diaspora, and our subsequent assimilation into a variety of cultures, we see that Hebrew still finds its way into our everyday language. **Djudeo-Espanyol** and Yiddish are just two examples. Here are just some of the Hebrew words that are used regularly in our **Djudeo-Espanyol**. How many more can you think of?

adam - man
afilu - even though
alef beth - alphabet
Alhad - Sunday

balabai - boss
barminan - heaven forbid
behor - first born
benadam - human being
beraha - blessing
bethahaim - cemetery
birkat mila - circumcision

darsar - to orate
daenou - enough

gan eden - paradise
gazoz - soda water
geinam - hell

hames - unleavened
hanukiah - menora for Hanuka
Hava - Eve, Adam's wife
haya - beast
heshbon - sum, account

kal - shul
kasher - kosher
kavod - honor, respect

lashon - language, chat

malah - angel
mamzer - bastard
mazal - luck
menora - any candelabra
minyan - quorum of 10
Misrayim - Egypt
misva - good deed
moed - holiday

neder - vow

rahamim - mercy, pity
rasha - wicked, evil

sedaka - charity
Sefarad - Spain
shabat - Sabbath
simha - happy event

tanith - to fast
taleth - talis
teva - reader's stand
trefa - unkosher

zahuth - good deed

HEBREW WORDS COMMONLY USED IN YIDDISH

Like **Djudeo-Espanyol**, many Hebrew words are still used regularly in the Yiddish language. Some are used in our **Djudeo-Espanyol**, some are not. Below is a partial list of Hebrew words that I have heard used in conversations between ***Yidishim***. Check them out with some of your friends.

agada - Passover ritual
alavay - it should happen
amotsi - blessing for bread

balabus - the boss
behavod - with honor
beraha - a blessing
betsim - eggs

cala - bride

emet - the truth
erev - eve of a holiday

ganav - thief
goy - gentile

haham - rabbi
hala - challah, bread
hametz - leavened bread
harosets - mixture for passover
heshbon - an accounting
hasid - hasidim
Hava - Eve, Adam's wife
haya - an animal
hora - a dance
hupa - wedding canopy
hutzpa - gall, nerve

kapara - penitential slaughter
kasher - kosher
ketuba - marriage contract

mahn - man
mamzer - bastard
mazel - luck
megila - a scroll
melamed - teacher
metsia - a find, a bargain
mikve - ceremonial bath
minyan - a quorum of ten
mishpaha - family
mitsva - a good deed
mohel - circumciser

rahamunis - rahamin, pity

sedaka - charity
sehel - brains
shamus - sexton
shekel - coin
shiva - mourning period
shohet - slaughterer
simha - happy occasion

taam - taste
tifilin - phylacteries
trefa - not kosher

TURKISH WORDS USED EVERY DAY IN OUR DJUDEO-ESPANYOL

Here is a small sampling of Turkish words that have found their way into our everyday language over the course of five centuries. A more complete list will be found in the glossary.

adjami - amateur
ama - but
achilear - to illuminate
adjile - hurry
aksi - cranky
aman - please
araba - wagon
arkadash - pal, sidekick
ashlik - allowance
astar - coat lining
ayde - go ahead

bakal - grocery store
balta - axe
barsak - cow's intestine
bashtoone - with pleasure
bela - trouble
bereket - abundance
bezelya - peas
bouz - ice
boya - paint
boyadji - painter
bouchouk - half, twin
bozdear - spoil
boudala - stupid
boulanik - cloudy
bouyroun - join us (mealtime)

chai - tea
chourouk - broken
churapes - socks, stockings

dava - lawsuit
dalga - sea wave
dip - bottom
diz - knee
djam - glass, pane
dolashear - coming around
doumouz - pig
douz - smooth
douman - smoke, as in fire

eech - none, zilch
embatakar - to soil
evala - thank God

fasla - chip on a dish
ferrahli - relaxed
furcha - a brush
fusta - a skirt

gazep - troublemaker

hal - plight
halis - true, real
hamal - laborer
hanoum - upper class lady
harif - sharp, clever
hatir - as a favor to
houvarda - generous

innat - stubbornness

kadar - amount
kalem - pencil
kaymak - cream
kapak - lid, cover
karisheyar - to stir, mix, mix in
karpooz - watermelon
kibrik - match, phosphorus
kira - rent
kolaye - easy
kimur - coal
kiyoshe - corner
kousour - left over, the rest
kiyoupree - bridge
kumardji - gambler

lakirdi - discussion

mavi - the color blue
maitop - scorn, mock
mashalla - may God preserve, God has willed
meana - saloon
merhaba - hello
metalik - Turkish coin, small coin
meze - hors d'oeuvre
minder - sofa-like settee
miskin - filthy, foul
musafir - visitor, guest
mushama - linoleum, floor covering
mushteri - customer

naalet - troublemaker
nargile - turkish water pipe
nazar - evil eye

palto - coat
paras - money

sakat - crippled
sira - a line, your turn

tavla - wood
tefter - a book
tekme - a kick
tokmak - a mallet, a dope
toutoun - tobacco

vitrina - store window

yaka - collar
yakishear - suitable, becoming
yene - again

zor - hard, difficult
zavali - poor thing

GLOSSARY

A complete Glossary of **L**adino, **T**urkish, **H**ebrew, **G**reek, **F**rench, **I**talian, and **E**nglish words as used throughout this book. The origin of all the words, except the Ladino words, will have a letter alongside designating their origin. A combination of two letters designates the use of that word in both languages.

Have some fun with your friends, use the list to jog their recollection to see how many of these words bring back memories of their loved ones.

A

abashada		- a cold
abatir		- to humble
abechar	*E*	- to bet
abokar		- to bend over
aboltando		- turning
aboltar		- to turn
abolto		- turned
abramilas		- prunes
abrasar		- to hug
abufado		- swollen
achunkate		- sit down
achiliado	*T*	- enlightened
adelantado		- advanced
adelantre		- ahead, forward
adjami	*T*	- novice
adjideate		- have pity
adjile	*T*	- hurry
adovar		- to mend
adurmesido		- numb
afito	*T*	- it happened
afirum	*T*	- a praise
afuera		- out, outside
agayas		- tonsils
agensia	*E*	- agency
agora		- now
agristada		- lemon & egg sauce
agua		- water
agujas		- needles
aharvar	*H*	- to hit
ahir	*T*	- animal enclosure
Ahptahn	*E*	- uptown
ajena		- foreign
ajo		- garlic
akavidate		- take care
akeyo		- that thing
aki		- here
akodrando		- remembering
akodrar		- to remember
akodrate		- remember!
akodro		- remembered
aksi	*T*	- cranky
alargar		- to lengthen
alavar		- to praise
albondigas		- meat patties
aldikerra		- pocket
alegre		- happy
alegria		- happiness
algunas		- some, a few

Alhad *H* - Sunday
alkunya - surname
almastiga - chewing gum
almendra - almond
aluenga - tongue
amadores - lovers
aman *T* - please
amante - a lover
amanyana - tomorrow
amargo - bitter
amatar - to extinguish
ambezamos - we learn
ambezar - to learn
ambiertura - hunger
ambre - hungry
amigo - friend
amistad - affection
amoudisyon *T* - silence!
amor - love
amoustrando - showing
anarshista *E* - anarchist
ande - where
animales - animals
ansina - like this, this way
ansyas - woes
antiguedad - antiquity
antiguos - old ones
anyo - year
aogar - to choke
apanyar - to catch
aparejar - prepare
aparejate - get ready!
apreta - squeeze
apretasion - pressure
apreto - tight spot
apurado - agitated
Arap *T* - Arab (black)
araba *T* - a wagon
arankar - pull up, out
arapar - to shave
araskar - to scratch
arastar - to drag
atar - to tie up
arazgar - to tear
arbole - a tree
arelumbra - shines
arena - sand
aresvalar - put on airs
ariento - inside
arina - flour
arkadash *T* - a friend, pal
arrondjar - to toss out, push
arroz - rice
arto - full, not hungry
ashlik *T* - an allowance
ashugwar *T* - hope chest
asker *T* - soldier
askeyo - revulsion
asolado - lonely
asta - until
astar *T* - coat lining
atado - tied
atavanado *T* - crazy
atemado - scared
atras - back, behind
avagar - slowly
aver - air
avikas - beans
avlando - talking
avlar - to talk
avlastina - gabby
avre - open
avrio - opened
aya - there

ayde	*T*	- go ahead
ayedados		- aged ones
ayer		- yesterday
ayi		- there
Ayifto	*H*	- Egypt
ayuda		- help, enema
ayudando		- helping
ayudar		- to help
azelo		- do it
azer		- to do, to make
azetunas		- olives
azeyte		- oil
aziendo		- doing, making
azno		- donkey, jackass

B

bailar		- to dance
bakal	*T*	- grocery store
bakalava	*T*	- delicacy
Balkanas		- the Balkans
bamyas		- okra
bandera		- flag
banyo		- bath
barato		- inexpensive
baril		- barrel
barminan	*H*	- heaven forbid
baruhaba	*H*	- welcome
bashetiko		- shorty
basho		- short, low life
bashtune	*T*	- with pleasure
bastante		- plenty, enough
batakchi	*T*	- dead beat
batal	*T*	- unemployed
bavajada		- nonsense, frivolous
bayat	*T*	- stale
baylar		- to dance
bedahaim	*H*	- cemetery
bela	*T*	- trouble
benadam	*H*	- human being
bendicho		- blessed
bendision		- blessing
bendizimos		- we bless
berendjena		- eggplant
bever		- to drink
bevienda		- beverage
bezelyas		- peas
beziko		- a little kiss
bien		- good, well
bilibis		- roasted chickpeas
bilyetes		- tickets
bimbriyo		- quince
birra		- anger
biskocho		- biscuit
bivda		- widow
bive		- live
bivimos		- we live
bivir		- to live
bivo		- I live
blanko		- white
bloko	*T*	- block, street
blusa		- blouse
boda		- wedding
bogo	*T*	- bundle
bohor	*H*	- first born
boka		- mouth
boracho		- drunk
borachones		- drunkards
botones		- buttons
bouchouk	*T*	- half, twin
boureka	*LT*	- a turnover
boulanteez	*T*	- nausea
bouyendo		- boiling

bouyroon *T* - welcome
bouz *T* - ice
boverias - nonsense
bovo - a dope
boy *T* - stature
boya *T* - paint
boyadji *T* - painter
boyero - pastry maker
boz - voice
bozeyar *T* - to spoil
braso - an arm
buendad - goodness
bueno - good
bukles - curls
bulanik *T* - cloudy
burako - hole
burlando - jesting
burmuelos - pastries
bushka - seek
butika - a shop

C

chadir *T* - umbrella
chalgi *T* - music
chamashir *T* - underwear
chanta *T* - handbag
chapeyo - hat
chapeteado - flushed
chapkin *T* - rascal
chaptear *G* - to hit
charshi *T* - marketplace
chibouk *T* - cigarette holder
chika - small
chikez - one's childhood
chikiniyar *T* - to hesitate
chikur *T* - shoelace, string
chilibi *T* - gentleman
chini *T* - plate, dish
chiro *G* - dried fish
chourouk *T* - crooked
chudjuk *T* - children
chuflete - a whistle
chupar - suckle
churapes *T* - stockings

D

Dahntan *E* - Lower East Side, downtown
dainda *H* - yet **(adayin)**
dame - give me
damla - a drop
danyo - harm, damage
dar *T* - to give
daoul *T* - a drum
dava *T* - lawsuit
debaldez - gratis
dedos - fingers
defendido - prohibited
defender - to defend
degoyar - to slaughter
dehiyar - to delay
delantre - ahead
demanda - ask, demand
demando - asked
deportado - deported
derritir - to melt
desaparaser - disappear
desatado - untied
desayuno - baked goods
desdenyar - to disdain, scorn
deseyo - desire
deshar - to leave

deskansar		- to rest
desmudo		- naked
despues		- later
desrepozado		- ill
detras		- behind
detuvo		- held back
devda		- debt
dezir		- to say
dezmayar		- to faint
dezmazalado		- luckless
dezmodrar		- to cause disarray
dia		- day
diamante		- diamond
dientes		- teeth
diez		- ten
difisil		- difficult
digame		- tell me
digidon	*H*	- backside
dinero		- money
dio		- gave
dip	*T*	- the bottom
dirito		- privilege
disho		- he/she said
diskutir		- discuss
diz	*T*	- knee
djam	*T*	- glass, pane
djenem	*T*	- hell
djente		- people
djep	*IT*	- pocket
Djudeo		- Jew
Djueves		- Thursday
djugar		- to play
djuntos		- together
djusdam	*T*	- changepurse
djustisia		- justice
doblado		- doubled
dodje		- twelve
doktor		- doctor
dolares	*E*	- dollars
domesilyo		- domicile
dormir		- to sleep
douz	*T*	- smooth
douzdear	*TL*	- to put in order
dravear	*E*	- to drive (a car)
dulses		- sweets
dulsor		- sweetness
duman	*T*	- smoke
durmete		- go to sleep
duro		- hard, difficult
dushman	*T*	- enemy
Dyo		- God

E

Ebreyo	*H*	- Hebrew
echar		- throw, expel go to bed
echado		- ill, in bed
echo		- made, done, job
edad		- age
eech	*T*	- nil
ejemplo		- example
ekmek	*T*	- bread
elevo	*F*	- student
embarasa		- to be sorry
embasho		- on the floor
embatakar	*T*	- to soil
embiyar		- to send
emburujate		- cover up
emborachar		- to get drunk
emigrantes		- immigrants
empesar		- to start
empeso		- started
emplear		- to shop

emprestar		- lend
enamorado		- in love
endenyar		- to deign
enderechar		- straighten
endevinar		- foretell
endjoyar	*EL*	- to enjoy
endjuntos		- together
enfasyar		- fed up with
enforkar	*T*	- to hang
engenara		- artichoke
englenear		- to entertain
englutir		- to swallow
engrandeser		- to raise
enkantado		- enchanted
enkashar		- stick in, insert
enkolgar		- to hang
enkontrar		- to meet
enkorajar		- encourage
ensembrar		- to plant
ensima		- over, on top
ensupito		- suddenly
entender		- to understand
entendido		- understood
entero		- all, total
enterrar		- to bury
entezar		- freeze
entonses		- therefore, then
entosigar		- to poison
entra		- enter
ermana		- sister
ermanastra		- stepsister
ermano		- brother
ermosa		- pretty
es		- is
eskapar		- to finish
eskarinyo		- to miss someone
eskarvar		- dig
eskaso		- a miser
esklavo		- slave
eskluido		- excluded
eskonder		- to hide
eskova		- a broom
eskrito		- written
eskrivir		- write
eskuralicha	*LT*	- earring
eskuro		- dark
espandir		- to stretch out
espantar		- to scare
espanto		- a scare
espantoso		- 'fraidy cat'
espejo		- mirror
espera		- wait
esperansa		- hope
espeso		- thick, pest
estavan		- they were
estimado		- esteemed
estofa	*EL*	- stove
estomago		- stomach
estores		- window shades
estremeser		- shudder
estrenar		- to wear the first time
estreya		- star
evalla	*T*	- thank God
eyelak	*T*	- out of work

F

facha	*LI*	- face
fakturia		- factory
falso		- false
fama		- fame
famiya		- family
fanela		- flannel
fant	*T*	- jack, in cards
faroujento		- rusty

fasha		- sash, bandage
fea		- ugly
fez	*T*	- Turkish head wear
fiede		- stinks
fierro		- iron
fijones		- beans
fil	*T*	- elephant
fila		- thin dough
fildjan	*T*	- demi-tasse cup
fin		- until, end
flako		- thin
flamas		- flames
flosho		- loose
folar	*GL*	- Purim pastry
fostan	*T*	- a dress
fortuna	*LT*	- storm
foya		- a grave
fraguar		- to build
franfooree	*E*	- hot dog
fregadero		- a sink
frente		- forehead; front
fresko		- fresh
fridjide	*E*	- refrigerator
frio		- cold
fruta		- fruit
fuego		- fire
fuente		- faucet
fuir		- flee
furcha	*T*	- a brush
furiente		- raging, furious
fusta	*T*	- a skirt
fustoukes	*T*	- peanuts in a shell
fuyo		- fled
fyongo		- bow of ribbon

G

galut	*H*	- exile
gameo		- camel
ganansyas		- winnings
ganar		- to win
gana		- desire
garganta		- neck
garon	*H*	- throat
garvansos		- chickpeas
gaste		- expense
gato		- cat
gayina		- chicken
gayo		- rooster
gazep	*T*	- troublemaker
gazeta	*F*	- newspaper
gazoz	*H*	- soda water
geinam	*H*	- hell
gizar		- to cook
godro		- fat
golor		- odor
gomitando		- vomiting
gostar		- to taste
gota		- a drop, a stroke
gozar		- enjoy
grasia		- grace
gravata	*FL*	- necktie
gritar		- yell
guadrar		- to hide, watch over
guantes		- gloves
guayas		- woe
guerko		- devil
guerra		- war
guesmo		- aroma
guevo		- egg
guizando		- cooking
guzano		- worm

H

haber	*T*	- news
hadras		- put on airs
haftuna	*T*	- a whipping
haham	*H*	- rabbi
hal	*T*	- plight
halis	*T*	- truly, true
halva	*T*	- sesame pastry
hamal	*T*	- a porter
haminado	*H*	- hardboiled (egg)
handrajo		- rag
hanoum	*T*	- pretty lady
haragan		- lazy
harem	*T*	- harem
harif	*TH*	- sharp, clever
hatir	*T*	- favor
haver	*H*	- partner
haya	*H*	- animal
hazino		- sick
hazinoura		- sickness
hedek	*EL*	- headache
henoza	*H*	- graceful
hermana		- sister
hermano		- brother
heshbon	*H*	- sum, account
highvan	*T*	- animal
highvane	*T*	- corral
hodja	*T*	- teacher
hohma	*H*	- wisdom
houvarda	*T*	- generous
hora		- hour
horo, hora	*GH*	- Israeli, Greek dance

I

ichizera		- witch
idiotos		- idiots
igual		- equal
ija		- girl, daughter
ijo		- boy, son
ilo		- thread
inche		- fill
indiana		- a turkey
indo		- going
ingles		- English
inmoral		- immoral
innat	*T*	- stubbornness
insanidad		- insanity
intensyone		- intention
ir		- to go
istoria		- history

K

kavesa		- head
kada		- each
kadar	*T*	- amount
kadem	*T*	- luck
kademsis	*T*	- luckless
kadena		- chain
kafe	*GTL*	- coffee
kalem	*T*	- pencil
kaimahk	*T*	- cream
kal	*H*	- synagogue
kalavasa		- squash
kale		- must
kaleja		- street
kalmante		- tranquilizer
kalpak	*T*	- head gear
kalsados		- shoes
kalsetones		- socks
kalyentura		- fever
kamareta		- a room

kamina - walk
kamino - path
kamisa - shirt
kanape - couch
kandela - candle
kandil *T* - drunk
kandireyar *T* - to fool, to dupe
kansado - tired
kantador - singer
kanyamazo - dishrag
kapak *T* - cover, lid
kapandja *T* - rat trap
kaprichoso - stubborn
kara - face
karabalik *T* - a mob
karisheyar *T* - mix, mix in
karne - meat
karpooz *T* - watermelon
kartikas - cards
kashkas - shells
kashon - drawer
kassap *H* - butcher
katife *T* - velvet
kavalyero - gentleman
kavane *T* - coffee house
kavesa - head
kavesal - pillow
kaveyo - hair
kavzar - cause
kawre *E* - quarter
kayado - quiet
kayer - to fall
kayes - streets
kayik *T* - a boat
kayisee *T* - apricot
kaza - home
kazado - married
kazal *T* - town, hamlet
kazar - to marry
kazik *T* - post-like stake
ke - what
kebar *T* - reserved
kehila *H* - temple
kemado - burned
kemar - to burn
kepazel - shameful
kerrer - want
kerhane *T* - whore-house
kerida - dear one
keshar - complain
ketuba *H* - marriage contract
kezo - cheese
kibrik *T* - match, phosporous
kien - who
kierro - I want
kilipoor *T* - low class
kimoor *T* - coal
kinyentos - five hundred
kira *T* - rent
kirbach *T* - a whip
kismet *T* - fate
kitar - to remove
kyoopri *T* - a bridge
klavos - nails, cloves
kodja *T* - large, big
kodrero - lamb
kol - cabbage
kolay *T* - easy
kolor - color
kolorado - red
kombidar - invite
komer - eat
kompanyero - companion
kompletar - to finish
komporto - behavior

kon - with
konklusion - conclusion
konoser - recognize
konsejas - tales
konsejo - advice
konsider *E* - consider
kontado - counted, famous, money
kontajiosa *E* - contagious
kontra - against
koudouriyar - misbehave
koukouvaya *T* - owl
koulo - ass, backside
kousour - the rest
korason - heart
korriendo - running
kortijo - courtyard
kosa - thing
kosuegros - in-laws
kourshoum *T* - lead, bullet
kosho - cripple
koustiyas - ribs
kovijate - cover yourself
kovrar - charge, fee
koza - thing
kreyer - to believe
kreyon *E* - crayon
kriador - creator
kriaturas - children
kriminal - criminal
krudo - raw
kualkier - whoever
kualo - what
kuando - when
kuanto - how much
kuatro - four
kuchara - spoon
kuchiyo - knife
kudyado - care, worry
kuedra - rope
kuerro - leather
kuento - a count (sum)
kueshko - fruit pit
kukla *G* - doll
kulpa - fault
kulpavle - at fault
kumar *T* - gambling
kumardji *T* - gambler
kumbara *T* - piggy bank
kundurya *T* - shoe
kunduryadji *T* - shoemaker
kunushear *T* - to talk
kuriyar - to wind
kurnaz *T* - sly
kushak *T* - waistband, strap
kushkiyas - ticklish
kusir - sew
kustumbre - custom
kusur *T* - the remainder
kuti *T* - box, carton
kuzina - kitchen
kyoftes *T* - hamburger patties
kyoutouk *T* - hard wood, hard head

L

Ladino - Judeo-Spanish
ladron - thief
lagrimas - tears
lakerda *G* - raw salted mackerel
lakirdi *T* - conversation
largo - long

lashon	*H*	- language
lavorante	*I*	- worker
lavoro	*I*	- work
lazdrar		- strive
leche		- milk
Lehli	*T*	- Polish, from Poland
lentejas		- lentils
lenyo		- wood
leshos		- distant
levantar		- to lift
ley		- law
liberado		- liberated
librik	*T*	- coffee pot
libro		- book
limon		- lemon
limpyo		- clean
liviano		- light (weight)
lodo		- mud
loko		- insane, crazy
lonso	*LT*	- a bear, stupid, dummy
lugar		- room, place
luna		- moon
Lunes		- Monday
luto		- mourning
luvya		- rain

M

mabul	*H*	- flood
madrasta		- stepmother
madre		- mother
maho		- meek, mild
mahpul	*T*	- unusual delight
mavi	*T*	- the color blue
maitop	*T*	- mock, scorn,
malah	*H*	- angel
malahim	*H*	- angels
malatia		- malady
maldad		- meanness
maldicho		- cursed
male	*T*	- district
malogrado		- wicked
malonesto		- dishonest
mamzer	*H*	- bastard
mandar		- send
mandarina		- mandarin
maniya		- bracelet
mankando		- missing
mano		- hand
manseves		- time of youth
mansevo		- young person
mantel		- table cloth
mantener		- maintain, support
manya		- habit
manyana		- tomorrow
manziya		- pity
mareado		- dizzy
marido		- husband
Martes		- Tuesday
mas		- more
masa		- matsas, dough
masapan		- marzipan
mashala	*T*	- God has willed
mashina	*E*	- machine, car
mashkar		- to chew
mazal	*H*	- luck
mazalozos	*H*	- lucky ones
mazalto	*H*	- high luck
meana	*T*	- saloon
medio		- middle
mejor		- better
meldado		- memorial reading

meldar		- to read
melezina		- medicine
meneyar		- to move
menester		- necessary
menesterozo		- needy one
mentiras		- lies
mentirozo		- liar
merced		- respect
mereser		- deserve
merekiya		- worry
merkado		- purchased
merkar		- to buy
mes		- month
mesez	*T*	- hors d'oeuvre
metalik	*T*	- Turkish coin
meter		to place
meyoyos		- brains
meza		- table
mezada		- monthly stipend
mezura		- measure
migaja		- little bit
miel		- honey
miembro		- member
Mierkoles		- Wednesday
mio		- mine
minder	*T*	- sofa-like settee
mira		- look
mirando		- looking
mishpaha	*H*	- family
mismo		- same
mitad		- half
miyatad		- half
moda		- fashion
modrer		- bite
moneda		- money, coin
moompich	*E*	- movies
moosho		- lip
morena		- dark
morir		- to die
mortaja		- shroud
mosa		- maid
moshka		- a fly
moso		- servant
mosotros		- we
mudante		- underwear
muelas		- molars
muerte		- death
mues		- walnut
muestras		- ours
mueve		- nine
muevo		- new
mujer		- wife
munchas		- many
muncho		- much
mundo		- world
murio		- died
musafir	*T*	- visitor, guest
mushama	*T*	- linoleum
mushteri	*T*	- customer
mustacho		- mustache
musho		- lip
muy		- much

N

nada		- nothing
nadar		- swim
naalet	*T*	- troublemaker
nalgas	*T*	- buttocks
nariz		- nose
nasyo		- was born
nasi		- I was born
navaja		- pocket knife
nazar	*T*	- evil eye
nekochera	*G*	- woman of the house

negro		- black, bad
ninguno		- no one
noche		- night
nombre		- name
nona	*IF*	- grandma
nosotros		- we
novelas		- novels
noventa		- ninety
novia		- bride
novio		- bridegroom
nunka		- never

O

ocho		- eight
ofisyo		- profession
ofresio		- offered
oidos		- ears
oir		- to hear
ojo		- eye
okupasion	*E*	- occupation
olvidar		- to forget
ombligo		- navel
ombre		- man
onesto		- honest
onze		- eleven
ood	*T*	- lute
ooti	*T*	- iron, press
ora		- hour
orasion		- prayer
orejas		- ears
ormiga		- ant
orno		- oven
oro		- gold
ospital	*LGE*	- hospital
otel	*E*	- hotel
otro		- other
ovligado		- obligated
oy		- today
oya		- stew pot
oye		- listen
oyendo		- hearing, listening

P

pacha		- leg
paga		- pay
pagamiento		- payment
pahk	*E*	- park
palavra		- word
palo		- stick
palomba	*I*	- a dove
palto	*T*	- coat
pandero		- tambourine
pantalon		- trousers
pantuflas	*T*	- slippers
papaz	*T*	- priest
papel		- paper
papelera		- paper bag
papon		- big eater
parientes		- parents, relatives
parir		- give birth
parlak	*T*	- shiny
pasado		- past
pasajero		- passenger
pasar		- to pass
pasensia		- patience
pasharo		- bird
pastra		- casino
patata		- potato
patla	*T*	- burst
patladear	*T*	- to burst
patlidjan	*T*	- eggplant

pato		- goose
patrones		- bosses
paz		- peace
pecho		- bosom
pedaso		- piece
pedredor		- loser
pedrer		- to lose
pedrido		- lost
pekado		- sin
pena		- labor
pendola		- fountain pen
pensa		- think
penseryo		- deep thought
peor		- worse
perdes	*T*	- curtains
perla		- pearl
perro		- dog
Pesah	*H*	- Passover
pesgado		- heavy, a bore
piadoso		- helpful
piedras		- rocks, stones
piedrita		- loss
pila		- a sink
pimentona		- bell pepper
pimienta		- pepper
pinaka	*E*	- pinochle
pipino		- cucumber
pipita		- sunflower seed
piron	*IG*	- fork
pishar		- to urinate
pishin	*T*	- right away
pishkado		- fish
pishman	*T*	- rueful
pishtamal	*T*	- bath towel
piye		- foot
plazer		- pleasure
pleto		- fight
pokeriko	*E*	- poker
poko		- little
polegamisto		- polygamist
pountozo		- touchy one
por		- for
porke		- why
portokal	*T*	- orange
postema		- woe, problem
pozo		- a well
pranso	*I*	- special meal
prasa		- leak
preferida		- preferred
prenyada		- pregnant
preparado		- prepared
presyado		- precious
presyos		- prices
presto	*I*	- quickly
preto		- black
primero		- first
primo		- cousin
prishil		- parsley
privada		- toilet
prizyon		- prison
problemas		- problems
profesores		- teachers
prometo		- promise
prostela		- apron
provechoso		- lucky one
provedad		- poverty
prove		- poor
proverbios		- proverbs
pudra		- powder
pudrido		- rotten
puede		- can do
puerko		- pork, pig
puerpo		- body
puerta		- door
pujar		- to grow
pul	*HT*	- postage stamp

pulgas		- fleas
punto		- point
punyado		- fistful
putana		- prostitute
putines	*T*	- shoes

R

raash	*H*	- earthquake
raki	*T*	- Turkish whiskey
rasa		- race
rasha	*H*	- wicked, evil
raton		- rat
ratonera		- mouse trap
ravano		- radish
rayer		- grind
redoma		- a bottle
refranes		- proverbs
regalo		- gift
reir		- to laugh
remeter		- to recuperate
renombrado		- famous
reposado		- at rest
reposo		- rest
repotrear		- languish
resivir		- receive
reskatado		- ransomed
respondyo		- answered
restoran	*E*	- restaurant
reushir	*I*	- to succeed
rey		- king
reyna		- queen
rezyo		- healthy
richina		- castor oil
riko		- rich
riye		- he laughs
riza		- laughter
rogando		- praying
romper		- break
roumatizmo	*E*	- rheumatism
ropa		- clothing
rouda		- medicinal plant

S

saber		- to know
sabido		- learned
sabroso		- tasty
savana		- bed sheet
saksi	*T*	- flower pot
sal		- salt
salata		- salad
salida		- exit, diarrhea
salir		- depart, leave
saltar		- to jump
salud		- health
saludar		- to greet
salvasion		- salvation
saman	*T*	- straw
samarra	*T*	- fur
sandjurwela		- leech
sano		- healthy
sarnudar		- sneeze
saviya		- knew
sedaka	*H*	- charity
seesterhoo	*E*	- sisterhood
segundo		- second
seguro		- sure, positive
sehora	*H*	- fear, fright
seko		- dry
selozo		- jealous
semana		- week
semanada		- salary
semeja		- looks like

semejante		- similar
semplees	*E*	- samples
sena		- dinner
sensya		- sense
senyora		- lady
Sefarad	*H*	- Spain
ser		- thirst
serka		- near
serra		- shut
sertifikado		- certified
sesh		- six
sesta		- basket
sevoya		- onion
seyado		- sealed
Shabat	*H*	- Saturday, Sabbath
shapear	*E*	- to shop
shakeka		- headache
shalvar	*T*	- bloomers
shamar		- slap
sharope	*T*	- white confection
shastre	*T*	- tailor
shavdo	*T*	- tasteless
sheeshit	*T*	- variety
shiftili	*T*	- peach
shimistra	*T*	- chemistry
shoozes	*E*	- shoes
si		- yes
sielo		- sky
siempre		- always
siento		- I feel
sierko		- garbage
siete		- seven
sigariko		- cigarette
siniza		- ashes
sinko		- five
sinkuenta		- fifty
sinsero		- sincere
sira	*T*	- turn, next-in-line
sirvir		- serve
sivdad		- city
siya		- chair
sol		- sun
soledad		- solitude
solitreo	*L*	- a script
solombra		- shadow
sousyedad		- dirt
sos		- you are
sosyeda	*E*	- society
spina		- fish bone
sudor		- perspiration
suegra		- mother-in-law
suenyo		- dream
sufrir		- suffer
sujeko		- subject
suluk	*T*	- breath
supo		- knew
suvrino	*L*	- nephew, cousin
suvyo		- climbed
suzyo		- dirty

T

tadre		- late
taksa	*E*	- tax
taled	*H*	- talis, shawl
tambien		- also
tanti		- aunt
tapado		- covered
tapete		- carpet
taralikos	*I*	- round cookies
tavan	*T*	- ceiling
tavla	*T*	- tray, wood
tavli	*T*	- backgammon
tefter	*T*	- a book

tejado *T* - roof
temeridad - temerity
temprano - early
tenekedji *T* - tinsmith
tener - to have
tengere *T* - pot
tengo *T* - I have
terbie *T* - discipline
tia - aunt
tiempo - time
tiene - has
tierra - earth
tifsin *T* - baking tray
tijerra - scissors
tikiya - tuberculosis
timarana *T* - insane asylum
tino - in mind
tio - uncle
tiralanya - spider web
todo - all
tokmak *T* - thick head
toma - take
tomat - tomato
tomi - I took
toutoun *T* - tobacco
topa - find
torno *EL* - turn
torpe *T* - dumb
tosigo - poison
tovaja - towel
travar - to pull
trayer - to bring
trazera - backside
tredje - thirteen
treno - train
trenta - thirty
tres - three
tresalido - delighted
tripa - stomach
triste - sad
tristeza - sadness
troka - change
trushieron - they brought
tuerto - twisted
tufenk *T* - gun
tuyendo - hurting

U

ugur *T* - luck
ugursoos *T* - luckless
universelle *F* - universal
unos - some
untar - to dunk; to bribe
unyas - finger nails
usos - customs

V

vamos - let's go
vate - leave
vazo - glass
vedrad - truth
vendedor - seller
vendiendo - selling
venir - to come
ventana - window
ventosas - cups
ventura - luck, fortune
ver - see
verano - summer
veras - you'll see
verdad - truth
verguensa - shame

vestido		- suit
vezino		- neighbor
vida		- life
vidrio		- glass
viejez		- old age
viejo		- old person
vijita		- a visit
vijna	*T*	- bing cherry
vinagre		- vinegar

Y

yagli	*T*	- oily
yaka	*T*	- collar
yakisheya	*T*	- becoming
yama		- call
yaprakes	*T*	- grape leaf patties
yaves		- keys
yene	*T*	- again
yeno		- full
yerno		- son-in-law
yerrado		- in error
yerva		- grass
yorrar		- to cry

Z

zabit	*T*	- army officer
zahood	*H*	- good deed
zampara	*T*	- woman chaser
zavali	*T*	- poor thing
zahuth	*H*	- good, merit
zingano		- gypsy